AHMANSON · MURPHY
FINE ARTS IMPRINT

THE AHMANSON FOUNDATION

has endowed this imprint

to honor the memory of

FRANKLIN D. MURPHY

who for half a century

served arts and letters,

beauty and learning, in

equal measure by shaping

with a brilliant devotion

those institutions upon

which they rely.

THE PUBLISHER GRATEFULLY ACKNOWLEDGES THE GENEROUS
SUPPORT OF THE ART ENDOWMENT FUND OF THE UNIVERSITY OF
CALIFORNIA PRESS FOUNDATION, WHICH WAS ESTABLISHED BY A
MAJOR GIFT FROM THE AHMANSON FOUNDATION.

THE AUTRY NATIONAL CENTER OF THE AMERICAN WEST GRATE-
FULLY ACKNOWLEDGES THE GENEROUS SUPPORT OF THE CARYLL
AND WILLIAM MINGST/THE MILDRED E. AND HARVEY S. MUDD
PUBLICATIONS FUND.

EMPIRE AND LIBERTY

EMPIRE AND LIBERTY

The Civil War and the West

EDITED BY

Virginia Scharff

Exhibition curated by Carolyn Brucken

AUTRY NATIONAL CENTER OF THE AMERICAN WEST

in association with   UNIVERSITY OF CALIFORNIA PRESS

University of California Press, one of the most distinguished university
presses in the United States, enriches lives around the world by advancing
scholarship in the humanities, social sciences, and natural sciences. Its
activities are supported by the UC Press Foundation and by philanthropic
contributions from individuals and institutions. For more information, visit
www.ucpress.edu.

University of California Press
Oakland, California

Library of Congress Cataloging-in-Publication Data

   Empire and liberty : the Civil War and the West / edited by Virginia
Scharff, exhibition curated by Carolyn Brucken.
     pages   cm
   Includes bibliographical references and index.
   ISBN 978-0-520-28126-4 (cloth)
   1. West (U.S.)—History—Civil War, 1861–1865.   I. Scharff, Virginia,
editor.   II. Brucken, Carolyn, 1966– curator.
   E470.9.E47   2014
   978′.02—dc23   2014037764

Manufactured in the United States of America

23 22 21 20 19 18 17 16 15
10 9 8 7 6 5 4 3 2 1

To Carolyn Brucken, sage of the storyboard

CONTENTS

ILLUSTRATIONS

FIGURES

ACKNOWLEDGMENTS

Writing a book requires substantial tolerance for one's own company. Producing an edited volume compels the lone wolf writer to spend a little more time with the pack. And combining that work with curating a museum exhibition launches the misanthropic scribe into the whirling dance of teamwork. This book represents the conjunction of all three fascinating enterprises, and the work and creativity of many people.

Let me begin with the incredible crew at the Autry National Center, led by Rick West, President and CEO, Vice President of Curatorial and Exhibitions Shelby Tisdale, Director of the Autry Institute David Burton, Belinda Nakasato-Suarez, administrator in the Autry Institute, and Western History Chair Stephen Aron. Steve, along with John Gray, now Director of the National Museum of American History, first recruited me to work at the Autry more than ten years ago, and I continue to be inspired and energized and rather daunted by their curiosity, friendship, and vision.

Our exhibition team includes Andi Alameda, project manager; Patrick Frederickson, Eugene Wyrick, and Alan Konoshi, exhibit designers; Laura Purdy, media; Erik Greenberg, education; Sara Signorovitch, collections; Maren Dougherty, communications/marketing; Victor Phillips, membership; Robyn Hetrick and Ben Fitzsimmons, programs; and Marlene Head, publications. I can't thank them enough for their patience, their persistence, their talent, and their dedication to doing great museum work. I also thank Daniel Lynch and Annie Powers, doctoral students at UCLA who served as research assistants on this project, a title that doesn't begin to convey their contributions.

Even as we have drawn on the marvelous collections at the Autry, this book and exhibit benefit from the generosity of people who provided objects and images: Cindy Brown, Wyoming State Archives; Susan Ogle of the Drum Barracks and the West Coast Civil War Collectors; and especially Wayne Sherman, all deserve a shout-out for all their support. Marilyn Van Winkle, Peg Brady, and Sarah Signorovitch at the Autry also assisted in photographing artifacts and getting permissions for the book.

At the University of California Press, Niels Hooper and Kim Hogeland have provided fine editorial guidance and thoughtful criticism, as have three anonymous readers and the ever generous David Wrobel. Copyeditor Bonita Hurd provided wise and meticulous treatment of all these essays and immeasurably improved our work. Project editor Dore Brown saw the book through its final stages. This is the third book I've published with the press, and I have come to depend on their thorough and professional reviewing process, their devotion to lovely design, and their willingness to hustle in the face of looming deadlines.

All the contributors to this book have put in an immense amount of time, labor, and cheer, not only in working on their own essays but also in working together as a group. Adam Arenson and Brenda Stevenson were instrumental in generating the ideas for the exhibition, and along with Bill Deverell, Dan Lynch, and Joan Waugh, they attended an initial meeting that got us started on a productive path. Adam Arenson and Andrew Graybill, editors of our brother volume on the Civil War and the West, have contributed greatly to this one as well. The Center for the Southwest at the University of New Mexico hosted a workshop to discuss the first drafts of the essays in this book, attended by most of the contributors, which offered a wonderful collaborative experience, as well as a chance for our group to enjoy some great New Mexico hospitality. Jen McPherson, graduate assistant in the Center for the Southwest, masterminded the workshop and is the brains of the operation in the CSW. Jen is a dream planning partner, a graceful and gracious smoother of paths and producer of solutions, and a fountain of great ideas. I have taken shameless advantage of her leadership and organization skills, even as I have delighted in watching her scholarship blossom. I also thank Matt Rembe and Nancy Kinyanjui and the staff at Los Poblanos Inn and Conference Center for their support of the Center's work, and for their loving care of the most enchanting place in the Land of Enchantment.

Charlie Steen and Melissa Bokovoy, successive chairs of the history department at the University of New Mexico, have granted me a course release to finish this book, and I am profoundly grateful to them, as well as to the always amazing history staff, Yolanda Martinez, Dana Ellison, Barbara Wafer, and Emily Wainwright.

Chris Wilson, my dear husband, unstintingly lends his expertise and insight to all my work and has a gift for hospitality that makes every colleague and collaborator welcome in our home. I am wildly grateful for his love and support.

I save for last the person to whom this book owes the most. Carolyn Brucken is much, much more than my co-curator on this exhibition. When it comes to making the magic happen in a museum exhibition, I am the tail of her comet. She has expertly sought out and secured every object, brokered every transaction, wrangled the project as a whole, shaped every idea that lies behind this book and exhibition, handled all the images and permissions, read drafts, attended meetings and workshops, made comments, and spent countless hours in front of computer screens and storyboards, teaching me to think with my eyes, to see the possibilities of doing history in real 3-D spaces, to understand the ways in which objects tell compelling stories. For a dozen years now, I have relied on her wisdom and wit, her courage and curiosity, her great company, and her stunning versatility and intellectual nimbleness. The opportunity to work with Carolyn has made me a better scholar, opened my mind to the many ways and places for doing history, and just been immense fun. I dedicate this book to her.

INTRODUCTION

Virginia Scharff

Most of us who studied American history, in elementary school or high school or even in college, learned to think of the nation's past as a grand series of epic moments. We started when the English landed at Jamestown, watched the Pilgrims found their city on a hill, then fast-forwarded to the Revolution, the democratizing age of Jackson, the rising conflict over slavery, and then the cataclysmic Civil War. Once the bloodshed had ended and the states had been reunited, we turned to the opening of the West, that region across the Mississippi famed in song and story and the instrument of the reunification of American purpose. By 1890, the frontier closed and the brawny continental nation got about the task of steaming and clanging its way into an urban, industrial, and decidedly modern world.

If this sounds like a "greatest hits" version of American history, it is still pretty much a sketch of what most Americans know about their past, if they think about that past at all. The problem, however, is that this story isn't true. A history like this treats the tangle of human events like a movie, with jump cuts and a clear progression from scene to scene, with heroes and villains, lead characters and walk-on parts, and with a beginning, middle, and end. But history doesn't work like that. Episodes that seem separate turn out to overlap. Characters who are supposed to appear in one scene sometimes wander into others, and one scene's marginal players turn into heroes—or is it villains?—in the next. People and things and places get mixed up, to the point where it gets hard to sort out who and what mattered, where and when. Off-screen events drive the action in myriad directions. Major plot lines intersect and fly apart, creating opportunities and obstacles, conflicts and consequences, that we can explain only by thinking about big themes and letting our imaginations range across multiple places, people, causes, and outcomes. And at all times, as historians have learned, there are more characters on- and offstage, acting with greater skill and knowledge, than we had once imagined.

So it is with the problem of slavery and freedom, and with the continental expansion of the nation. This volume is the companion to an exhibition on the Civil War and the West co-curated by Carolyn Brucken and Virginia Scharff. In that exhibition, we use objects to tell a story composed of many stories, a tale of diverse people and events. Our narrative brings together two epic subjects in American history, the story of the struggle to end slavery and extend liberty that reached a violent climax in the Civil War, and the story of the westward expansion of the United States, from Atlantic to Pacific. We twine the strands of these seemingly self-contained tales together because we believe they were never really separate in the first place. To put it plainly, we hold that you cannot understand the Civil War without addressing the significance of the West to the creation and development of the United States, and you cannot understand the West without taking into account the causes, contingencies, and consequences of the nation's cataclysmic Civil War. Instead of focusing on the conflict between the free North and the slave South that culminated in a civil war, we consider that epic struggle across a longer time and a larger field. And instead of imagining westward expansion as something akin to a force of nature, we take into account the many moments and forms of conquest by violence. The nation's defining debates and battles over freedom, race, land, and the rights of individuals took place amid, and because of, the territorial expansion of the American empire.

From the moment of its birth, the United States was a creature of imperial expansion into fully inhabited country, as well as an entity grappling with the presence of human bondage even as it avowed its dedication to human liberty. Indigenous nations had long practiced various forms of enslavement, often involving prisoners taken in the bloody enterprise of raiding. Those human spoils of war might end up being adopted into a clan or village, making the journey from captives to cousins.[1] But Spanish expansion from the South, and American settlers' quest for more land, added layers of violence onto existing conflict, as native peoples who were pressed from the east and south moved into already occupied terrain.

After 1800, most Americans did not question the wisdom or the necessity of national expansion, though they disagreed vehemently about which American institutions ought to go west. To complicate the picture further, Americans of the time were perfectly capable of declaiming their dedication to liberty even as they tolerated or ignored or lived off the labor of enslaved Americans. Thomas Jefferson, the slaveholding son of a westering slaveholder, wrote the stirring words in the Declaration of Independence that assert, "All men are created equal, and endowed by their creator with certain inalienable rights" including life, liberty, and the pursuit of happiness. Jefferson embraced territorial expansion as the engine of an "empire for liberty," though Jefferson's fellow slaveholders more often envisioned an empire for slavery. Simultaneously, the agents of American empire, whatever their views on slavery, imagined that history or cultural superiority or destiny or divinity entitled them to occupy the West. American leaders generally had little regard for the life, liberty, or pursuit of happiness of the original inhabitants of the continent, or for that matter, of the descendants of the Spanish and indigenous peoples who had for generations lived in the West. But as Jefferson himself well understood, western lands were occupied by people whose ideas about land and liberty and labor diverged, often sharply, from those of the would-be conquerors.

Slavery and liberty and empire commingled at the most iconic moments of the American past. In 1803, when Meriwether Lewis and William Clark led Jefferson's Corps of Discovery into the newly purchased Louisiana Territory, they were ambassadors of liberty and agents of conquest, promising peace and freedom while asking for submission from the people they met. One member of the traveling party was a man of African ancestry named York, held as a slave by William Clark. Another was a Shoshone woman named Sacagawea, wife or slave (or in some other way not quite free) to the mixed-blood translator and voyageur Toussaint Charbonneau. In the traveling caravan that represented the infant democracy, American slavery mingled with indigenous captivity and forced labor. As they traveled among the peoples of the West, the men and woman of the Corps of Discovery embodied the variations in liberty that accompanied empire, and they often misunderstood the practices and viewpoints of those they encountered, the very people upon whom they often depended for their survival.[2]

Throughout our nation's history, every lunge toward the west carried with it the questions of how to deal with the people already in place, as well as how to negotiate the humanity of Americans held in slavery. How, indeed, could Jefferson have spoken of an "empire for liberty" when the persistence of slavery depended on territorial expansion, and when continental conquest implied not only the dispossession of previous occupants but also the spread of brutal bondage?[3] Who had the right to claim space? Who counted as American citizens? What rights ought citizens to possess to property and territory they had claimed long before the Americans arrived, or even to their own bodies, their labor, and the fruits of their labor? How should the government of the United States assert its authority in places where power was very much up for grabs? And when was violence, even to the point of genocide, justified?

Before independence, Native nations exercised dominion over most of what would eventually become the United States, with Spain nominally in charge (though hardly in control) in the future American Southwest. And even then, the inhabitants of North America had diverse histories reaching into the deep past and spanning the globe.[4] The British government had attempted to limit British colonies' westward expansion with the Proclamation of 1763, drawing a line along the crest of the Appalachian Mountains. But even at that time, Americans like Benjamin Franklin already claimed lands that British authorities meant to remain in indigenous hands. Even before the Constitution was adopted, the government that had been established by the Articles of Confederation passed the Northwest Ordinance of 1787, banning slavery in territory north of the Ohio

River. But the framers of the Constitution saw fit to recognize the institution of slavery, and to politically empower slaveholders, in the infamous Three-Fifths Compromise. Jefferson's Louisiana Purchase doubled the size of the nation and led inevitably to disputes over the personal and property rights of indigenous people, the status of those enslaved, and the freedom of slaveholders to carry their human property wherever they would.

Every congressional attempt at a compromise raised the stakes. Slaveholders insisted that their political power be maintained in the Senate, that every free state admitted be balanced by a new slave state. Americans seeking western lands insisted that indigenous occupants be exterminated or relocated west of the Mississippi. After the passage of the Indian Removal Act of 1830, Southeastern tribes, like the Cherokees and Choctaws, who had so successfully assimilated to Southern society that they had, on a par with their non-Indian neighbors, adopted the all-American practice of chattel slavery, were forced to walk a trail of tears west to Oklahoma. How would such people respond when forced to choose sides in a war that pitted the government, which had sent them into exile, against the former neighbors who had seized their homelands?

American empire-building inevitably provoked multiple conflicts over race and rights. Westward-moving agents of that empire trumpeted their peaceful intentions and democratic ideals, and those who were invaded or exploited fought to claim their own lands and liberties. The West had always been a place of incredible cultural diversity and fluidity, a place understood as much by the rules and relations of family and kinship as by politics and policies.[5] But as more and more emigrants moved in, from Asia and Latin America as well as from Europe and the United States, struggles over who counted as a person, as a potential property holder, and as a citizen occurred in many places, along many lines of friction and fracture. Turning our eyes to the West of the antebellum period, the war, and the period of Reconstruction, we see how many ways the diverse inhabitants of the expanding nation worked to claim a home place and a legitimate voice.[6] We cannot tell all their stories, but in this volume we use the inspiration of fascinating objects to unpack and explore complicated and meaningful moments, as well as the experiences of diverse people, in the strange American coupling of empire and liberty.

American territorial expansion meant tragic loss for people who came west in bondage. As Brenda Stevenson's essay reveals, Southern slaveholders viewed Texas as both a land of opportunity and a safe haven once their right to human property was threatened. For those enslaved, however, emigration meant wrenching separation from loved ones, physical privation, hard labor, and brutal discipline. Working from bills of sale, the kind of documents that apply a veneer of soullessness over the cruelty, Stevenson shows us the broken hearts and beleaguered bodies of men, women, and children treated as pieces of portable property.

Others, who went west by choice, found themselves inevitably involved in struggles over empire and liberty, none more so than the larger-than-life hero and magnificent failure John Charles Frémont, incisively profiled here by John Mack Faragher. When Frémont planted his personal flag, sewn by his gifted and ambitious wife, Jessie Benton

Frémont, atop the crest of the Continental Divide, he claimed the West for the nation and meant to claim a large part of American history for himself. The man who became famous as "the Pathfinder" would capture California and suffer court-martial for insubordination; gain and lose a fortune in the California goldfields; run for president in 1856 as the first candidate of the Republican Party, under the banner of "Free Soil, Free Men, and Frémont"; and, as commanding general of the Department of the West, issue the nation's first (and quickly rescinded) emancipation proclamation. Following Frémont's oscillating fortunes, we see the many lines of convergence between the drive for continental conquest and the conflict over slavery and freedom.

In the context of a unified story of empire and liberty, it makes perfect sense that the first shots of the Civil War were fired in the West. Jonathan Earle gives us a vivid tale of the arms race in a region that had so recently been a "permanent" home to multiple indigenous peoples—some areas of which were still claimed by native powers—soon to be infamous as Bleeding Kansas. Earle explains how the guns that fired those shots came to be in the hands of advocates and opponents of legalizing slavery on the Kansas frontier. As proslavery Missourians, armed to the teeth, flooded into Kansas, antislavery partisans like the zealot John Brown and his sons vowed to greet violence in kind. Those who perpetrated the sack of Lawrence and the Pottawatomie Massacre did not disagree that men like themselves should occupy the land wrested from native people. They came to bloodshed, however, over whether such men should have the right to bring along other people they claimed to own.

At the time of the firing on Fort Sumter in South Carolina, in April 1861, most of what would become the American West was still contested terrain. That would begin to change as the Union mobilized men and arms on a massive scale. It was no coincidence that Abraham Lincoln, the Great Emancipator, was also the most ruthless and effective commander in chief in American history. Durwood Ball's masterful account of the Union army's western campaigns against indigenous people shows us how seamlessly the United States used technologies of communication as various as the telegraph and the bugle to support military might in forms ranging from elegant pistols to artillery, to fight enemies—Confederates and native resisters—in the name of consolidating its control over territory in the South and the West. As Ball shows us, the West was not one place when the army launched its effort to defeat Confederate Texans, decimate Dakota warriors in Minnesota, and dispossess and relocate the Navajo people in the Southwest. U.S. control of the continent was by no means secure in 1865. Indigenous people continued to defend their homelands and their sovereignty, even as the government pursued its efforts to force them into submission and dependency.

At times it seems nearly impossible to capture the story of that struggle for sovereignty on a shifting terrain, where resolution through violence was more often the rule than the exception. As Kent Blansett reveals, the Cherokee Nation, once thriving in the Southeastern United States, had strained to the breaking point in the 1830s over the terrible choice of removal. The Cherokees took their battles to their new home in Oklahoma as they faced the nearly impossible dilemma of how to protect their sovereignty with the coming of the American Civil War. Slaveholding Cherokee leaders like Stand Watie and John Ross hoped to protect both their national independence and their human and territorial property, but they disagreed bitterly over how to achieve those ends. Their choices, always as double-edged as the bowie knife Watie received for his service as a colonel in the army of the Confederate States of America, were shaped by a quest to claim both sovereignty and slavery amid almost constant warfare.

For some of the descendants of proud Spanish-Mexican soldiers who had settled in Alta California, the Civil War provided an opportunity to demonstrate valor and patriotism. In Daniel Lynch's meditation on the sword that belonged to Juan de la Guerra of California's Native Cavalry, we experience the complex loyalties of those whose ancestors had come to the Americas as conquerors. Now, those descendants found themselves absorbed into someone else's empire. Lynch offers up a rich history of de la Guerra's saber, an instrument of death and symbol of honor, virtually putting the weapon into our own hands as he transports us to the remote posts where Union soldiers fought boredom as well as opposing forces.

While the war continued in the West, politicians and their supporters in the East were already looking for ways to put the conflict behind them. President Ulysses S. Grant dealt with the Reconstruction of the South and the continuing resistance of native peoples, as men like the illustrator John Gast and the publisher George Crofutt imagined the West as a grand arena for reconciliation. Gast's widely reproduced painting, *American Progress*, seems almost timelessly iconic, with its multiple symbols of an inevitable, peaceable American civilization spreading ever westward. But in Adam Arenson's fine-grained examination of post–Civil War politics, we discover that Gast's painting represented the ideas of the Liberal Republican Party, an ephemeral political movement that rapidly rose and fell at a time of enormous contention. Liberal Republicans, as they called themselves, were eager to end the federal occupation of the South, effectively abandoning freed people attempting to claim their rights in the face of a campaign of terror and repression by former Confederates already under way. As Arenson shows, *American Progress* was a document designed to persuade the nation to ignore the unfinished business of liberty and to foreground the civilizing march of empire, a painting more about forgetting than remembering.

Images like *American Progress* evaded the dirty work of empire building, but ordinary Americans picked up their shovels and hoes, their rolling pins and washtubs. It was still not clear, in far-flung territorial outposts of the nation, who was in charge, who counted as American, who enjoyed the rights of citizenship. The Fourteenth Amendment to the Constitution guaranteed to freed men the privileges and immunities of citizenship, but the amendment explicitly withheld those rights from both women and "Indians not taxed." The country that had always been, and still was, home to diverse native peoples, and that for centuries had been home to the descendants of the Spanish and Mexicans, now saw an influx of thousands of immigrants. These were Chinese and Irish men laboring to build the transcontinental railroad that was then inching its way eastward from California and westward from Nebraska, as well as former soldiers from both sides looking to make a new start or, all too often, fleeing authority; freed people claiming their liberty; and families from everywhere hoping to get a little land, make a little stake, make a home.

This diverse and fluid mix of people could be found in some of the most remote places in the West, including the town of South Pass City. In my essay, I follow one woman, Janet McOmie Sherlock Smith, who had come from Scotland to the United States with a party of Mormon immigrants, walked across the country to Utah, and found her way to the mining boomtown of South Pass City, Wyoming. As a woman, Janet Sherlock Smith made choices that were circumscribed by marriage and motherhood. But like so many women of her time, the vagaries of fortune and the deaths of both her husbands often threw her on her own resources. Her two wedding dresses represent a life of determination and adaptation, privation and persistence. Over more than half a century of tough living, Janet and her children held on in South Pass City, long after the mining boom busted. Without "stickers" like Janet Sherlock Smith to lay claim to the remote reaches of vast space, the dream of the American empire would have remained an abstraction, perpetually besieged.

As women like Janet Smith began to claim their rights in the West, forms of unfree labor persisted in that region as well as in the South. White Southerners hurried to replace chattel slavery with restrictions that gave black Southerners not much more freedom than they had enjoyed before the war. As Maria Montoya's essay reveals, long-standing and incredibly complex forms of not-quite-free labor, mingling the vestiges of captivity and kinship, persisted in the Southwest too, well into the twentieth century. A family photograph, a painting, and a santo testify to the murky relationships along a spectrum of kinship and freedom in New Mexico villages. At the same time, Chinese immigrants came to the United States under oppressive work contracts, and certain documents, such as a certificate of residence, show us how the Chinese struggled to assert their rights as free people. Freedom, it seems, eluded some of those who had newly arrived in the empire seeking liberty, as well as some with deep roots in Western soil.

The trauma of the Civil War reshaped the West in many ways, just as the West served as both catalyst and catharsis for the nation's crisis. Some of those most grievously affected sought healing in the West. As William Deverell's moving essay demonstrates, some veterans, including members of the notorious Brown family, sought to heal the anguish of Antietam with the peace of Pasadena. Inspired by one of the weirdest objects in the Autry collection, a lamp made from the carved halves of a steer's horns, Deverell finds the human stories that unite seemingly separate images and narratives.

Sometimes, such objects bring the past very much into the present. Jennifer Denetdale's essay mingles the personal, the familial, the scholarly, and the historical currents that came together when she brought to the Navajo Nation, from the Autry collections, the blanket and dress that had belonged to her great-great-great-grandmother, known as Juanita, and whose Diné name was Asdzáá Tł'ógi (Lady Weaver). As members of Denetdale's family came together to view and talk about the textiles, they shared stories, added to the scholar's knowledge and understanding, and deepened their connections to one another and to their collective history. Denetdale's story shows us how past events live on in memory and reflection and in the possibilities of the future.

The essays in this volume, and the objects that inspired them, do not encompass the entire history of the long struggle over land and freedom, nationhood and citizenship, justice and power, diversity and unity. They cannot tell the tangled tale of continental conquest that spawned a national cataclysm. Not by a long shot. Neither does this volume resolve the dilemmas of empire or achieve the dream of liberty. But in bringing these stories together, we hope to create a more capacious and complicated American story, told across a broader battlefield, moving in many directions, an ongoing story in which all Americans can find a place.

NOTES

1. See James F. Brooks, *Captives and Cousins: Slavery, Kinship and Community in the Southwest Borderlands* (Chapel Hill: University of North Carolina Press, 2001). See also Juliana Barr, *Peace Came in the Form of a Woman: Indians and Spaniards in the Texas Borderlands* (Chapel Hill: University of North Carolina Press, 2007); Ned Blackhawk, *Violence over the Land: Indians and Empires in the Early American West* (Cambridge, MA: Harvard University Press, 2008); Pekka Hämäläinen, *The Comanche Empire* (New Haven, CT: Yale University Press, 2009); Brian DeLay, *War of a Thousand Deserts: Indian Raids and the U.S.-Mexican War* (New Haven, CT: Yale University Press, 2009).

2. James P. Ronda, *Lewis and Clark among the Indians* (1984; bicentennial edition, Lincoln: University of Nebraska Press, 2002).

3. Adam Rothman, *Slave Country: American Expansion and the Origins of the Deep South* (Cambridge, MA: Harvard University Press, 2005); Walter Johnson, *River of Dark Dreams: Slavery and Empire in the Cotton Kingdom* (Cambridge, MA: Harvard University Press, 2013).

4. Daniel K. Richter, *Facing East from Indian Country: A Native History of Early America* (Cambridge, MA: Harvard University Press, 2003); Daniel K. Richter, *Before the Revolution: America's Ancient Pasts* (Cambridge, MA: Harvard University Press, 2011); Colin Calloway, *One Vast Winter Count: The Native American West before Lewis and Clark* (Lincoln: University of Nebraska Press, 2006).

5. Anne F. Hyde, *Empires, Nations, and Families: A New History of the North American West, 1800–1860* (Lincoln: University of Nebraska Press, 2011).

6. See Elliott West, "Reconstructing Race," *Western Historical Quarterly* 34, no. 1 (Spring 2003): 6–26; Heather Cox Richardson, *West from Appomattox: The Reconstruction of America after the Civil War* (New Haven, CT: Yale University Press, 2007); Adam Arenson, *The Great Heart of the Republic: St. Louis and the Cultural Civil War* (Cambridge, MA: Harvard University Press, 2011); Stacey L. Smith, *Freedom's Frontier: California and the Struggle over Unfree Labor, Emancipation, and Reconstruction* (Chapel Hill: University of North Carolina Press, 2013); D. Michael Bottoms, *An Aristocracy of Color: Race and Reconstruction in California and the West, 1850–1890* (Norman: University of Oklahoma Press, 2013).

1

THE PRICE OF SLAVERY
ACROSS EMPIRE
Family, Community, and Loss in Texas

Brenda E. Stevenson

William Garrett made a tremendous purchase in 1851, even for a wealthy cotton planter. The Tennessee-born Texas slaveholder bought 11 women and children for $2,500—an amount of labor worth approximately $1 million in today's economy.[1] His expenditures for slave labor were not the actions of an irrational or naive spendthrift. Indeed, Garrett got quite a bargain, and he must have known it. He, like so many white Southerners who poured into Texas during the 1830s, 1840s, and 1850s, believed that his future financial security was intimately tied to the production of sizable cotton, corn, sugar, and grain harvests, and that those harvests, in turn, depended on fertile soil and slave labor. These were truisms that Garrett bet on; and he won that bet, even during the recession of the 1850s. Having arrived in the 1820s with his father, Jacob, who was one of the first white Americans to settle on the Brazos River in the east Texas vicinity of San Augustine, William had served, in 1836, in the militia commanded by William Kimbrough, which had helped gain Texas's independence from Mexico. Over the course of the next three decades, Garrett had amassed substantial wealth in land and slaves. In 1850, the thirty-eight-year-old possessed real estate worth $14,700 and 22 slaves. Ten years later, he owned 132 bondspeople.[2] On the eve of the Civil War, William Garrett could look back over his life as a child of a pioneering settler, his career as a "founding" Texan and planter, and his status as a namesake of a local municipality and be assured that he had managed to create a fortune in, and by, his slaves. His receipts for slave purchases included in this exhibition are a lasting testimony to sound investments made during a time when cotton was king and African slaves still were being smuggled into Texas via Cuba and New Orleans.

9

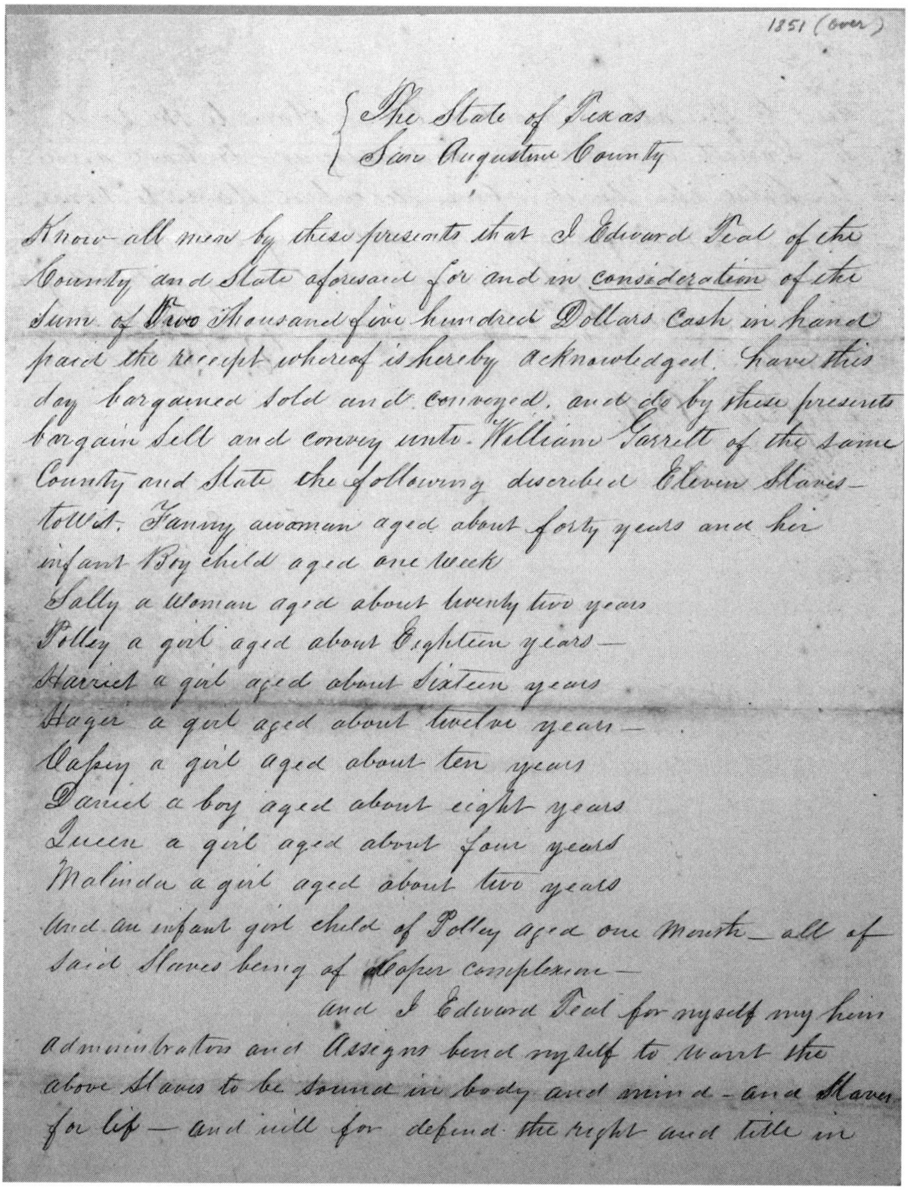

1851 (over)

The State of Texas
San Augustine County

Know all men by these presents that I Edward Teal of the County and State aforesaid for and in consideration of the sum of Two Thousand five hundred Dollars Cash in hand paid the receipt whereof is hereby acknowledged, have this day bargained sold and conveyed, and do by these presents bargain sell and convey unto William Garrett of the same County and State the following described Eleven Slaves— to wit: Fanny a woman aged about forty years and her infant Boy child aged one week

Sally a Woman aged about twenty two years
Polley a girl aged about Eighteen years—
Harriet a girl aged about Sixteen years
Hager a girl aged about twelve years—
Casey a girl aged about ten years
Daniel a boy aged about eight years
Queen a girl aged about four years
Malinda a girl aged about two years
And an infant girl child of Polley aged one Month— all of said Slaves being of Coper complexion—

and I Edward Teal for myself my heirs administrators and Assigns bind myself to warrant the above Slaves to be sound in body and mind— and Slaves for life— and will for defend the right and title in

FIGURE 1.1
William Garrett's bill of sale for eleven slave men, women, and children, 1851. Rosenstock Collection, Autry Library Collection, Autry National Center, 90.253.4100.32. For a color version of this image, see plate 1.

But these symbols of a rapidly amassed fortune that was foundational for the Garrett family meant just the opposite for the slaves who were sold, rented, bequeathed, bred, and stolen to fulfill the labor needs of ambitious farmers and planters like Jacob and William. Sales such as those documented in the receipts of the Garretts meant destabilization and, often, destruction of slave families. William seemed to prefer to purchase young, fertile women who would increase his slave property as they reached adulthood. According to the sale receipt from 1851, for example, he purchased only bits and pieces of slave families and communities: 40-year-old Fanny and her infant son, and 18-year-old Polly and her baby, were the only family ties delineated. The others he bought—22-year-old Sally, 16-year-old Harriet, 12-year-old Hagar, 10-year-old Massey, and the even younger Daniel, Queen, and Marinda—could have been part of an extended family, the children and grandchildren of Fanny. That would be the best scenario. But even if that were the case, still glaringly absent were Fanny's husband—the children's father and grandfather—and other community members. Perhaps William was following the example set by Jacob, who, for instance, purchased an enslaved woman, Hagar, and her child, Hannah, in March 1842, but not other members of that family.[3] Additional blacks William bought in the 1840s came singly or in smaller, probably more fractured, groups. On December 11, 1840, for example, Garrett acquired, for one thousand dollars, Polly and her twin children, but no one else. Another receipt, dated August 19, 1841, indicates that William purchased eight-year-old Madison for three hundred dollars, but none of the boy's family. Garrett, a typical slaveholder, bought blacks in "lots," not as couples, families, or communities.[4] Commodification of the black body—the essence of the enslavement of Africans and those of African descent in the American South and Southwest—severed physical ties with blood, marital, and extended kin time and time again, leaving many to feel, as did Adeline Marsh, who had been purchased as a baby and taken to Texas without her family members, that "black folks jes' raise up like cattle in de stable."[5]

The price of slavery was exorbitant for black family and community life in Texas, where bondspeople arrived in the thousands during the last decades before the Civil War, causing the slave population to almost quadruple between 1850 and 1860 alone. Most had been forced to leave kin and community behind or shed their families while on their journeys south and west. While creole slaves were the majority sold in or moved to Texas, others, perhaps thousands, were new arrivals from across the Black Atlantic, brought in clandestinely in violation of federal and international laws. Acquiring strong workers and fertile bodies was a sure way to make a fast buck if you were a trader, or to invest in a lucrative agricultural enterprise if you were a planter like William Garrett. The prices paid in cash, cotton, land, and other property, as indicated by the bills of sale found in this exhibition, varied according to the designs of the market, buyer criteria, and a slave's personal attributes. The price of slavery for the enslaved, however, was remarkably stable across the generations—a devastatingly high toll on family and communal life. The Civil War exaggerated this cost as thousands of slaveholders raced to Texas with only their most valuable slaves, leaving behind, or selling to others, their property's kin and friends.

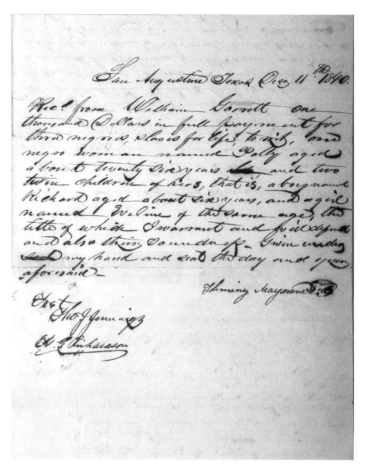

The notion that Texas was a safe haven for slavery while the United States fought a war that fundamentally threatened the institution proved to be an especially severe blow to slave family stability.

THE EVOLUTION OF A PECULIARLY TEXAN INSTITUTION

Texas was, indeed, the last frontier of antebellum Southern slavery, the institution having endured hundreds of years of Spanish, Mexican, and finally U.S. attempts at crafting an American empire in what would become the West. The Lone Star state had a history of colonial occupation and slavery that reached back to the early sixteenth century, when the Moroccan slave Estevanico arrived with his master, Andres Dorantes de Carranza, at a location near present-day Galveston in 1528. Estevanico was among the first Atlantic world explorers and slaves to travel in what is today the American Southwest but what was then the northwest frontier of the Spanish American empire. Sold as a child without parents or kin in 1513 by Portuguese slave traders to Carranza, Estevanico, as a slave, eventually journeyed to Florida, Texas, Mexico City, and the Gulf of California, before being killed by the Zunis in 1539. Like many of the slaves of Anglo whites in Texas who would arrive in the 1800s, Estevanico was sold multiple times on the western frontier he traversed.[6]

For the next three hundred years, Texas, as a part of the Spanish empire, and then in 1821, as a part of the new republic of Mexico, was the site of black slavery.[7] Under Spanish control, the institution largely was centered in and around the towns of San Antonio, Nacogdoches, and Goliad (Bahia).[8] Colonial Texas slavery was, however, extremely marginalized—numerically and in terms of economic impact—when compared to the African presence and influence in other parts of the empire, particularly Hispaniola (later Santo Domingo), Venezuela, Peru, Puerto Rico, and Cuba, and even when compared to other areas of New Spain, such as Mexico City, Veracruz, Guerrero, Oaxaca, Morelos, Michoacán, and the Yucatan.[9] Historian L. B. Rout Jr. calculates that a total of 1.5 million Africans arrived in these areas during the entire Spanish colonial era (1500–1810),[10] while Herman Bennett estimates that almost 680,000 blacks (slave and free) resided in all of Mexico in 1796.[11] In 1790, however, only 37 slaves lived in what would become Texas.[12] Documents from these eras indicate that black slaves served in a variety of roles in the colonial economies of New Spain—working in gold and silver mines, on agricultural estates and livestock ranches, as pearl divers, in textile factories, at missions, in cities as domestics of all sorts, and as skilled artisans, sex laborers, and teamsters, and even as part of the local militias.[13]

Prices of African slaves and slaves of African descent in New Spain could be steep.[14] A record from as early as the mid-sixteenth century, for example, is remarkably reminiscent of William Garrett's 1851 purchases.[15] This 1554 receipt indicates that the widow Velez Rascon, of the Mexican city of Puebla, was willing to pay 1,110 pesos of "pure gold" for six slaves—two men, two women, and two children—an inflated price, since most adults typically cost about 150 gold pesos at the time.[16] Regardless of cost, Rascon's bill of sale reveals consequences for slave family life that were also evident in William Garrett's bill of sale three hundred years later: dislocation and separation of at least some vital members of the kinship group. Although the Catholic Church expected slaves in the Spanish empire to convert to Christianity, and their owners to allow them to take on the sacrament of marriage, most masters acted out of the belief that blacks were morally and intellectually inferior, good only for work and the production of future workers. The countervailing forces of racism and economic expediency in Spanish America (including Texas) eroded, and often openly desecrated, slave marriage and family life.[17]

It is ironic that black slavery began to grow and actually flourish in Texas just as Mexico was poised to end it. Independent Mexico outlawed slavery in 1829.[18] In the eight years between independence and abolition, however, Moses and Stephen Austin had managed to gain permission to settle a colony of U.S. Anglos in Texas. Immigrants such as William Garrett's father, Jacob, rushed in to claim fertile land and establish plantations.[19] By 1825, there were 444 slaves in Austin's colony alone—24 percent of that settlement's population.[20] In 1834, reportedly 1,000 bondspeople resided in Brazos, and another 1,000 in Nacogdoches.[21]

The tension over the ability of U.S. citizens to settle in and bring slaves to Mexico's Texas, as well as the right of masters already there to maintain their human property, fueled great political, economic, cultural, and, eventually, military tension.[22] When the war for Texas independence finally broke out in 1835, there seemed little doubt that, if the "revolutionaries" prevailed, black slavery would be guaranteed. And so it was.[23] Even as the war was being fought, traders were smuggling bondspersons into Galveston.[24]

In fact, once Texas became part of the United States, the rush by new Anglo migrants to purchase slaves boosted their prices greatly, from close to $345 each in 1845 to about $800 in 1860.[25] Even on the brink of the Civil War, it still was not unheard of for Texas slaveholders to buy prime male hands for $1,500 or even $1,800, and prime females for $800.[26] William Garrett, as noted earlier, obviously happened onto a bargain in 1851 when he purchased eleven slaves for $2,500. Although only five were prime workers, his average price of $227 was a steal by any measure.[27]

SLAVE LIFE IN LATE-ANTEBELLUM TEXAS

The cost of being purchased was, for slave men, women, and children in Texas, familial loss and emotional devastation. Even by age eight, as documented in William Garrett's 1841 receipt for the purchase of the boy Madison, children were being forced to leave their parents and vice versa. The autobiographical accounts of former slaves are replete with examples of painful separations related to the developing institution of chattel slavery in Texas, an institution that included only 40,308 slaves in 1848, but which had expanded to 169,166 by 1861.[28] This tremendous growth, mostly a result of the domestic slave trade, placed great pressure on slave family life.

Unlike many former Texas slaves who knew, or remembered, little of their family history, Silvia King was certain of her personal history. She had been born in Morocco, where she was married and had three children. That was before she was sold as a slave and taken to Bordeaux, France, trained as a chef, and sold again to traders smuggling human cargo into New Orleans. There, a trader going to Texas purchased her.[29] Silvia had had to leave her Moroccan family, and then leave what community she had acquired in France. Others affected were the children left behind or who were part of the trade themselves. Tom Robinson of Cass County, Texas, recalled, for example: "I can just barely remember my mother. I was not 11 when they sold me away from her."[30] Sarah Ashley recounted that she had been born in Mississippi but sold as a child to someone in Texas. Her sisters and father were sold in Georgia. "Us family was sep'rated," she explained.[31] Mandy Tucker revealed, "I was large enough to know when they took my parents to Texas, but I didn't know how serious it was till they was gone. . . . They left me

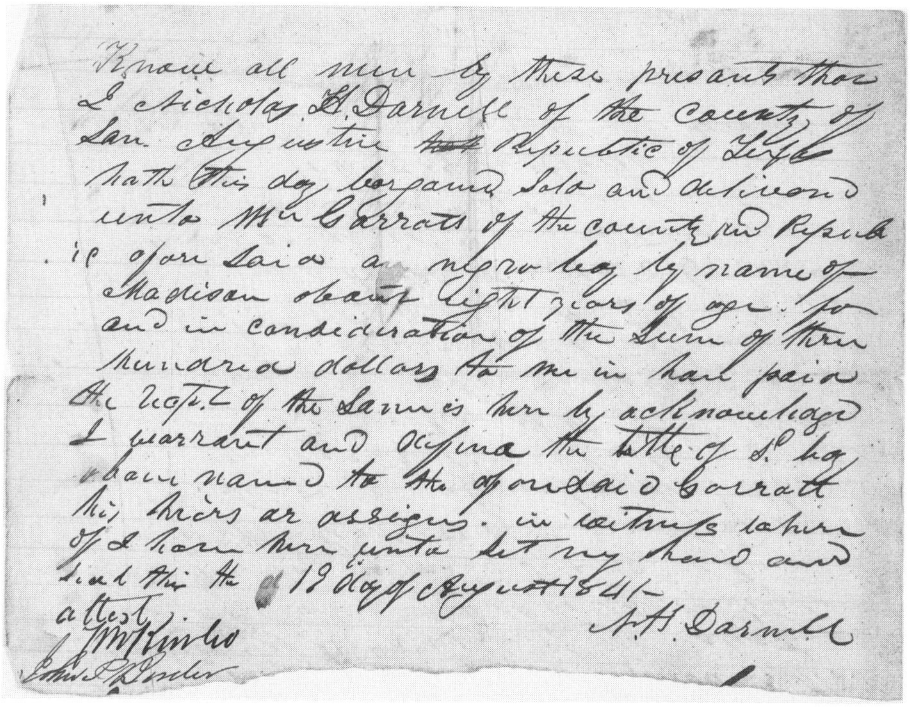
Know all men by these presents that I Nicholas H. Darnell of the County of San Augustine ~~and~~ Republic of Texas hath this day bargained sold and delivered unto Mr Garrett of the county and Republic aforesaid a negro boy by name of Madison about eight years of age. for and in consideration of the sum of three hundred dollars to me in hand paid the receipt of the same is here by acknowledged I warrant and defend the title of sd boy above named to the aforesaid Garrett his heirs or assigns. in witness whereof I have here unto set my hand and seal this the 19 day of August 1841—
N.H. Darnell
attest
J M Kimbro

FIGURE 1.3
William Garrett's bill of sale for eight-year-old Madison, 1841. Rosenstock Collection, Autry Library Collection, Autry National Center, 90.253.4100.25.

with the old doctor woman."[32] "They sold Grandma's daughter to somebody in Texas," Luke Dixon remembered. "She cried and begged to let them be together. They didn't pay no 'tenshion to her."[33]

Movement of slave property was an expensive enterprise for owners and a physically and emotionally brutal experience for the enslaved. Mariah Robinson was given away as a wedding gift. She traveled by steamship and stagecoach to Waco.[34] Others came in wagons, and many walked. Henrietta Ralls, for one, walked as a child from Mississippi to Arkansas and then to Texas.[35] Hezekiah Steel also walked. So too did Ben Simpson of Georgia, along with his mother and sister. Along the way, Simpson's sadistic master killed Ben's mother because she could not keep up with his pace.[36]

Movement during the Civil War era took on an even more intense speed. Many slaveholders believed that Texas was the last and best hope for retaining their bondspeople even if freedom came to other parts of the South. Henrietta Ralls recalled, "The owners was tryin' to hide the colored people. Our white folks took us clear out in Texas to keep the Yankees from gettin' 'em."[37] J. L. Smith explained that his owners "were running from one place to the other to keep the Yankees from freeing the slaves."[38] Senia Rassberry remembered that "our white folks took us to Texas during the War. . . . My mother died

FIGURE 1.4
Photograph of Sarah Ashley, a former Texas
slave sold as a child, May 28, 1937. Library of
Congress, Manuscripts Division.

there with a congestive chill."[39] George Robertson of Tennessee recounted, "They took my mama off when I was a baby to keep the Yankees from gettin' her."[40] William Hamilton lost his family while being moved to Texas by a trader during the war: "Dat trader was on his way south with my folks and a lot of other slaves, takin' 'em somewhere to sell." He left William by himself on the Buford plantation.[41] Elvira Boles lost her child on the trail to Texas: "Marster said dey was runnin' us from de Yankees to keep us, but we was free and didn' know it. Died at Red River and we left it. . . . Dey say we'd never be free iffen dey could git to Texas wid us."[42]

Those persons who arrived in Texas in the 1840s and 1850s, like the Garretts who had come in the 1830s, settled mainly in the east; but slavery eventually flourished in most of the state. San Augustine, Brazoria, and Matagorda Counties had particularly heavy slave concentrations in 1840; by 1850, nineteen counties had more than a thousand slaves each; and in 1860, large numbers of enslaved persons could be found everywhere except in west Texas and a few areas north.[43]

Most late-antebellum slaves lived in the Texas countryside. The initial economic outlay for the land, slaves, equipment, seed, and work animals was high, and slaveholders held their black laborers to a rigorous work routine, reaping fast profits.[44] The impact on slave bodies and families could be destructive. Edgar Bendy recounted that he rarely spent time with his parents after he was hired out as a nurse in town while his parents

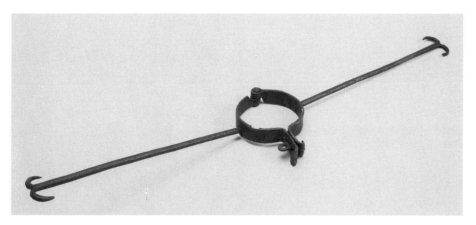

FIGURE 1.5

Slave collar used for punishing fugitive slaves, mid-nineteenth century. Autry National Center, 98.8.1.

worked on his master's cotton and sugar plantation.[45] William Rimm of San Patricio recalled that his father had to work despite illness. "Dey wants you to work if you can or can't," Rimm explained. "My pappy have de back mis'ry, and many de time I seed him crawl to de grist mill. Him am buyed 'cause him an de good millhand."[46] Elvira Boles worked in her master's brickyard, doing the same work as the men. "I toted brick back and put 'em down where dey had to be. Six bricks each load all day. . . . Ise worked to death."[47] Adeline Marsh recalled that her owner and his drivers were relentless: "All de time whippin' and stroppin' de niggers to make dem work harder. Didn't make no difference to Cap'n how little you is, you goes out to de field mos' soon's you can walk."[48]

Owners used powerful incentives to make their slaves work as intensely, and consistently, as possible. Sarah Ford from West Columbia explained that her owner allowed their black driver to work and whip his slaves harshly. "Uncle Big Jake sho' work de slaves from early mornin' till night. When you is in de field you better not lag none. . . . Massa Charles run dat plantation jus' like a factory."[49] Slaves complained about not only cruel masters but also cruel mistresses. Julia Banks in San Antonio, for one, remembered one woman who was so cruel to a female slave that "she would make the men tie her down, and she had what they called cat-o-nine tail, and after she got the blood to come, she would dip it in salt and pepper and whip her again. Oh, she was mean!"[50] Banks noted that her own mistress "wasn't good" either. She would try to force her husband to beat the women, but he often refused. "He would say, 'Them are your slaves. You whip them.'"[51]

Slaves responded to overexertion, extreme punishment, starvation, and other forms of abuse with consistent, but diverse, resistance strategies. Many stole; some fought back; others ran away; some even committed suicide. One ex-slave explained that an elderly man on her plantation killed himself after being whipped. The next morning they saw "old Beans, what's so old he can't work good no more . . . hangin' from a tree back of de quarters.

FIGURE 1.6
Photograph of Adeline Cunningham,
age eighty-five, former Texas slave
woman, circa 1936–38. Library of
Congress, Manuscripts Division.

He done hang himself to 'scape he mis'ry!"[52] Walter Rimm remembered that "when massa start to whip him [Bob Love] he cuts his throat and dives into de river. He am dat scairt of a whippin' dat he kilt himself."[53] Walter's father and another slave named John were serial fugitives. Walter assumed that John eventually escaped to Mexico, "where a lot of de slaves runs to."[54] Lavinia Bell, who was held near Galveston, repeatedly tried to escape. She eventually made it to Canada, but the toll her resistance took on her was extreme. According to Bell and the Montreal physician John Reddy, who examined her, the price of slavery that she paid was cut, burnt, broken, and beaten into her body—slit ears, broken-out teeth, a broken jaw, skull fractures, large brands on her abdomen and hand, scars and marks covering her back and most of her body, and a finger that had been cut off.[55] Adeline Cunningham recalled that a slave who ran away in Lavaca County was blinded for his efforts.[56]

Certainly, not all enslaved individuals were treated as barbarically as Bell or those known by Cunningham. Slaves were, after all, valuable property. There is even evidence that some owners, such as Cynthia Ewing, supported the desire of their most "favored" slaves to gain freedom. Ewing petitioned the Texas legislature in 1847, for example, to allow Delilah, her cook, to purchase herself. More than eighty other Houston whites signed Ewing's petition.[57]

The bills of sale given to William Garrett, and found in this exhibition, leave few clues to how his slaves lived. What one can discern from these receipts and the lists of his slaves found in federal census records, however, is that Garrett was particularly interested

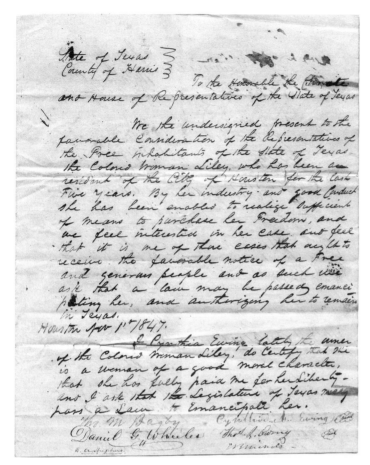

FIGURE 1.7
Petition for the Emancipation
of Liley, November 1, 1847.
Courtesy of Texas State Library
& Archives Commission.

in expanding his slave property. This suggests that he probably did not sell slaves unless they proved to be particularly problematic, because they were runaways or were disruptive, or because they were infertile or unable to work.

As noted earlier, Garrett seemed especially interested in purchasing female slaves who were fertile, as documented by his 1840 and 1851 receipts. He may have paired these women, whether they were willing or not, with some of the many men he owned. In 1860, for example, William Garrett had 29 women of childbearing age; 40 men between the ages of 15 and 50; and 51 youth between the ages of 1 and 14 years.[58] Certainly most of these children belonged to the women, and at least some of the men, on his plantation. Others undoubtedly had fathers on neighboring properties; but Garrett, as the owner of the mother, would be these children's master. One cannot know whether Garrett, or his father Jacob, invested in slave breeding.

Still there is much evidence to suggest that antebellum Texas, probably because it was the frontier of a thriving slave economy in which the price of slaves continued to rise, was the site of much forced slave coupling. Rose Williams was clear about the pressure her Texas owner put on her to "marry" Rufus, a man she despised because he was a bully. When she refused to have sex with Rufus, her owner told her flat out: "Woman, I's pay big money for you and I's done dat for de cause I wants yous to raise me chillens. I's put yous to live with Rufus for dat purpose. Now, if you doesn't want whippin' at de stake, yous do what I wants."[59] Sarah Ford recalled that "de white folks don't let de slaves what works in de field marry none, dey jus' puts a man and bredin' woman together like mules. Iffen the woman don't like the man, it don't make no difference, she better go or dey gives her a hidin'."[60] Julia Moore of Lockhart, Texas, noted that her father was "made de husbands of lots of women on de place, 'cause he de big man."[61] Silvia King's owner asked her if she was married in her "old country," but when the Moroccan slave woman answered yes, it was no deterrent to her master marrying her to another slave man. Women's fertility often was measured by their girth— big women were assumed to be more fertile. Silvia's owner bought her because of her size. King noted, "When Marse Jones seed me on de block, he say, 'Dat's a whale of a woman.'" He married her to Bob, who was in charge of their owner's oxen teams.[62]

Sexual labor and the production of additional enslaved laborers were part and parcel of what owners expected from their enslaved females, and males. William Garrett purchased women who were young enough to have numerous children, who would then belong to him. Census records from 1860 indicate that Mr. Garrett had no mulatto women or children among his slave property, which strongly suggests that he did not demand sexual liaisons with his slave women. Certainly other Texas slaveholders did. One former slave spoke openly about the "No Nation" (neither black nor white, she explained) slaves on her plantation: "I hear say he [the master] don't have no wife, but a black woman what stays at de house. Dat de reason so many 'No Nation' niggers around."[63] Sarah Ford also recalled the African woman named Rose who had been a concubine for both her master and, later, her master's brother. "Massa Kit have a African woman from Kentucky for he wife, and dat's de truth," she explained. "I ain't sayin' iffen she a real wife or not, but all de slaves has to call her 'Miss Rachel.'"[64]

Undoubtedly, Texas slaves belonging to William Garrett and others struggled to maintain some semblance of family and community life, despite the tremendous pressures of labor, the daily humiliations, the constant threat of sale or punishment, and sometimes even being forced into sexual relations and marriages or made part of breeding schemes. While most who survived to tell their histories offered overwhelming evidence that life on the Texas frontier was harsh and sometimes unforgivably, even horrifically, cruel, they also offer glimpses of family and community life that, at least for some period of time, made their existence bearable. Some, for example, spoke of having fun at corn huskings, quilting bees, hog-killing time, hunting parties, and secret church meetings, as well as during the Christmas holidays, when most were off for at least a few days and had extra food rations.[65] C. B. McRay of Jasper fondly recalled playing marbles and "town ball" and having his mother sing to him the lullaby "Bye-o Baby Buntin'."[66] Many also recounted the camaraderie and sense of community borne of group resistance or trying to help runaways or family members.[67]

Harrison Beckett was a slave of I. D. Thomas in San Augustine County, where William Garrett resided. Frederick Law Olmsted commented on San Augustine and its surrounding plantations when he passed through it. Perhaps together, Beckett's recollections and some of Olmsted's observations can shed light on what it might have been like for Garrett's slaves.

Olmsted was none too impressed with the county or town of San Augustine, noting its large number of poor whites, scantily clad slaves, and dilapidated slave cabins.[68] Former slave Beckett recalled that life had been difficult, but that he had had the opportunity to reside with his parents and older siblings, all of whom were field-workers. Both parents had been bought as individuals by Texans, but had not been sold after they married and had children for Thomas. Their slave community was somewhat smaller than that of William Garrett's slaves, with about a hundred bondspeople spread across two farms of approximately 150 acres each. Harrison explained that his mother worked long hours for Thomas, only coming "in from de field at nine or ten o'clock at night," and that often "she be all wore out and too tired to cook lots of times." Still, she prepared dinner for the family, and then "she's so tired she go to bed without eatin' nothin' herself." Beckett's family had lived in typical slave lodgings: "pole houses and some in split log houses, with two rooms, one for to sleep in and one for to cook in." Furnishings were sparse and spare, but all included some form of bedding. Clothing was minimal and usual. As a boy, Harrison wore shirttails that came down below his knees, and sometimes he wore pants in the winter. Full hands received pants, shirts, dresses, shoes, and coats in the winter; and in the summer they were given hats and scarves, along with another set of clothes. Beckett's owner did allow the women to "pick up cotton from de ground" during "ginning time" and make mattresses and quilts. A slave weaver made most of the slave cloth, but Beckett's owner also bought cloth for slave seamstresses to make into clothing. Harrison did not complain bitterly about the whippings he received, noting that sometimes his master would allow Harrison's father to whip him—a rare indication of slave patriarchal authority. The boy's work was to take care of his master's stock and help the domestic slave women. "Old Massa he care for he hands purty well, considerin' everything," Beckett concluded.

Still, at the end of the Civil War, Harrison lost a key member of his family. His father, who initially had been sold away from his kin in Florida, returned to them, leaving Harrison, his Texas wife, and other children behind. Harrison's mother, who was from Georgia, remained in Texas, deciding not to claim her former kin.[69] The price of slavery was indeed much higher for the enslaved than indicated by the prices written on the bills of sale belonging to Jacob and William Garrett and included in this exhibition. It was a bill they continued to pay long past emancipation.

NOTES

1. Bill of sale to William Garrett, c. 1851, San Augustine County, folder 21, San Augustine, Texas, Papers, 1783–1937, Institute for the Study of the American West, Autry National Center

(hereafter Garrett Papers); MeasuringWorth.com provides a formula for assessing the present-day value of past currency. See also Randolph B. Campbell, *An Empire for Slavery: The Peculiar Institution in Texas* (Baton Rouge: Louisiana State Press, 1989), 275; Laurie E. Jasinski, "Garrett, William," *Handbook of Texas Online,* Texas State Historical Association, modified on October 24, 2013, www.tshaonline.org/handbook/online/articles/fga57, published by the Texas State Historical Association.

2. 1850 U.S. Census, San Augustine, TX, roll M432_914, page 336A, image 322, Ancestry .com; *1860 U.S. Federal Census—Slave Schedules,* online database, Provo, UT, 2010; U.S. Bureau of the Census, *Eighth Census of the United States, 1860* (Washington, DC: National Archives and Records Administration, 1860), M653, 1,438 rolls. The data is also found in the online database *Texas, Land Title Abstracts, 1700–2008,* Ancestry.com, http://search.ancestry.com /cgi-bin/sse.dll?db=1860slaveschedules&indiv=try&h=2404763&requr=294915&ur=0&dny ref=1, accessed March 28, 2013.

3. Bill of sale to Jacob Garrett, March 15, 1842, Garrett Papers.

4. Work Projects Administration, *Texas Narratives,* pt. 3, in vol. 16 of *Slave Narratives: A Folk History of Slavery in the United States from Interviews with Former Slaves,* Kindle edition (Washington, DC: Work Projects Administration, 1936–38), Kindle location 542–68 (hereafter *Texas Narratives*).

5. See, for example, J. L. Smith, "Chenango Plantation," Brazosport Archeological Society, Life on the Brazos River website, http://lifeonthebrazosriver.com/Chenango%20Plantation .htm, accessed March 28, 2013.

6. Campbell, *An Empire for Slavery,* 10; Donald E. Chipman, "Estevanico," *Handbook of Texas Online,* last updated November 5, 2013, www.tshaonline.org/handbook/online/articles /feso8, published by the Texas State Historical Association; "Estevanico, the Black Conquistador," PBS, n.d., www.pbs.org/opb/conquistadors/namerica/adventure2/a10.htm, accessed March 28, 2013.

7. It is not certain if enslaved blacks participated in the failed attempt by René-Robert Cavelier, Sieur de La Salle, to establish a French colony between 1685 and 1688 at what is today Inez, Texas. See, for example, volume 2 of *The Journeys of Rene Robert Cavelier, Sieur de La Salle,* ed. Isaac Cox (New York: Allerton, 1905), available at the University of North Texas Libraries, http://texashistory.unt.edu/ark:/67531/metapth6103/.

8. Campbell, *An Empire for Slavery,* 11.

9. Herman Bennett, *Africans in Colonial Mexico: Absolutism, Christianity and Afro-Creole Consciousness, 1570–1640* (Bloomington: Indiana University Press, 2003), 27. Most of these Africans came from Senegambia and Guinea in the sixteenth century; but primarily they were born in Angola and the Kingdom of Kongo, and some were born in the Gold Coast, Senegambia, and the Bights of Benin and Biafra in the seventeenth century, when approximately two thousand arrived annually. M. Malowist, "The Struggle for International Trade and Its Implications for Africa," in *Africa from the Sixteenth to the Eighteenth Century,* ed. B. A. Ogot, vol. 5 of *General History of Africa* (Berkeley: University of California Press, 1992), 8–9; J. E. Inikori, "Africa in World History: The Export Slave Trade from Africa and the Emergence of the Atlantic Economic Order," in Ogot, *Africa from the Sixteenth to the Eighteenth Century,* 106; Douglas W. Richmond, "Africa's Initial Encounter with Texas: The Significance of Afro-Tejanos in Colonial Tejas, 1528–1821," *Bulletin of Latin American Research* 26, no. 2 (April 2007): 4–6;

Lorena Madrigal, "The African Slave Trade and the Caribbean," *Human Biology of the Afro-Caribbean Populations* (Cambridge: Cambridge University Press, 2006), 3, http://assets .cambridge.org/97805218/19312/excerpt/9780521819312_excerpt.pdf.

10. Inikori, "Africa in World History," 81.

11. Bennett estimates that 151,018 lived in New Spain fifty years earlier, in 1646 (*Africans in Colonial Mexico,* 19); Inikori, "Africa in World History," 96, 103–4.

12. Campbell, *An Empire for Slavery,* 11.

13. Bennett, *Africans in Colonial Mexico,* 17–19; Matthew Restall, "Manuel's Worlds: Black Yucatan and the Colonial Caribbean," in *Slaves, Subjects, and Subversives: Blacks in Colonial Latin America,* ed. Jane Landers and Barry M. Robinson (Albuquerque: University of New Mexico Press, 2006), 147–74.

14. On the coasts and in the hinterlands of Africa, Portuguese and then Dutch and Flemish traders bartered for their human property, using copper, iron and brass bars and wire; firearms and ammunition; Indian textiles; cowries from the Maldives; silver coins; gold; glass beads; liquors; paper; and horses. Paul E. Lovejoy, *Transformations in Slavery: A History of Slavery in Africa,* 2nd ed. (Cambridge: Cambridge University Press, 2000), 107–10; Robin Law, *The Slave Coast of West Africa, 1550–1750: The Impact of the Atlantic Slave Trade on an African Society* (Oxford: Oxford University Press, 1990), 45–58; Inikori, "Africa in World History," 106.

15. An excerpt from the sixteenth-century receipt read: "I the widow Catalina Velez Rascon do hereby promise to pay to you, Diego de Villanueva, alderman of this City of los Angeles, 1,100 pesos of pure gold . . . for six slaves (piezas de esclavos), to wit: the Negro Lorenzo, *ladino,* born on the Island of Tercera (in the Azores), his wife Antonia, Negress, born in Biafara, with a young mulatto daughter of hers Maria, plus a Negro called Manuel, born in Zapa, and a Negress Catalina, born in Portugal, with a young Negro daughter of hers named Paula, making six slaves in all, all of whom were disposed of in public auction as part of the estate of Francisco Munoz, deceased, In two lots, and were sold to my son-in-law don Juan de Zuniga, bidding on my behalf. . . . Given in this city of los Angeles on the 16th day of July in the year of the birth of Our Savior Jesus Christ 1554." Quoted in Peter Boyd-Bowman, "Negro Slaves in Early Colonial Mexico," *The Americas* 26, no. 2 (October 1969): 134. Rascon's bits and pieces of purchased families included an individual (Manuel); a nuclear/blended family group (husband, wife, and stepdaughter—Lorenzo, Antonia, and Maria); and a matrifocal family unit (mother and daughter—Catalin and Paula). This early bill of sale also indicates many important attributes of the institution in colonial Mexico—some females owned slaves (even though a male member of Rascon's family actually appeared in public, at the auction, to purchase her slaves); slaves often were racially mixed; and slaves were supplied from various locales, in this case from the Azores and Biafra in Africa, from Portugal, and locally. Perhaps most important, both bills of sale indicate that, regardless of their place and cultures of origin, enslaved men and women believed that the creation and maintenance of family—nuclear, matrifocal, stem, extended, and so on—were vitally important. They persisted in their desire for family even in the face of great hostility to family stability.

16. Most of the slaves available for sale, and sought after, were young and male. Skilled males typically garnered the highest prices. Children commanded fifty-five pesos or less, and women might be priced slightly higher if they were mixed race, spoke Spanish well, were skilled, or were going to be employed as prostitutes or concubines. Ibid., 134, including n. 4.

17. Richmond, "Africa's Initial Encounter with Texas," 5–6.

18. Sean Kelley, "'Mexico in His Head': Slavery and the Texas-Mexico Border," *Journal of Social History* 37, no. 3 (Spring 2004): 711–13.

19. Indeed, Stephen Austin and other promoters argued forcefully to Mexican officials throughout the 1820s and 1830s that his new colony would be doomed if both the slave trade and the institution were outlawed. While Austin's diplomatic efforts bought only tenuous agreements and exceptions from the Mexican government to allow slavery in Texas, substantial growth in the number of planters and the slave population still occurred. Jacob Garrett, for example, arrived in 1822. Jared E. Groce migrated from Alabama, also in 1822, with 90 slaves, creating a cotton plantation on more than four thousand acres along the Brazos River. Six years later, Groce had 131 slaves and was Texas's largest slaveholder. Campbell indicates Groce was from Georgia (*An Empire for Slavery*, 16); Kelley states he was from Alabama ("'Mexico in His Head,'" 713).

20. Campbell, *An Empire for Slavery*, 19.

21. Some estimates even state the number as twice that amount—meaning that slaves would have been 20 percent of the nonnative population. Ibid., 31, 33.

22. Regarding the variables that led to the creation of the Republic of Texas, see ibid., 10–34; Kelley, "'Mexico in His Head,'" 713–17; Paul D. Lack, "Slavery and the Texas Revolution," *Southwestern Historical Quarterly* 89, no. 2 (October 1985): 181–202; Eugene C. Barker, "The Influence of Slavery in the Colonization of Texas," *Mississippi Valley Historical Review* 11, no. 1 (January 1924): 3–36.

23. The Texas Constitution of 1836 stated, "Congress shall pass no laws to prohibit emigrants from bringing their slaves into the republic with them, and holding them by the same tenure by which such slaves were held in the United States; nor shall congress have power to emancipate slaves; nor shall any slave holder be allowed to emancipate his or her slave or slaves without the consent of the congress." Campbell, *An Empire for Slavery*, 46–47.

24. Ibid., 46; also see Kelley, "'Mexico in His Head,'" 710, regarding the price of Texas slaves during this era.

25. Campbell, *An Empire for Slavery*, p. 71, table 2.

26. Ibid., pp. 72 and 73, table 4; Samuel H. Williamson and Louis P. Cain, "Measuring Slavery in 2011 Dollars," MeasuringWorth.com, www.measuringworth.com/slavery.php, accessed February 18, 2013; Robert E. Evans, "The Economics of American Negro Slavery," in *The Aspects of Labor Economics*, ed. Universities National Bureau (Princeton, NJ: Princeton University Press, 1962), 212.

27. The seller, Edward Ford, must have feared that he would not be able to sell the large parcel of mostly women and children for more; or perhaps Garrett was willing to pay in cash as an incentive for the low price.

28. Indeed, the number of slaves in Texas increased, on average, more than ten thousand persons per year, each year between 1850 and 1860, rendering Texas the state with the most growth in slaves, by far, in the nation that decade. Campbell, *An Empire for Slavery*, p. 56, table 1.

29. *Texas Narratives*, pt. 2, Kindle locations 3272–81.

30. Work Projects Administration, *Arkansas Narratives*, pt. 6, in vol. 2 of *Slave Narratives: A Folk History of Slavery in the United States from Interviews with Former Slaves*, Kindle edition

(Washington, DC: Work Projects Administration, 1936–38), Kindle location 679–85 (hereafter *Arkansas Narratives*).

31. Sarah Ashley, *Texas Slave Narratives*, http://freepages.genealogy.rootsweb.ancestry .com/~ewyatt/_borders/Texas%20Slave%20Narratives/Texas%20S/Ashley,%20Sarah.html, accessed March 25, 2013.

32. *Texas Narratives*, pt. 2, Kindle locations 3503–6.

33. National Humanities Center, 2009, http://nationalhumanitiescenter.org/pds/; Luke Dixon, "Born in Slavery: Slave Narratives from the Federal Writer's Project, 1936–1938" (full text [as digital images] of the WPA narratives is found in American Memory, Library of Congress, http://lcweb2.loc.gov/ammem/snhtml/snhome.html, accessed March 13, 2013). Also see the eighteenth- and nineteenth-century narratives at Documenting the American South, University of North Carolina at Chapel Hill Library, http://docsouth.unc.edu/index.html. Complete image credits are found at *The Making of African American Identity, Vol. 1, 1500–1865*, National Humanities Center, http://nationalhumanitiescenter.org/pds/maai/imagecredits .htm, accessed March 25, 2013.

34. *Texas Narratives*, pt. 3, Kindle location 2687–700.

35. *Arkansas Narratives*, pt. 6, Kindle location 177–83.

36. Ben Simpson, *Texas Slave Narratives*, http://freepages.genealogy.rootsweb.ancestry .com/~ewyatt/_borders/Texas%20Slave%20Narratives/Texas%20S/Simpson,%20Ben.html, accessed July 20, 2014.

37. *Arkansas Narratives*, pt. 6, Kindle location 177–83.

38. Ibid., 1950–52.

39. Ibid., 217–20.

40. Ibid., 600–602.

41. *Texas Narratives*, pt. 2, Kindle location 1326.

42. *Texas Narratives*, pt. 1, Kindle location 1175–78.

43. Campbell, *An Empire for Slavery*, 57–58.

44. Randolph Campbell, speaking of slave profitability in antebellum Texas, concludes that "slavery was the key to an agricultural economy in antebellum Texas that was profitable, self-sufficient in food production, and growing. Moreover, it performed numerous functions that, while not appearing in the profit-or-loss column on a balance sheet, were of great benefit to many Texans." Ibid., 95.

45. *Texas Narratives*, pt. 1, Kindle location 753–55.

46. *Texas Narratives*, pt. 2, Kindle location 2641–45.

47. *Texas Narratives*, pt. 1, Kindle location 1158–62.

48. *Texas Narratives*, pt. 3, Kindle location 542–68.

49. *Texas Narratives*, pt. 2, Kindle location 639–41.

50. *Texas Narratives*, pt. 1, Kindle location 1041–43.

51. Ibid.

52. *Texas Narratives*, pt. 3, Kindle location 542–68.

53. Ibid., Kindle location 2644–54.

54. Ibid.

55. Reddy described Lavinia Bell's wounds: "A V shaped piece has been slit out of each ear; there is a depression on the right parietal bone, where it has been fractured, and is now very

tender to the touch; the corresponding spot on the opposite side, has a large scar uncovered by hair; there is a large deep scar, 3 ½ inches long, on the left side of the lower jaw; several of her teeth are broken out; the back of her left hand has been branded with a heated flat-iron; the little finger of her right hand, with a portion of bone that it connected with, has been cut off; the abdomen bears the mark of a large letter 4 inches long in one way and 2 ½ inches in another, also branded with a hot iron; her ankles are scarred, and the soles of her feet are all covered with little round marks apparently inflicted by some sharp instrument, which she accounts for by stating that she was obliged to walk over hackles used for hackling flax; her back and person are literally covered over with scars and marks, now healed, evidently produced by the lash." John Blassingame, ed., *Slave Testimony: Two Centuries of Letters, Speeches, Interviews and Autobiographies* (Baton Rouge: Louisiana State University Press, 1977), 341–43.

56. *Texas Narratives*, pt. 1, Kindle location 2881.

57. "Petition for the Emancipation of Liley, November 1, 1847," Texas State Library and Archives Commission, last updated August, 29, 2011, www.tsl.state.tx.us/treasures/earlystate /delila-01.html.

58. *U.S. Federal Census—Slave Schedules*, online database, Ancestry.com, http://search .ancestry.com/cgi-bin/sse.dll?db=1860slaveschedules&indiv=try&h=2404763&requr=29491 5&ur=0&dnyref=1&nreg=1, accessed March 20, 2013.

59. "On Slaveholder's Sexual Abuse of Slaves: Selections from 19th and 20th Century Slave Narratives," *National Humanities Center Resource Toolbox: The Making of African American Identity: Vol. I, 1500–1865*, National Humanities Center, http://nationalhumanitiescenter.org /pds/maai/enslavement/text6/masterslavesexualabuse.pdf, accessed March 10, 2013.

60. *Texas Narratives*, pt. 2, Kindle location 618–19.

61. *Texas Narratives*, pt. 3, Kindle location 532–33.

62. *Texas Narratives*, pt. 2, Kindle location 3272–82.

63. *Texas Narratives*, pt. 3, Kindle location 542–68.

64. *Texas Narratives*, pt. 2, Kindle location 624.

65. *Texas Narratives*, pt. 1, Kindle location 1171–72.

66. *Texas Narratives*, pt. 3, Kindle location 488–518.

67. Blassingame, *Slave Testimony*, 342; *Texas Narratives*, pt. 2, Kindle location 612–14; *Texas Narratives*, pt. 3, Kindle location 2644–54.

68. Frederick Law Olmsted, *A Journey through Texas: Or, a Saddle-Trip on the Southwestern Frontier; with a Statistical Appendix*, 64–69, Making of America Books, http://quod.lib.umich .edu/m/moa/aaw3927.0001.001/107?page=root;size=100;view=image.

69. Harrison Beckett's autobiographical account is found in *Texas Narratives*, pt. 1, Kindle location 621–58.

2

THE FRÉMONTS
Agents of Empire, Legends of Liberty

John Mack Faragher

John Charles and Jessie Benton Frémont arrived at the Southern Pacific Depot in Los Angeles on Christmas Eve 1887. Pleading exhaustion after their transcontinental journey, they left a small crowd of greeters on the platform and caught a hack to the Hotel Oxford on North Main Street, near the city's old plaza. There, forty-one years before, after signing a treaty that ended the American war of conquest in California, Frémont had ordered the five hundred men of the California Battalion to pitch their tents. The *Los Angeles Times* reminded readers of that accomplishment in a note of welcome to the elderly couple. General Frémont had "done as much to make a pathway for empire across the continent as any man in the history of the country," the *Times* declared. "The gray old soldier, will see a marvelous change in this southern land. What then existed here only as an idea, an intangible dream for the future, he will now discover is an accomplished fact."[1]

A few weeks later city fathers staged a celebration of Frémont's seventy-fifth birthday. Hundreds of electric lights illuminated Armory Hall on South Main, its walls hung with patriotic bunting and a banner proclaiming, "Welcome to the Pathfinder." Several hundred men—retired army officers, bankers, citrus growers, and real estate agents—listened as Frémont delivered a short address. He and his wife, he told them, had gratefully accepted the gift of a small house in the new community of Inglewood, where they planned to retire. "Time and again I made efforts to establish myself here, but circumstances were against me," he said. "I determined that this time, at least, I would succeed—unless the rider on the pale horse should cut me down."[2]

The Frémonts reveled in the welcome, for in truth their relocation to Los Angeles had been a last resort. During the previous half century the two of them had played a leading role in some of the era's most important events. But the passage of time had not been kind to the Pathfinder. His victorious entry into Los Angeles in 1847 had been the high point of his career. In the decades since, he had suffered through a court-martial for mutiny, a failed political career, a controversial turn as Civil War general, and the loss of a fortune to risky speculation. Formerly accustomed to magnificent California estates and elegant Manhattan townhouses, the Frémonts had been reduced to living in a succession of cheap, rented cottages. For at least a dozen years Jessie Benton, as the author of popular books and magazine articles, had been the sole support of the family, which included the couple's unmarried daughter, Lily. John Charles was broke, despondent, and suffering from chronic bronchitis. Warned by her husband's doctor that he might not survive another eastern winter, Jessie Benton had appealed to their old friend, railroad magnate Collis P. Huntington, who had provided money and passes for the rail journey to Los Angeles. The charity of friends was their last remaining asset. "God and events were against Frémont," writes historian Bernard De Voto. "He tried to be a great man, but something always happened." The checkered careers of John Charles and Jessie Benton Frémont, characters who were simultaneously larger than life and less than they claimed, track the similarly checkered career of that unique American construction, an empire for liberty.[3]

John Charles Frémont's initial rise to fame and fortune by pluck and luck might have been imagined by Horatio Alger. He was born in 1813 in Savannah, Georgia, illegitimate son of a young woman from the planter class who abandoned a loveless marriage to an elderly husband and ran off with her French instructor, a ne'er-do-well who died before John Charles was old enough to remember him. His mother, outcast and impoverished, raised him and two siblings in Charleston, South Carolina. Biographer Andrew Rolle suggests that the early loss of his father and the absence of extended family deprived Frémont of the ability to trust others and contributed to a lifelong contempt for authority. There is plenty of evidence for the contempt, whatever its cause, and it would result in no end of trouble. But other biographers note that young Frémont—gifted with native curiosity, quick intelligence, and considerable charm—also would demonstrate a knack for attracting the support of influential older men, who opened many doors for him.[4]

Completing grammar school at the age of thirteen, he went to work, clerking for a local law firm. Impressed with the boy's talent, his employer agreed to sponsor Frémont's continuing education at a local preparatory school. Three years later Frémont entered the College of Charleston on a charity scholarship. He excelled in mathematics and science, although his teachers complained of his love of adventure novels and his tendency to skip class in favor of hiking or sailing, often accompanied by a girlfriend. College trustee Joel Roberts Poinsett, sensing something special about the young man, took Frémont under his wing. Born into Charleston aristocracy, Poinsett was educated in the North and traveled extensively abroad. When he met Frémont, he had just returned from a four-year term as American minister to Mexico—bringing back the Christmas plant with red bracts that still bears his name. Poinsett was a man of strong views, and deeply influenced young Frémont. Despite owning slaves himself, Poinsett believed that slavery was an inefficient labor system, holding back the economic and social progress of the South. The nation's future greatness, he believed, would result from western expansion, the creation of the "Empire for Liberty" envisioned by Thomas Jefferson. Slavery would not be able to compete with free labor in the West, and that would eventually transform the South itself. Poinsett was a committed Unionist, opposing all talk of Southern secession. Young Frémont idolized his mentor and adopted the man's views as his own. "I was one of his devoted adherents," he later wrote. "I joined the party of Mr. Poinsett and gave unwavering allegiance to the union."[5]

When it came time for Frémont to pursue a career, Poinsett secured him several appointments, including an assignment surveying the homeland of the Cherokee Indians, who were about to be dispossessed and forced onto the Trail of Tears. Poinsett supported the project of Indian removal enthusiastically, declaring that "civilized man has the right to take from the savage the land which the latter does not know how to use." Frémont agreed, believing that removal was "a wise and humane measure." But the purpose behind the fieldwork meant less to him than the experience itself, which he loved—the wandering life, the great outdoors, the rough sociability of the crew. "Here," Frémont later recalled, "I found the path which I was destined to walk."[6]

In 1837, Poinsett became secretary of war in the cabinet of newly elected President Martin Van Buren. His principal assignment was supervising the ongoing course of Indian removal, a process that involved the exploration and mapping of the territory west of the Mississippi River. For that purpose he reorganized the Army Corps of Topographical Engineers and recruited Joseph Nicolas Nicollet, a distinguished émigré scientist from France, to head up the western surveys. Poinsett did not neglect Frémont, securing his appointment as a second lieutenant in the corps, assigned as Nicollet's assistant. It proved a perfect pairing. Young Frémont, fluent in French, charmed Nicollet, who reciprocated with paternal affection. In Saint Louis, where they outfitted the expedition, Nicollet introduced Frémont to his circle of French-speaking friends, including the Chouteaus, a powerful trading family with a network of contacts throughout the West, as well as many of the frontiersmen they employed. For Frémont the expedition amounted to a crash course in what he hoped would be his life's work. Nicollet praised his assistant for "the talents which he displayed for this branch of service." In early 1840, following two seasons in the field, the two men repaired to Washington to begin work on a series of precise maps of the western country.[7]

When Senator Thomas Hart Benton of Missouri stopped by their rooms to inspect the progress of the mapping, Frémont met the man who more than any other would determine the course of his life. Powerful chair of the Senate Military Affairs Committee,

Benton was Washington's most outspoken advocate of continental expansion. In 1825, during his first term, he introduced the bill that authorized the federal government to survey and map the Santa Fe Trail. In 1840 he wanted the same done for the trail to Oregon, and he spoke with Nicollet and Frémont of the imperative need for such an expedition. "The thought of penetrating into the recesses of that wilderness region filled me with enthusiasm," Frémont later recalled. "This interview with Mr. Benton was pregnant of results and decisive of my life." Nicollet was suffering with a chronic bronchial infection, probably tuberculosis, that would result in his early death, and Benton naturally turned to Frémont, Nicollet's heir apparent. Soon the young man was a regular participant in the informal salons Benton held at his family residence in Washington.[8]

It was there Frémont met Jessie Anne Benton, the senator's daughter. Their relationship has long fascinated Americans. In addition to numerous scholarly biographies of him, there are two of her, as well as two studies focusing on their marriage and relationship. There are also a number of historical novels, including two best sellers, Irving Stone's *Immortal Wife* (1944) and David Nevin's *Dream West* (1984). Both novels play up the romance, but Nevin's is the bodice-ripper: "She had thought his kiss would be tender, ... but instead it swept her like fire. Heat flared red behind her closed lids. Her mouth opened. ... *Oh my God!*" A TV miniseries soon followed, with John Charles played by Richard Chamberlain and Jessie Benton by Alice Krige, *en décolleté*.[9]

To be sure, in real life these two young people were strongly attracted to one another. She was a vivacious and willful sixteen-year-old, he a dashing and eligible bachelor of twenty-seven. She was flirtatious, and he had enjoyed his flings. Biographer Allan Nevins writes that Frémont "was impetuous in matters of the heart as in everything else." He acted impulsively with Jessie Benton, and she responded in kind. When Benton and his wife noticed the budding attraction, they declared their opposition. She was too young; he was too poor and of dubious background. But strong-willed, like her father, Jessie Benton refused to give John Charles up.[10]

There was more going on here than mere physical magnetism. John Charles was also powerfully drawn to the warm and affectionate family life in the Benton home, something he had never previously experienced. Biographer Pamela Herr puts it well: "The warm and lovely Jessie, the intimacy of the family circle, the exciting talk of western exploration with the powerful senator from Missouri, all must have been dazzling indeed." For her part, Jessie Benton was fascinated by the prospect of sharing in Frémont's promising career. Not only was she her father's pet, but she was also his aide, translating documents for him (she was fluent in French and Spanish) and transcribing his dictation. She may have glimpsed the possibility of continuing a similar collaboration with Frémont, a man who might actually carry out her father's expansionist vision. "Perhaps she already knew," writes Herr, "that she had found a hero-worth-the-making in John Charles Frémont."[11]

The couple eloped in the fall of 1841. The Bentons reacted angrily but soon got over it, and by Christmas the couple were living as husband and wife in a rear apartment at the Benton residence. A few weeks later, in early 1842, they received the news that the Army Corps of Topographical Engineers, now known as the Army Corps of Engineers, had authorized a topographic expedition of the country west of the Missouri River under the command of Lieutenant John Charles Frémont.

Even before that news arrived, Jessie Benton had figuratively sealed her partnership with John Charles by presenting him with a large flag she made herself. Anticipating that an expedition of the Far West would likely cross into Mexican territory, Frémont realized he could not risk carrying or flying the official national flag. His bride solved that problem by creating a banner of her own design, made from a plain-weave cotton fabric, incorporating the basic elements of thirteen alternating red and white stripes and an upper quadrant of stars, but adding her hand-painted image of a bald eagle, the national emblem, clutching a cluster of arrows in its left talon and, in its right, in place of the traditional olive branch, a calumet, or peace pipe, a symbol of Frémont's peaceful intentions with the Indian tribes. To the reverse she attached a large guidon made from material cut from her silk wedding dress, embroidered with the phrase "Rocky Mountains 1841" and including the image of a butterfly. The butterfly was not merely decoration. It was Jessie Benton's personal icon, appearing over the course of her life on her seal ring, her stationery, and both the cover and the title page of her first independently authored book. In Victorian imagery the butterfly could stand for the soul, and embroidered on fabric from her wedding dress it may have had the connotation of "soul mate."[12]

Frémont carried Jessie Benton's flag with him when he set out in June with two dozen men for a scientific survey of the Platte River valley, following its course to the South Pass of the Rockies, then indulging himself with a side trip to the Wind River Range of Wyoming, where he climbed a commanding peak and unfurled the flag. Returning home in October he presented it to his wife. "This flag was raised on the summit peak of the highest point of the Rocky Mountains," he told her, and "I brought it to you." During the expedition, Frémont fully demonstrated his scientific training, compiling detailed research notes on the flora and fauna and using astronomical instruments to determine latitude and longitude. But it would be his grandstanding on the summit of the Rockies that would be most remembered.[13]

That was because of the publication, in 1843, of his *Report on an Exploration of the Country Lying between the Missouri River and the Rocky Mountains*. If the flag symbolized the promise of collaboration between John Charles and Jessie Benton, the report was the first harvest of their efforts. Jessie Benton later explained how it came about. "The horseback life, the sleep in the open air, had unfitted Mr. Frémont for the indoor work of writing—and second lieutenants cannot indulge in secretaries. After a series of hemorrhages from the nose and head had convinced him he must give up trying to write his report, I was let to try, and thus slid into my most happy life-work." They developed a routine in which he dictated and she transcribed, sometimes asking for more detail, sometimes editing to speed up the narrative, precisely the kind of assistance she had provided for her father.

FIGURE 2.1

Above: Frémont expedition flag, circa 1841–42. Gift of Elizabeth Benton Fremont. Southwest Museum of the American Indian Collection, Autry National Center, 81.G.5A. For a color version of this image, see plate 2. *Below:* Fragment of Jessie Benton Frémont's wedding dress attached to the Frémont expedition flag. Gift of Elizabeth Benton Fremont. Southwest Museum of the American Indian Collection, Autry National Center, 81.G.5.

There is some controversy among the biographers about Jessie Benton's contribution. On one side Allan Nevins insists, with a hint of male defensiveness, that the report was "nine-tenths his." On the other, Pamela Herr counters that without Jessie Benton's "sharp eye for a good story, the report, if completed at all, would have been another dry treatise to be filed and forgotten." But perhaps Jessie Benton's most important contribution to this and later narratives of her husband was the way in which she framed Frémont as an authentic American hero, encouraging readers to see him through her admiring eyes. Measuring up to that standard would present innumerable difficulties for the real-life man.[14]

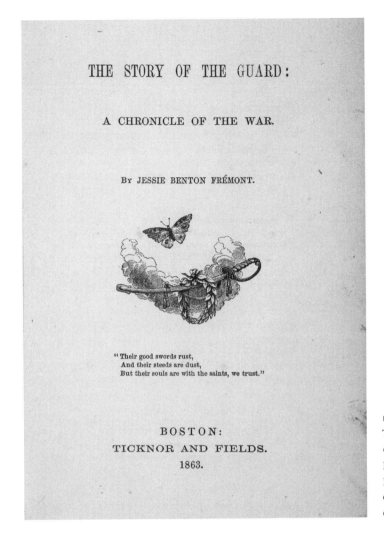

THE STORY OF THE GUARD:

A CHRONICLE OF THE WAR.

By JESSIE BENTON FRÉMONT.

" Their good swords rust,
And their steeds are dust,
But their souls are with the saints, we trust."

BOSTON:
TICKNOR AND FIELDS.
1863.

FIGURE 2.2
Title page of *The Story of the Guard*, showing Jessie Benton Frémont's butterfly icon, 1863. Braun Research Library Collection, Autry National Center, 92F872j, F73j.

The *Report* of 1843 was a best seller, as was a subsequent publication that narrated Frémont's second expedition, extending the survey across the Rockies all the way to the Oregon Country. These books were among the most widely read of their day. Congress ordered the printing of thousands of copies, as well as a series of maps, and the narrative was serialized in newspapers and reprinted by commercial publishers in the United States and abroad. Over the next twenty years, thousands of emigrants would travel the Overland Trail, guided by Frémont's narrative and his map.

The most widely admired passage in the *Report* detailed Frémont's ascent of the Rockies and his raising of Jessie Benton's flag. There, at the summit of the Continental Divide, he offers a figurative view of the entire continent, in what biographer Tom Chaffin calls a "bravura affirmation of American nationalism." As he admires the view, "a solitary bee (*bromus, the humble bee*) came winging his flight from the eastern valley, . . . and we

COL. FREMONT

PLANTING THE AMERICAN STANDARD ON THE ROCKY MOUNTAINS.

FIGURE 2.3

Frémont planting the American standard on the Rocky Mountains (New York: Baker & Godwin, circa 1856). Proof made for banner or poster for John Frémont's campaign as the Republican presidential nominee. Library of Congress, Prints and Photographs Division.

pleased ourselves with the idea that he was the first of his species to cross the mountain barrier—a solitary pioneer to foretell the advance of civilization." The bee as the symbol of advancing American settlement had appeared earlier, in William Cullen Bryant's poem "The Prairies" (1834) and Washington Irving's *A Tour of the Prairies* (1835), and its celebrated appearance in Frémont's *Report,* Chaffin writes, suggests "the degree to which John, or Jessie—or, more likely, both of them—possessed a pitch-perfect sense of their audience." The reports, celebrating American expansion, made Frémont one of the most famous men in the United States.[15]

On Frémont's third expedition, surveying in advance of settlement gave way to overt conquest. His official instructions authorized a survey of the southern Rockies, but within the inner circles of Washington, D.C., it was well understood that he was headed for California. The United States had annexed Texas the year before, creating a diplomatic crisis with Mexico, which refused to recognize the independence of that breakaway province. President James Polk sought to use the political crisis as a means of acquiring

California as well, and he wanted Frémont and his party of armed men on the Pacific Coast, where they might prove useful as he attempted to maneuver Mexico into firing the first shot.

The story of Frémont and the conquest of California has been told many times. The stand on Gavilán Peak, where he raised the flag (Jessie Benton's banner, by some accounts) in defiance of Californio authorities; his meeting with a special envoy carrying "secret instructions" from the president; his encouragement of the Bear Flag rebellion; his organization of the California Battalion of Mounted Riflemen. Historian Cardinal Goodwin puts it succinctly: "Frémont, an explorer, acting on the discretion which he believed had been given him, abruptly terminated his explorations and ultimately assumed the leadership of a filibustering expedition in a foreign country." Frémont's impetuosity and recklessness were on full display. Fortunately for him, American naval forces arrived at Monterey and San Francisco and, anticipating the outbreak of war between the United States and Mexico, raised the American flag and declared the official seizure of the territory. Frémont and the California Battalion were mustered into official service.[16]

When he entered Los Angeles at the conclusion of the conflict in January 1847, Frémont was operating under the authority of Commodore Robert Stockton of the navy. He found, however, that General Stephen Watts Kearny had arrived with a regiment of mounted dragoons after an overland march across the desert Southwest, bearing orders from President Polk to organize a civilian government for California. Stockton and Kearny were locked in a dangerous struggle over who would be in charge. Frémont's clear obligation was to General Kearny, his superior officer in the army. But Stockton appointed him military governor of California. Frémont choose Stockton. It was an impulsive and disastrous decision at the moment of his greatest triumph. Refusing a direct order from Kearny, he set himself up as *jefe político* at Los Angeles. Once reinforcements arrived in the form of the Mormon Battalion and a volunteer regiment from New York, Kearny had the power to enforce his authority. He had Frémont arrested and escorted him back across the continent to face a court-martial in Washington. Frémont was convicted of mutiny. President Polk offered to commute the sentence, but a prideful Frémont resigned his commission. This fiasco was entirely of Frémont's making. Although he and Jessie Benton would enjoy years of fame and fortune afterward, from this point on nothing ever turned out right for Frémont. His confrontation with General Kearny proved to be the watershed moment of his life.

Of course, it did not appear that way at the time. Jessie Benton and her father were by his side during the court-martial, and afterward he and Benton planned a fourth surveying expedition, organized with private capital this time, intended to mark out a railroad passage through the southern Rockies. Frémont was to end up in California, where he would meet his wife and daughter, who were coming by way of the Isthmus of Panama. The couple had just buried a baby boy, their second born. They had agreed on a new beginning, hitching their wagon to California's rising star. But Frémont's expedition, which attempted a crossing of the southern Rockies in winter, was a complete disaster, claiming the lives of ten men. "There is no more shocking or more unnecessary failure in the exploration of the West," writes historian Bernard De Voto. Jessie Benton and eight-year-old Lily also suffered through a horrendous journey, which began soon after the first word of the gold strike in California reached the East. They arrived in Panama on an overcrowded sailing ship, traversed the isthmus on mules, then waited for several weeks for passage up the coast, delayed because of the shortage of vessels. Jessie Benton fell seriously ill with fever before they finally boarded a steamer headed north. She and John Charles were reunited in San Francisco in the spring of 1849.[17]

Before leaving California in 1847, Frémont had arranged for the purchase of a plot of land in San Francisco. In a mix-up, he instead acquired title to an undeveloped grant known as "Las Mariposas" in the foothills of the southern Sierra. The mistake turned to windfall when alluvial gold was discovered on his property. Frémont hired two dozen Sonoran miners to work the claim, and soon they found a fabulous vein of gold in the quartz rock. Frémont refused an offer of a million dollars for his claim, believing it to be worth far more. The mine promised wealth and happiness, but it brought nothing but trouble and disappointment. Its development demanded investment and management skills Frémont did not possess. The possibility of great wealth, writes Allan Nevins, "filled the sanguine Frémont with an unfortunate conviction that he could be a highly successful business man."[18]

John Charles Frémont was not a cautious man. Not only did he undertake the management of a mining operation, but he also jumped into politics, another field for which he had neither the training nor the aptitude. In the fall of 1849, Californians elected delegates to a convention that drafted a state constitution, then appealed to Congress for immediate statehood. Pending congressional approval, voters elected a complete slate of government officials and legislators, and Frémont was chosen to be one of the prospective state's first two senators. The Frémonts returned to Washington glorying in their vindication. A book of portraits of "illustrious Americans," published soon after their arrival, included a brief biographical sketch, quite possibly written by Jessie Benton herself, summing up her view of things. "Frémont was made the victim of a quarrel between two American commanders," it read. "Like Columbus, he was brought home a prisoner." But the voters of California had "reversed the judgment of the court-martial, and Frémont was made the first senator of the golden state. It was a noble tribute to science and heroism."[19]

Frémont stepped onto the political stage at the moment of the greatest crisis in a generation. The acquisition of the Far West, which he had done so much to promote, raised the controversial question of whether that territory would enter the Union as a slave or free state. That was not the way it was supposed to work. Expansion into new territory was supposed to be the great ameliorative of the American system. "Extend the sphere," James Madison had argued in the *Federalist Papers*, "and you take in a greater variety of parties and interests; you make it less probable that a majority of the whole will have a common motive to invade the rights of other citizens." This was an article of faith in American politics. There had been trouble in 1819 when Missouri sought admission as a slave state, but the fever of disunion broke after the passage of the Missouri Compromise, which drew a line at 30°30', north of which slavery could not go. The faith was reborn during the age of Jackson. Expansion, Frémont's political mentor Joel Roberts Poinsett explained, "multiplies political interest, and weakens the spirit of party by dividing it." Expansion, said William Wilkins, Poinsett's successor as secretary of war, "multiplies counteracting interests and lessens the danger of its influence." New territory would offer new lands, new farms, new cities, new industry, and new opportunity. Poinsett trusted that the South would see the light about free labor.[20]

But that did not happen. Poinsett was scorned in South Carolina and became something of a political pariah. The South demanded that territories be open to slavery in the land won from Mexico. The issue fractured American politics along sectional lines after David Wilmot, a Democratic congressman from Pennsylvania, offered an amendment to a spending bill in the late summer of 1846 that would have prohibited slavery in any of the territory ceded to the United States by Mexico. The amendment was defeated, but the issue would not go away. Territorial expansion became the cause, not the cure, of political conflict.

Every politician had to take a stand on the issue. "My personal sentiments," Senator Thomas Hart Benton declared, "are against the institution of slavery and against introduction into places in which it does not exist. If there was no slavery in Missouri today, I should oppose its coming in; if there was none in the United States, I should oppose its coming into the United States; as there is none in New Mexico or California, I am against sending it to those territories, and could not vote for such a measure." That was Frémont's position as well. California statehood got caught up in the struggle, and it was months before Congress was able to agree on a series of measures, known collectively as the Compromise of 1850, that admitted California as a free state. Frémont aligned himself with the "free soil" wing of the Democratic Party. He was a listless legislator, although he voted to ban the traffic in slaves in the District of Columbia and to weaken enforcement of the Fugitive Slave Act. His actions alienated the Democratic Party in California, dominated by proslavery forces, and at the end of his term he was not reelected.[21]

Frémont preoccupied himself with the management of the gold mine at Las Mariposas, which became increasingly complicated and costly by the month, "a perfect Pandora's Box of complications," in the words of Allan Nevins. But politics came as a kind of rescue in 1856, when Frémont was recruited to become the first presidential candidate of the newly organized Republican Party, rallying under the banner "Free Soil, Free Men, Frémont!" "I am opposed to slavery in the abstract and upon principle," he declared, and "while I feel inflexible in the belief that it ought not to be interfered with where it exists, under the shield of state sovereignty, I am as inflexibly opposed to its extension on this continent beyond its present limits." That was Benton's view as well, although he refused to break ranks with the Democrats and refused to endorse Frémont. Benton died soon after the campaign, which was particularly nasty. Frémont's adversaries raked up all the muck they could find or invent.[22]

Jessie Benton served as a behind-the-scenes advisor in what some termed the "John and Jessie" campaign. Lily Frémont, fourteen at the time, later recalled the slurs and slanders of the campaign deeply affecting her father. "He was used to life in the open and wanted a square fight, not one filled with petty innuendoes and unfounded recriminations," she wrote. "So at the outset it was agreed that he should not read his mail during the campaign, nor read the newspapers until they had been blue penciled by my mother—a promise he religiously kept during all the excitement of that year." Jessie Benton not only managed her husband's correspondence but also actively assisted editor John Bigelow of the *New York Evening Post* in researching and writing the official campaign biography.[23]

It was the first time a candidate's wife had played such a role. "What a shame that women can't vote," exclaimed woman's right's activist Lydia María Child. "We'd carry 'our Jessie' into the White House on our shoulders, wouldn't we." One man later recalled seeing the couple during a campaign rally in New York City. "Frémont and Jessie appeared on the balcony, and when we caught sight of the romantic couple, in the light of the flaming torches, they seemed to be the ideal specimens of manly vigor and womanly grace. We rent the air with our plaudits and our salutations were returned by the twain, who looked supremely happy." Campaign portraits, painted by the fashionable American artist Thomas Buchanan Read, captured the couple at their best, he appearing strong and assertive, she attentive and luminous.[24]

When Frémont lost the election to James Buchanan, it marked the end of his short political career. John Bigelow, who advised Frémont during the campaign, came to feel afterward that his candidate "might have proved a disastrous failure as President." Bigelow based his opinion in part on his discovery that party bosses had purchased the silence of a "French mistress" who had threatened to expose a dalliance with Frémont during the campaign. It was neither the first nor the last time such rumors would surface, and because Jessie Benton was so intimately involved, it proved impossible this time to keep the story from her. Although she never wrote or spoke of her husband's infidelities, and remained his most valiant defender to the end of her days, their relationship was transformed by this experience, according to biographer Sally Denton. The Frémonts had always spent considerable time apart because of his expeditions and the slowness of travel, but after 1856 the periods of separation grew, along with Jessie's own independence.[25]

In the spring of 1858 the Frémont family—including fifteen-year-old Lily and the couple's two sons, John Charles and Francis Preston—returned to California. At Las Mariposas, where they took up an isolated residence, hundreds of squatters challenged Frémont's ownership, and there were some frightful standoffs. After two hard years he purchased a house in San Francisco, at a location known as Black Point, on the bluffs near the Golden Gate (a name bestowed by Frémont himself in 1846), and the family relocated there. The neighborhood was home to a small but influential group of social and political reformers

Thomas Buchanan Read, *John Frémont*, 1856, oil on canvas. Sons of the Revolution in the State of California.

FIGURE 2.5

Thomas Buchanan Read, *Jessie Benton Frémont,* 1856, oil on canvas. Gift of Elizabeth Benton Fremont. Southwest Museum of the American Indian Collection, Autry National Center, 81.G.2.

who befriended Jessie Benton. Emulating her father, she opened her home to a small circle of the city's writers and intellectuals, including minister Thomas Starr King, poet Bret Harte, and photographer Carleton Watkins. Frémont was mostly away, fretting over affairs at Las Mariposas. Jessie Benton remained at Black Point for only a year, but it may have been her happiest.

The aggregate liabilities on Las Mariposas—taxes, debts, and legal fees—continued to mount. In 1859 Frémont reported annual revenues of a quarter million dollars, but that barely covered operating expenses and debt service. By 1860 his obligations on the property had ballooned to more than a million dollars. He contracted with Carleton Watkins to produce a set of large-format photographs of the entire operation, and in the fall of 1860 he left for Europe, where he hoped to attract investors with the images. He was in London in the spring of 1861 when he learned of the firing on Fort Sumter. Sometime later he received word that President Lincoln had appointed him one of four major generals of the Union Army, in command of the Army of the West. He notified Jessie Benton by mail, and in late July they arrived together at army headquarters in Saint Louis.

Missouri was in danger of being overrun by secessionists. Confederate forces massed on the border with Arkansas and threatened to sweep up the Mississippi. If they gained control of the river town of Cairo, Illinois, at the mouth of the Ohio River, there was a realistic prospect that Kentucky might join the Confederacy. Frémont had to organize, arm, and supply raw volunteers; he had to hold Saint Louis, with its large population of rebel sympathizers; and he had to pacify the violent guerrilla struggle taking place in the countryside. As Allan Nevins puts it, "All this had to be done by a man who had never commanded forces of more than a few hundred."[26]

Moving gunboats south, he fortified Cairo, putting Union forces in a position to force their way south. But almost simultaneously the Confederates advanced in the southwestern corner of the state, defeating a Union force at the Battle of Wilson's Creek. In an attempt to gain control of the deteriorating situation, Frémont issued a proclamation at the end of August, declaring martial law, providing for the summary execution of rebel guerrillas found under arms, confiscating the property of disloyal owners, and emancipating their slaves. Frémont made this bold move precipitously, without consulting President Lincoln.

The president wired Frémont immediately after receiving a copy. "Should you shoot a man according to the proclamation," he wrote, "the Confederates would very certainly shoot our best men in their hands in retaliation," and he countermanded that provision. In regard to the emancipation of slaves, Lincoln worried that it would "alarm our Southern Union friends and turn them against us; perhaps ruin our rather fair prospect for Kentucky," and he asked Frémont to modify the order himself. "This letter is written in a spirit of caution and not censure," the president concluded. But Frémont refused. "If I were to retract of my own accord," he responded, "it would imply that I myself thought it wrong, and that I had acted without the reflection which the gravity of the point demanded. But I did not. I acted with full deliberation, and upon the certain conviction that it was a measure right and necessary, and I think so still." He dispatched Jessie Benton to Washington to carry his letter of refusal and make his case directly to the president.[27]

She and Lincoln met at the White House late one evening in early September. She gave him Frémont's letter, which he read, then he listened as she defended the thinking of her husband. "You are quite a female politician," the president said in a tone that was scornful, not ironic. The war was for union, he told her, and "General Frémont should not have dragged the Negro into it." It was clear, she later wrote, "that the President's mind was made up against General Frémont—and decidedly against me." Lincoln later

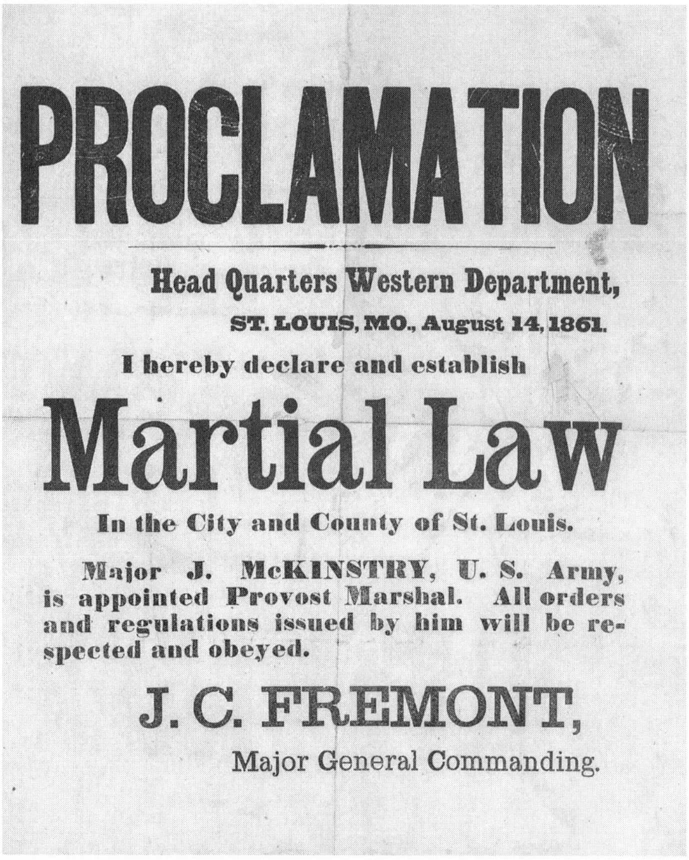

PROCLAMATION

Head Quarters Western Department,
ST. LOUIS, MO., August 14, 1861.
I hereby declare and establish

Martial Law

In the City and County of St. Louis.

Major J. McKINSTRY, U. S. Army,
is appointed Provost Marshal. All orders
and regulations issued by him will be respected and obeyed.

J. C. FREMONT,

Major General Commanding.

FIGURE 2.6
Broadside proclamation of martial law in the city and county of St. Louis by General Fremont, dated headquarters, Western Department, Saint Louis, August 14, 1861. Missouri History Museum, Saint Louis.

told his aides that Jessie Benton "tasked me so violently with so many things, that I had to exercise all the awkward tack I have to avoid quarreling with her." Suggesting that her husband knew better than the president, she had done his cause considerable harm. Lincoln revoked the proclamation and several weeks later removed Frémont from command, provoking a torrent of criticism from abolitionists.[28]

Radical Republicans largely took Frémont's side. Quaker poet John Greenleaf Whittier sent him these lines:

Thy error, Frémont, simply was to act
A brave man's part, without the statesman's tact,
And, taking counsel but of common sense,
To strike at cause as well as consequence.

The Republican press largely took Frémont's side, and for years afterward he enjoyed a heroic reputation among the radicals for righteous politics. In 1867 the fashionable artist Giuseppe Fagnani painted a portrait of Frémont reflecting this view. Dressed in the uniform of a major general, with scabbard and sword at hand, Frémont leans against a bookcase upon which the artist has included an image of John Quincy Adams Ward's small bronze casting of *The Freedman,* of which a small number were produced, one of them owned by Frémont. It was, perhaps, the single most important piece of American art commemorating the victory of emancipation. Several years after the conclusion of the war, Senator Charles Sumner of Massachusetts paid Frémont tribute. "I offer my homage to that great act of political wisdom and humanity," he said, "by which he declared emancipation at the head of his army. Had this measure been adopted at that early day, I cannot doubt that it would have hastened immensely the close of the war. But his be the honor forever more."[29]

Most historians have taken a different view, siding with Lincoln in the controversy, persuaded by his cautious approach. Putting that issue aside, it is clear that Frémont's "error" was not simply political, as Whittier suggested. It was congenital. A wiser man would have sought counsel before issuing his proclamation, would have treated Lincoln's request to modify it as an order rather than a suggestion, and would not have sent his wife, however talented she was, to represent him with the president of the United States. But Frémont was not that wiser man.

The Frémonts lived lavishly. They were millionaires and they acted the part, with a commodious New York City brownstone off Fifth Avenue and a country estate on the Hudson. In 1863, John Charles finally divested himself of Las Mariposas, cashing out with a million dollars or more. He might have purchased safe securities and guaranteed a generous lifetime income for his family, but that would not have been in character. Instead Frémont invested everything he had in western railroads. "With characteristic impetuosity," writes Nevins, "he hastened to throw not a quarter, not a half, but all his money into these enterprises."[30]

Like most elite Republicans, Frémont shifted his attention following the war to making money, mostly through speculation. That was what Reconstruction meant to him. His special project was a new transcontinental line on the southern route, through Texas, New Mexico, and Arizona. It ended in disaster. Bonds worth millions were sold in France under false pretenses, and in 1870 a French court convicted Frémont of fraud in absentia, sentencing him to five years in prison. The Frémonts never returned to France, a place they loved. The Riggs National Bank of Washington labeled Frémont "a poor and visionary speculator with not very strict moral principles." Whatever capital remained he lost in the Panic of 1873.

The luxurious days were over. In 1877 the Frémonts were forced to auction off most of their possessions, an event that was covered by the New York press. Crowds of people thronged the Kurtz Art Gallery to gawk at the display of objects. Portraits, including the one by Fagnani and the two by Read (the painting of Jessie Benton did not sell and remained in the family); dozens of canvases by American painters of the Hudson River school; sculpture, including the bronze casting of *The Freedman* by Ward; a fine set of Minton's china bearing the monogram "JCF"; Jessie Benton's Steinway grand piano; and books by the lot. "What has befallen the Pathfinder of late that his estate, or what remains of it, has been dispersed by auction?" asked the *New York Evening Express*. "We are not admirers of General Frémont, and never have been, but we are sincerely sorry that circumstances of any kind should have forced him to dispose of his personal belongings, which must be dear to him from the associations connected therewith." The auction marked the destruction of not only Frémont's fortune but his reputation as well.[31]

During the war Jessie Benton had been successful with her short book *The Story of the Guard* (1863), a defense of her husband's military record, and she had donated the royalties to the Western Sanitary Commission, a private agency ministering to wounded soldiers. With the collapse of Frémont's finances, she took up her pen again, this time to support the family. Over the next twenty years she turned out dozens of magazine articles and several books in a desperate effort to ward off poverty. Much of her work was reminiscence. *A Year of American Travel* (1878) told of the arduous trek she made to California with daughter Lily in 1849; *Souvenirs of My Time* (1887) focused on experiences from her youth and her European travels; *Far-West Sketches* (1890) was about life at Las Mariposas. This last collection, her best, included some memorable portraits of western women. "These patient pioneer women," she wrote, "knew that the men burned their ships and took no backward look—it is always the woman who looks lingeringly to what she is leaving, who watches for the last sight of her sinking ship with a sinking heart. Then, they rise to their work and do it patiently, bravely, cheerfully." Jessie Benton wrote from experience.[32]

Frémont appealed to Republican leaders for a position of some kind, and in 1878 he received a presidential appointment as territorial governor of Arizona. It is a measure of their poverty that the couple considered the salary of twenty-six hundred dollars a year a lifeline, although it barely covered their expenses in the capital of Prescott. Jessie Benton hated Arizona and left after only several months. Frémont served for three years but spent most of the time in the East, trying to drum up investors for Arizona mining schemes. In the judgment of Jay Wagoner, author of the standard history of the Arizona Territory, Frémont has the distinction of being the worst of the territorial governors. His neglect of his duties resulted in calls for his resignation, and in 1881 he complied and returned East.[33]

Frémont was a beaten man. Growing sentimental during one of several transcontinental railroad journeys during his gubernatorial term, he penned a poem, which he sent to Jessie Benton, saying in part:

> The buoyant hopes and busy life
> Have ended all in hateful strife
> And baffled aim.
> The world's rude contact killed the rose,
> No more its shining radiance shows,
> False roads to fame.

Yet old patterns continued. Most days, John Charles left their cottage on Staten Island and took the ferry into Manhattan "on business," while Jessie Benton remained at her desk working on her writing. "I can realize it to be a woman's duty to devote herself to her husband, maintain him, and do all she can to make him good and happy," an old friend wrote after a visit with her in 1883. "But to allow him to gamble away his own & their children's bread over & over again, . . . to do it that many times. And he too faithless even to pretend to live with her. . . . My idea of Jessie is that she belongs to him body & soul, & he does with [her] as he pleases."[34]

What that otherwise astute comment misses is the essential compromise Jessie Benton made years before. Talented and opinionated, sentimental and romantic, she invested everything she had in Frémont, and she was, more than anyone else, responsible for the Frémont myth. John Charles excelled as a leader of topographic expeditions, but he was not the hero Jessie Benton made him out to be. "She had wrapped her own identity so tightly around the heroic image she helped him to create," writes Pamela Herr, "that though it might be shattered in others' eyes, in hers it would always remain intact."[35]

In 1884 the Frémonts were paid a visit by Josiah Royce, a young instructor at Harvard College. A California native who had grown up in a gold-rush town, Royce knew from personal experience that the real history of the origins of his state was nothing like the myth. He was working on a book that, when finished, would explode a central part of that myth, the role Frémont had played in the conquest. Without exactly divulging his true purpose, he requested and was granted an interview. Royce found John Charles "a pleasing old gentleman, quiet, cool, self-possessed, patient, willing to bear with objections of all sorts," but frustratingly uncommunicative. It was Jessie Benton who took the lead during his visit. Royce described her as "very enthusiastic, garrulous, naively boastful, [and] grandly elevated above the level of the historical in most that she either remembers or tells of the past." Royce's final judgment was harsh but penetrating. "Can a man help it," he wrote of Frémont, "if, despite all, he is a fiction—a creature escaped from a book, wandering about in a real world when he was made for dreamland?"[36]

In late 1887, when the Frémonts came to Los Angeles, Southern California was in the midst of its first great real estate boom. In exchange for his endorsement of their development at Inglewood, the Centinela Land Company deeded the couple a house. But finding they didn't like isolated Inglewood, the Frémonts leased it out and rented a place in the West Adams district of the city. "The General is perfectly well," Jessie wrote a friend in the spring of 1888. "How can one fail to regain health here?" Within weeks, however, Frémont had left for Washington, D.C., where he spent several months lobbying for a military pension. Jessie Benton remained in Los Angeles with Lily, continuing her writing, which provided her only source of income. She began to redevelop the kind of independent life she had enjoyed in San Francisco, including relationships with local artists and writers. Frémont returned for a few weeks in the summer of 1889, and while he was in town she arranged for him to sit for a portrait by one of her protégés, the young artist John Gutzon Borglum, who would

FIGURE 2.7
Mrs. Jessie Benton Frémont at
home, 1892, gelatin silver print.
Gift of Mr. George Wharton
James. Braun Research Library
Collection, Autry National
Center, P.36493.

later become world famous for his creation of Mount Rushmore. Dressed in black, Frémont
looks to the side, his beady gaze emphasized by heavy eyelids. He looks exhausted. But at
summer's end Frémont departed again for the East, where "business" beckoned. Separation
had become part of their relationship, essential for them both.[37]

In the spring of 1890, Congress awarded Frémont a pension of six thousand dollars
a year. But barely three months later, on July 14, 1890, before he had received the first
payment, Frémont died of peritonitis in a second-class hotel in New York City. He was
seventy-seven years old. His son Charles Frémont, who lived in New York, was with him
at the end and sent a letter describing the scene to his sister Lily. Their father's last years
had been filled with such pain and burdened by such failure and humiliation, he wrote,
that "as I looked at him lying there so still and peaceful, . . . I could find no sorrow or pity
for him at all—but a feeling of relief that his life was over." He was glad their father's
struggle was over. But "what the effect is going to be on mother, I don't dare think."[38]

Jessie Benton could not afford the price of a ticket back East to attend the funeral. She
was forced to borrow from friends to meet immediate expenses. Press reports of her
poverty resulted in the passage in Congress of a special bill granting her a widow's pension of two thousand a year. A group of wealthy Los Angeles women built a lovely house

for her and daughter Lily not far from the campus of the University of Southern California, where they lived together for a dozen years, until Jessie Benton's death in 1902 at the age of seventy-eight. For a half century and more, her life had been dedicated to the construction and maintenance of the heroic image of John Charles Frémont as the man who pointed the way west for Americans. It had proved to be a path leading to the greatest conflict in the nation's history, and Frémont had been inadequate to the challenge. But, right up to the end, that was something Jessie Benton Frémont could not see, blinded as she was by the shining, heroic image of John Charles Frémont she had done so much to create.

NOTES

1. "General Fremont," *Los Angeles Times*, December 23, 1887; "General Fremont Arrives," *Los Angeles Times*, December 26, 1887; "Personal Mention," *Los Angeles Herald*, December 23, 1887. See also Pamela Herr and Mary Lee Spence, "'By the Sundown Sea': The Los Angeles Letters of Jessie Benton Frémont, 1888–1902," *California History* 71 (Winter 1991–92): 478–93.

2. "The Pathfinder: General Fremont's Future Home to Be Here by the Sea," *Los Angeles Times*, January 1, 1888; "General Fremont," *Los Angeles Herald*, January 1, 1888; "General Fremont: Grand Reception to Him at Armory Hall," January 22, 1888.

3. Bernard De Voto, *Across the Wide Missouri* (Boston: Houghton Mifflin, 1943), 457.

4. Andrew Rolle, *John Charles Frémont: Character as Destiny* (Norman: University of Oklahoma Press, 1991), 20; David Roberts, *A Newer World: Kit Carson, John C. Frémont, and the Claiming of the American West* (New York: Simon and Schuster, 2000), 115; Tom Chaffin, *Pathfinder: John Charles Frémont and the Course of American Empire* (New York: Hill and Wang, 2002), 23.

5. John Charles Frémont, *Memoirs of My Life* (New York: Belford, Clarke, 1887), 64; J. Fred Rippy, *Joel R. Poinsett: Versatile American* (Durham, NC: Duke University Press, 1935).

6. George Wilson Pierson, *Tocqueville and Beaumont in America* (New York: Oxford University Press, 1938), 652; Frémont, *Memoirs*, 24.

7. J. N. Nicollet, *Report Indented to Illustrate a Map of the Hydrographical Basin of the Upper Mississippi River* (Washington, DC: Blair and Rives, 1843), 106; Martha C. Bray, ed., *Joseph N. Nicollet on the Plains and Prairies: The Expeditions of 1838–39 with Journals, Letters, and Notes on the Dakota Indians* (Minneapolis: Minnesota Historical Society Press, 1993).

8. Frémont, *Memoirs*, 65; William Nisbet Chambers, *Old Bullion Benton, Senator from the New West* (Boston: Little, Brown, 1956).

9. Biographies of John Charles include Cardinal Goodwin, *John Charles Frémont: An Explanation of His Career* (Palo Alto, CA: Stanford University Press, 1930); Allan Nevins, *Frémont: Pathmarker of the West* (New York: Appleton, Century, Crofts, 1939); Ferol Egan, *Frémont, Explorer for a Restless Nation* (Garden City, NY: Doubleday, 1977); Rolle, *John Charles Frémont*; Chaffin, *Pathfinder*; David Miller, "'Heroes' of American Empire: John C. Frémont, Kit Carson, and the Culture of Imperialism, 1842–1898" (PhD diss., University of California, San Diego, 2007). Biographies of Jessie Benton include Catherine Coffin Phillips, *Jessie Benton Frémont: A Woman Who Made History* (San Francisco: J. H. Nash, 1935); Pamela Herr, *Jessie Benton*

Frémont: A Biography (New York: F. Watts, 1987). On the Frémont marriage, see Alice Eyre, *The Famous Frémonts and Their America* (n.p.: Fine Arts Press, 1948); Sally Denton, *Passion and Principle: John and Jessie Frémont, the Couple Whose Power, Politics, and Love Shaped Nineteenth-Century America* (New York: Bloomsbury, 2007). Best sellers about the couple include Irving Stone, *Immortal Wife* (New York: Doubleday, 1944); David Nevin, *Dream West* (New York: G. P. Putnam's Sons, 1983). *Dream West,* the miniseries, is available on DVD from Warner Archive.

10. Nevins, *Frémont,* 25.

11. Herr, *Jessie Benton Frémont,* 59–60.

12. Pamela Herr and Mary Lee Spence, eds., *The Letters of Jessie Benton Frémont* (Urbana: University of Illinois Press, 1993), 160, 307; Jessie Benton Frémont, *The Story of the Guard: A Chronicle of the War* (Boston: Ticknor and Fields, 1863); Carolyn Brucken, email to John Mack Faragher, March 12, 2013.

13. Herr and Spence, *Letters of Jessie Benton Frémont,* 12.

14. Ibid., 12; Nevins, *Frémont,* 118; Herr, *Jessie Benton Frémont,* 81–82.

15. Chaffin, *Pathfinder,* 145; John Charles Frémont, *The Exploring Expedition to the Rocky Mountains in the Year 1842, and to Oregon and North California in the Years 1843–'44* (Washington, DC: Blair and Rives, 1845), 69–70.

16. Goodwin, *John Charles Frémont,* 150.

17. De Voto, *Across the Wide Missouri,* 466.

18. Nevins, *Frémont,* 395.

19. *The Gallery of Illustrious Americans* (New York: J. Wiley, G. P. Putnam, D. Appleton & Co., 1850), 14.

20. James Madison, "Federalist No. 10," from *The Federalist Papers,* by Alexander Hamilton, John Jay, and James Madison, available at Project Gutenberg, www.gutenberg.org/ebooks/1404, accessed February 9, 2013; Joel Roberts Poinsett, conversation with Alexis de Tocqueville, see excerpts titled "Conversation with Mr. Poinsett, 13th, 14th, 15th January," Alexis de Tocqueville Tour Exploring Democracy in America, www.tocqueville.org/ga.htm, accessed February 9, 2013; Michael A. Morrison, *Slavery and the American West: The Eclipse of Manifest Destiny and the Coming of the Civil War* (Chapel Hill: University of North Carolina Press, 1997), 18.

21. John Ashworth, *Slavery, Capitalism, and Politics in the Antebellum Republic* (Cambridge: Cambridge University Press, 1995), 449.

22. Nevins, *Frémont,* 393; John Bigelow, *Memoir of the Life and Public Service of John Charles Frémont* (New York: Derby & Jackson, 1856), 449.

23. I. T. Martin, comp., *Recollections of Elizabeth Benton Frémont, Daughter of the Pathfinder General John C. Frémont and Jessie Benton Frémont, His Wife* (New York: Frederick H. Hitchcock, 1912), 77.

24. Herr and Spence, *Letters of Jessie Benton Frémont,* xvii; "Early Glimpses of Frémont," *Los Angeles Times,* January 27, 1888.

25. John Bigelow, *Retrospections of an Active Life* (New York: Baker, 1909), 142; Rolle, *John Charles Frémont,* 167; Denton, *Passion and Principle,* 264.

26. Nevins, *Frémont,* 484.

27. Ibid., 505–6.

28. Ibid., 516–17.

29. Chaffin, *Pathfinder*, 473; *Interesting Debate in the United States Senate, June 21, 1870* (Washington, DC: Chronicle Print, 1870), 16.

30. Nevins, *Frémont*, 587.

31. Rolle, *John Charles Frémont*, 239; *New York Times*, October 10, 1877; "The Fremont Sale," *New York Evening Express*, October 11, 1877.

32. Jessie Benton Frémont, *Far-West Sketches* (Boston: D. Lothrop, 1890), 174.

33. Jay J. Wagoner, *Arizona Territory, 1863–1912: A Political History* (Tucson: University of Arizona Press, 1970), 164.

34. Roberts, *A Newer World*, 290; Rolle, *John Charles Frémont*, 255.

35. Herr, *Jessie Benton Frémont*, 415.

36. Rolle, *John Charles Frémont*, 261.

37. Denton, *Passion and Principle*, 368.

38. Herr, *Jessie Benton Frémont*, 434.

3

BEECHER'S BIBLES AND BROADSWORDS
Paving the Way for the Civil War in the West, 1854–1859

Jonathan Earle

The long Civil War in the American West began with a stolen election. Not the election of Abraham Lincoln to the White House in 1860, which was by most accounts scrupulously honest (although the victor garnered just 39.7 percent of the popular vote and virtually no votes in the South).[1] The election that precipitated armed conflict among the nation's pro- and antislavery partisans was instead a relatively inconsequential one, on November 29, 1854, for the not-so-lofty office of nonvoting delegate to the U.S. Congress from the new territory of Kansas.

Staging a first election in a new territory was often a complex endeavor, especially in an era where heavy internal migration undermined the very notion that voting was tied to residence. Added to this was the uncomfortable fact that, as the so-called permanent habitat for thousands of Kickapoos, Sacs and Foxes, Shawnees, Delawares, Prairie Potatatomis and Miamis, Kansas, Ottawas, Wyandots, and Osages, not one square inch of the territory created by congressional statute on May 30, 1854, was legally available to sell. But Missourians residing close to the Kansas border—partisans of a "Southern rights candidate" named J. W. Whitfield—were so overzealous in their prosecution of the election in the neighboring territory that they began an arms race there that involved nearly every settler, squatter, legitimate tribal claim-holder, and speculator on up to the president of the United States. Frederick Starr of the new town of Leavenworth, Kansas, called the 1854 canvass "the greatest outrage on the ballot box ever perpetrated on American soil" as "some 1200 or 1400 Missourians armed with bowie knives & revolvers took to the polls," where they "brow-beat and intimidated the Judges, forced their own votes

into the ballot box for WHITFIELD, and crowded out and drove off all who were suspected of being in favor of any other candidate."[2]

A congressional investigation later concluded that nonresidents cast—fraudulently—more than 1,700 votes, making up a large percentage of Whitfield's 2,258 totals. Although shocking, the numbers were not enough to throw the election to another candidate, and the territorial governor let the election stand. After all, proslavery settlers from Missouri and the upper South likely did constitute a bona fide majority in the territory as of the fall of 1854. But the tide was changing fast.[3]

As ice on the waters of the Missouri River and its tributaries melted in early 1855, boatload after boatload of settlers from New England and other Northern states passed through Missouri's proslavery hotbeds, like Boonville, Lexington, and Independence, en route to Kansas. Fearing what might happen to their own slave property if the state were surrounded on three sides by free territory, the Missouri slaveholders took note of the emigrants with Yankee accents making their way to the new Kansas Territory towns of Lawrence, Topeka, and Osawatomie. Missouri's bombastic U.S. senator David Rice Atchison urged his supporters to repel the antislavery settlers as they would an invading army: "Money, time, private interest and all other things are but as dust, compared to [the slavery question] in its consequences; the Abolitionists are most energetically at work, we must meet and conquer them 'peaceably if we can forcibly if we must.'"[4]

The next election in Kansas Territory, for members of the territorial legislature, took place just four months later and made the canvass of the previous fall look tame in comparison. According to one scholar, unprincipled leaders at the head of a "motley, unwashed mob of ruffians, drunk with bad whisky and armed with cannon and every variety of small arms, overran the border and turned impending defeat into a glorious victory." According to the congressional report, Missouri residents cast 4,908 votes out of a total of 6,307, suggesting that just 22 percent of the votes were legitimate.[5]

After this "second Missouri invasion," free-soil leaders concluded they would never win Kansas for their side with numbers alone. Alongside population growth, money, and a righteous cause, they needed another, more immediately persuasive tool. They needed guns. Three days after the election of what was promptly called the "bogus legislature," Lawrence resident and free-soil leader Charles Robinson wrote to reformer Eli Thayer of Worcester, Massachusetts, the founder of the New England Emigrant Aid Company: "We want *arms.* . . . Give us the weapons and every man from the North will be a soldier and die in his tracks if necessary, to protect and defend our rights. . . . Cannot your secret society send us 200 Sharps rifles as a loan till this question is settled?"[6]

The answer to Robinson's question was an unequivocal "yes," and between 1855 and 1859—the period known as "Bleeding Kansas"—nine hundred to a thousand Sharps carbines were purchased by aid societies in the Northern states for use in the political movement to keep slavery out of the territory.[7] This volatile mix of ideology and state-of-the-art weaponry brought Americans on opposite sides of the slavery issue into armed conflict during the antebellum decade. The type of fighting that came to characterize the Kansas conflict—guerilla-style, retributive, house-to-house warfare that involved citizens as well as "soldiers" and frequently included raids on nearby plantations to liberate enslaved African Americans—was in many ways directly connected to the arming of the free-state side with "Beecher's Bibles" (famously so-called because the prominent clergyman Henry Ward Beecher said he "believed that the Sharps rifle was a truly *moral* agency, and that there was more moral power in one of those instruments . . . than in a hundred Bibles").[8] This type of warfare, perfected on the Kansas-Missouri border, would spread across the West and, eventually, the battlefields of the East and South.[9] In this way Missouri's Senator David R. Atchison, his gangs of "Border Ruffians," and Kansas settlers like Dr. Charles Robinson and the abolitionist "Osawatomie" John Brown became, arguably, the first combatants in the Civil War in the West.

To ensure that his request for Sharps rifles would be heard by his New England benefactors (who also provided equipment and machinery for saw and grist mills, as well as religious, scientific, and military books), Robinson dispatched an Emigrant Aid Company clerk named George W. Deitzler to Worcester and Boston to press his case. Deitzler, who later served as a brigadier general during the Civil War, recalled receiving an order for one hundred Sharps rifles within an hour of arriving in Boston on May 5. Deitzler made the quick trip to the Sharps factory in Hartford, the guns were packed the very next day, and he started back for Kansas on the morning of May 7, accompanied by a large box labeled "Books." Deitzler recalled, "Those rifles did good service in the 'border war.' . . . It was perhaps the first shipment of arms for our side and it incited a healthy feeling among the unarmed free state settlers, which permeated and energized them until even the Quakers were ready to fight."[10]

When the weapons arrived at their destination two weeks later, the antislavery settlers of Kansas Territory were well on the way to equaling and, finally, surpassing their proslavery rivals in the arms race and frequent skirmishes that quickly became a proxy war

FIGURE 3.2
One of the Sharps Model 1853 carbines purchased by the New England Emigrant Aid Company and shipped to Kansas, 1854–57. Donated by Mr. R. L. Wilson. Autry National Center, 87.104.1. For a color version of this image, see plate 3.

for the national battle over the expansion of slavery. Of the more than 150 violent deaths in Kansas during the territorial period, more than half were predominantly a result of the political divide over the slavery issue; it wasn't until President Franklin Pierce sent a new governor and more than thirteen hundred federal troops to Kansas that the violence subsided.[11] Both sides exaggerated the extent of the killings and atrocities committed in Kansas, but there is little doubt that the arming of the region's settlers—who already were living cheek-to-jowl in the territory's river valleys—virtually guaranteed the political violence that kept the conflict on the nation's front pages for nearly two years and paved the way for still more sectional strife.

The injection of breech-loading firearms into the cauldron of eastern Kansas Territory was initially met with consternation. Settlers from the Midwest, who tended to be less committed to the antislavery cause than their neighbors from New England, complained the Yankees might use force to crowd them off of land claims. James H. Lane, whose name later became synonymous with antislavery derring-do, but who, at the time, was a conservative Democrat from Indiana, urged the recipients of the new and lethal "books" to return them immediately to Massachusetts.[12] But the guns stayed.

Although partisans on both sides called the firearms "rifles," every known Sharps weapon delivered to the free staters in Kansas was actually a carbine—a shortened version of Sharps' full-sized rifle that fired the same ammunition, but at a lower rotational velocity. The carbine's smaller size and lighter weight made it easier to handle for many of the Kansas settlers, who were less well-trained and fought in mobile, guerilla-type bands, unlike regular soldiers.[13]

Owing to its use in the Civil War and in numerous cavalry battles with the first peoples of the Great Plains (as pictured in countless movies in the Western genre),[14] the rifles built by Christian Sharps's company were, along with Samuel Colt's revolver, *the* major innovation in firearms design in the antebellum decade. Compared to the muzzle-loading rifles of the day, the Sharps weapons offered far more firepower; recipients of the donated rifles were able to use the carbines as tools to make their political influence match their numbers. Not only were the Border Ruffians from Missouri often inebriated during their expeditions into the territory, but they were also usually armed with squirrel rifles and buffalo guns, along with the occasional army musket. Members of the free-soil movement in Kansas, aided with money and arms from their eastern benefactors, determined to create their own antislavery government with a "new code of laws called Sharps Revised Statutes."[15]

Almost immediately, free-state leaders began to angle for still more firearms; their eastern supporters, eyeing the near monopoly on intimidation held by the proslavery side, were eager to oblige. A list of subscribers dated August 24, 1855, found in the papers of Amos A. Lawrence (the industrialist and treasurer of the Emigrant Aid Company, whose name adorns Kansas Territory's most famous antislavery town), is a who's who of New England abolitionism and includes Wendell Phillips ($100), Gerrit Smith ($250), Samuel Hoar ($50), and Lawrence himself ($955). The "books" were rushed to Kansas Territory for use, if required, in the October 1855 election for delegates to the extralegal and antislavery Topeka Constitutional Convention, which proposed to form a separate and competing state legislature.[16]

Transporting Sharps rifles and other munitions to the free-state settlers in Kansas often proved difficult. A settler named David Starr Hoyt led a party in late 1855 to bring to the territory a massive arsenal, including four breech-loading cannons, one hundred Sharps carbines with saber bayonets, thousands of percussion caps (invented in the early nineteenth century to enable muzzle-loading firearms to fire reliably in any weather), and a large quantity of cartridges. After several weeks of winter travel, Hoyt's party split: two members traveled overland to Kansas City with the slides necessary to operate the weapons hidden in their baggage, while Hoyt and William B. Parsons, who recalled the incident years later, boarded the steamship *Arabia* with the rest of the shipment.

After the proslavery captain discovered a letter from Hoyt describing the precious cargo and read it aloud onboard, a mob gathered and demanded to see the guns. "I judge that not one of them had ever seen a breech-loading arm, and the surmises as to how the thing went off were ludicrous," Parsons remembered. When ordered to fire the weapon, Parsons told them they would have to send ahead to Lawrence and get a slide to stop the breech, a line deemed by one and all onboard a "d——d Yankee trick." When Hoyt refused to sign a document surrendering the arms, the *Arabia* tied up in Lexington, one of the most rabidly proslavery towns on the Missouri River, where the boat was "welcomed by a thousand natives armed with every conceivable weapon." Cooler heads prevailed after a large majority demanded a hanging; and in exchange for the arms, Hoyt was given a paper that read, "Taken from D.S. Hoyt the following described property, to be delivered to the order of Wilson Shannon, governor of Kansas Territory, or his successor in office," followed by a detailed schedule of the property. Hoyt later returned to Saint Louis and "libeled" the *Arabia* upon her return, and collected over 50 percent more than the cost of the goods in the first place; in 1857 many of the carbines were recovered.[17]

Things didn't end as well for Hoyt, however, because he was murdered a few weeks after the incident on the *Arabia* after parlaying in a "Border Ruffian fort" in southern

Douglas County while supposedly under the protection of the white flag. He was remembered as "among the earliest and the bravest of the Kansas martyrs."[18]

Meanwhile, the fraudulently elected pre-Sharps "bogus" legislature passed law after law designed to make the territory a haven for slaveholders, including one that incorporated into Kansas statute, and strengthened, Missouri's own slave code. The territorial legal code stipulated that only proslavery men would be allowed to hold office or serve on juries, and it outlined severe punishments for speaking out against slavery (five years at hard labor), helping runaway slaves escape (ten years in prison), and possessing books about slave rebellion or fomenting insurrection (death by hanging).[19]

Free-state settlers, including John Brown Jr., son of the not-yet-famous abolitionist, decided on a two-pronged response to the "bogus" legislature: meet in a separate convention to create an alternate (and antislavery) constitution for the territory, and fight back against attacks by the proslavery side.[20] The strategy produced mixed results, since the formation of the alternate (and extralegal) Topeka Legislature allowed the proslavery minority to claim the mantle of "law and order," and especially since President Franklin Pierce wholeheartedly backed all actions of the "bogus" legislature in Lecompton.

Like many Kansas immigrants from the free states, the Browns hoped to become permanent farmers in Kansas as well as soldiers on the front lines of the battle over slavery and its expansion. Brown's brothers Jason, Owen, Frederick, and Salmon, ranging in age from eighteen to thirty-three, emigrated with him, along with his Aunt Florella Brown Adair (John Brown Sr.'s half sister) and her husband, Samuel.[21] The place the family selected for their new home was north of Pottawatomie Creek, ten miles west of the antislavery town of Osawatomie. Despite the name of the creek (a name the Browns would soon make infamous), the site of Brown's Station was originally part of the Miami reserve. The abolitionist Brown clan was thus part of a wave of intruders onto Indian lands in the spring of 1855, a tide that one Indian agent described as "an absolute reign of terror." While federal Indian commissioner George Manypenny scrambled to renegotiate treaties with the tribes, President Pierce decided to allow the U.S. Army to expel intruders like the Browns from Indian reservations—but cautioned the officers in charge "to go very slow." The net effect of this "policy" was that settlers were allowed to occupy and control their claims on Miami, Shawnee, and Osage land indefinitely. As two historians of Indian Kansas have written, "Many of the intruders [including the Browns and Adairs] had journeyed thousands of miles to seek homes in Kansas; most were God-fearing heads of respectable families; winter was approaching, food was in short supply, children were sickly, and, since the intruders had 'no where else to go' . . . justice was deferred until the following spring." This, of course, effectively meant forever.[22]

John Brown Sr. at first declined to join the Kansas party, writing to his son that he felt "committed to operate in another part of the field." He added that if he "were not so committed, I would be on my way this fall."[23] By the middle of 1855, however, Brown had changed his mind. He had received several long letters from John Jr. asking for help procuring weapons for the fight against his aggressive proslavery neighbors. According to one:

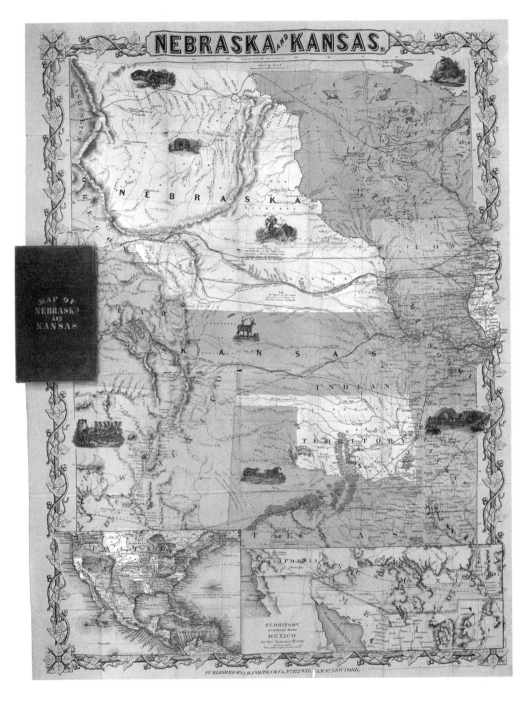

FIGURE 3.3

J. H. Colton & Company illustrated map of Nebraska and Kansas, circa 1855. Rosenstock Collection, Autry Library Collection, Autry National Center, 90.253.4179.

FIGURE 3.4
Photograph taken of John Brown in Kansas, 1856–57. Kansas State Historical Society.

"The friends of freedom are not one fourth of them half armed, and as to Military Organization among them it no where exists in this territory," the son wrote to his father. Another of the letters lamented that the free-state settlers "exhibit the most abject and cowardly spirit, whenever their dearest rights are invaded and trampled down." The letters struck exactly the right chord for the abolitionist, who had planned to confront the Slave Power (shorthand for the antislavery position alleging disproportionate and unfair political power wielded by slave owners in various branches of the national government) with violence, if necessary, and who seemed to struggle with exactly how and where to make his mark. So John Brown made plans to settle his wife, Mary, and a new baby, Ellen (his twentieth child), back at the Browns' Adirondack farmstead and strike out for Kansas, where he planned to rescue both his endangered family and the imperiled cause of freedom.[24]

On the way West, Brown returned to Akron, Ohio, where he procured some unusual weapons for his fight against the Slave Power in Kansas. Instead of the Sharps carbines and Colt revolvers so coveted by the free staters (which were expensive and heavy), Brown procured several swords from a compatriot named General Bierce, who had removed them from an old armory there. Included among these were about half a dozen "short cutlasses, or artillery sabers . . . straight and broad, like an old Roman sword," as well as "some curved swords" and some "old bayonets." These old-fashioned tools of war called to mind more ancient battles and would go a long way toward making John Brown into the antislavery warrior-prophet he had long imagined himself to be.[25]

Almost immediately after the elder Brown's arrival at Brown's Station, word arrived that a proslavery Virginian named Franklin Coleman had shot down the free stater Charles Dow in the road. Eyewitness testimony suggests that Coleman and Dow's disagreement was over a land-claim dispute, not politics (the two had reportedly never quarreled about slavery)—but in the tinderbox of antebellum eastern Kansas, politics and the slavery question overwhelmed everything else.[26] The incident emboldened citizens in the antislavery town of Lawrence, thirty miles north of Brown's Station, to hold a protest meeting in November 1855, where they explicitly agreed to Charles Robinson's plea to take up arms. In retaliation, the proslavery county sheriff and governor—informed that an armed force in Lawrence was in "open rebellion" against the laws of the territory—mobilized the militia and invited back the Missouri "visitors" from the previous spring. A large and rowdy mob gathered just south of town, on the banks of the Wakarusa River, spoiling for a fight.

The Browns arrived in Lawrence on December 7, 1855, guns and knives drawn (and the scary old bayonets rattling on the floor of the wagon), at one point bisecting a crowd of rowdy Missourians and silencing them with an intimidating display of personal armament. Both John Browns were given commands (John Brown's official title was captain in the First Brigade of Kansas Volunteers), but before the "Wakarusa War" could heat up, it was defused by an agreement between Charles Robinson and territorial governor Wilson Shannon. Open warfare was, for the moment, averted.[27]

The bitter Kansas winter briefly quelled the tensions of the previous fall. But when a Lawrence resident nonfatally shot the proslavery sheriff of Douglas County while the latter was attempting to arrest free-state settlers, events quickly reached a boiling point. On May 11, 1856, a federal marshal determined that free-state settlers were illegally obstructing justice (by preventing the sheriff from executing warrants on members of the extralegal Topeka Legislature) and declared that Lawrence's Free State Hotel constituted a military installation rather than mere lodging. Both accusations were true. Sheriff Samuel L. Jones amassed a posse of eight hundred Missourians to seize the town, disarm the citizens, wreck the town's antislavery presses, and destroy the Free State Hotel.

The sack of Lawrence was yet another example of the free-state side completely wilting under an aggressive armed assault by residents of another state. Although the free-state side was better armed by 1856, the force from Missouri was apparently intimidatingly strong. The latter also possessed artillery in the form of a cannon known as "Old Sacramento," one of ten cannons captured by Col. Alexander Doniphan in the Battle of Sacramento near Chihuahua, Mexico, on February 28, 1847. After the war the captured guns were taken to Missouri and kept in the arsenal at Liberty, near Doniphan's home. When things heated up in Kansas Territory in the next decade, "some zealous Missourians pillaged the arsenal to secure arms and munitions of war," and Old Sacramento was wheeled the fifty-five miles to Lawrence.[28]

When the town's free-state leadership heard of the size and armaments of the Missouri invaders, they effectively disbanded. Along with noting the American flag, witnesses remarked on a blood-red banner also mustered by the invading force and

inscribed with the words "Southern-rights."[29] Within minutes the town's two antislavery printing offices were looted, the presses destroyed, and the moveable type cast into the Kansas River. Next the invaders turned Old Sacramento on the Free State Hotel. The first shot was fired by none other than a U.S. senator from Missouri, David Rice Atchison, although the volley missed the target. Fifty shots (and several kegs of gunpowder) later, the walls still remained standing; an incendiary device, however, finally did the job and the town's most impressive structure was rendered smoldering and roofless. On their way out of town, forces torched Charles Robinson's house.[30]

The role in the assault by the old Mexican War cannon suggests two things about the escalating violence in Kansas Territory. The first is the use, by both sides in the conflict, of more sophisticated and more destructive weaponry to advance a political cause. Before the sack of Lawrence, weaponry on each side had been confined to carbines, shotguns, and pistols. Second is the constant reuse and salvage of weapons in the conflict, something common to the frontier and the West. Weapons constantly changed hands—in the case of Old Sacramento, from Mexican forces (perhaps even Spanish before that; the cannon's provenance is unknown) to the U.S. Army to Border Ruffians, and, finally, to free-state Kansans. Antislavery forces successfully captured Old Sacramento in an attack on a proslavery stronghold on August 12, 1856, turning it on its former possessors four days later in the Battle of Fort Titus. It was last used in battle on September 14, 1856, in the Battle of Hickory Point, before being transported to Lawrence, where it was used for the next forty years for celebratory occasions.[31]

John Brown and his allies were already en route from Brown's Station to defend Lawrence from the Missouri invasion when they met a rider who had escaped the sacking and shared the news. Witnesses described John Brown as in a "state of disbelief." How could Lawrence have been taken without a fight? Brown told his men: "We must fight fire with fire. . . . Something must be done to show these barbarians that we, too, have rights." Brown gathered four of his sons (Owen, Salmon, Frederick, and Oliver) and two new recruits, and loaded a wagon with carbines and revolvers. But before heading off into the night, Brown and his men sharpened the shortened artillery broadswords he had procured in Ohio and placed them in the wagon as well. "There was a signal understood,"

Owen Brown later recalled. "When my father was to raise a sword—then we were to begin."[32]

Later that same night (the day after South Carolina congressman Preston Brooks beat antislavery Massachusetts senator Charles Sumner bloody and unconscious for insulting his uncle and the South in a speech titled "The Crimes against Kansas"[33]), Brown and his war party awakened the family of proslavery settlers James and Mahala Doyle. Calling themselves the "Northern army," the men at the door announced they had come to take Doyle and his three sons prisoner. After successfully pleading for the freedom of her youngest son, John, Mahala Doyle watched the late-night visitors take her husband and two other sons into the night. As she later testified, "My husband and two boys, my sons, did not come back any more." The next stop for the war party was the home of Allen Wilkinson, who, like the Doyles, had emigrated from Tennessee but owned no slaves. Wilkinson, however, was an outspoken member of Kansas's proslavery legislature. He, too, was led, bound and unshod, from his home. Finally, the war party stopped at the house of "Dutch" Henry Sherman, who ran a rough tavern and store frequented by proslavery settlers. Henry was not at home that night, but the "Northern army" took away his brother William. The next morning residents of Pottawatomie Creek awoke to find the bodies of all of these men, slashed and mutilated by blades. Several of the corpses were missing fingers, limbs, and had their skulls split open.[34]

News of the killings spread quickly, and Jason Brown immediately confronted his father and demanded to know his role in the murders. "I did not do it, but I approved of it," the father told the son. "God is my judge. . . . We were justified, under the circumstances."[35] After this moment, John Brown rarely spoke of the night of the Pottawatomie massacre except in the vaguest of terms, admitting culpability without taking responsibility for shedding any blood. His family stuck to this story, too (although later Salmon admitted his father had fired a shot into the head of James Doyle, but after he was already dead, as a "signal"). The Browns' defenders explained the murders using almost identical language: that the attacks were a preemptive strike against dangerous men who intended to do harm to the antislavery settlers in the area, and that they were, therefore, acts of self-defense. All references to the bodies' mutilation were downplayed, with the defenders insisting that swords were used only to avoid noise and thus retribution, and that any unseemly wounds were merely the result of the victims' attempts to ward off the slicing blows of the broadswords.

Perhaps. John Brown's guilt for the murders has been endlessly relitigated by his contemporaries and by scholars, with conflicting verdicts handed down with virtually each attempt.[36] It is worth noting, however, that until the night Brown's "Northern army" visited Pottawatomie, the proslavery side held a virtual monopoly on actual violence in the territory, with countless acts of intimidation, six bona fide murders, and the destruction of Lawrence as the crowning example. As Brown had lamented, the defenders of Lawrence had put up little or no fight (as had Senator Sumner), and the batterers and killers of free-state men had largely gone free. What remains clear was Brown's overarching goal, no matter whether he led or actively participated in the massacre: to instill fear in the hearts of the proslavery settlers and make it clear that murder would be met with murder, Gideon-like. "LET SLIP THE DOGS OF WAR!" roared one Missouri newspaper. Kansas was, officially, bleeding, and at this turning point Brown chose to use antique cutlasses rather than Sharps carbines. But it would be guns, not swords, that turned conflict into war.[37]

Although most other free-state settlers condemned the actions at Pottawatomie, Brown's adoption of retributive violence gave voice to the despair and rage many antislavery Kansans experienced during the fifteen months after the election that created the "bogus" legislature. Coming so soon after the sack of Lawrence, the murders helped spur formerly peaceful settlers to act with force, even as their political leaders called for calm and negotiation. "Violence breeds violence," wrote James Hanway, who was shocked at the murders but continued to support Brown and to condemn the proslavery party. "They advocate assassination and now that five persons have been murdered on their side perhaps they will learn that such hellish sentiments when carried into effect, will work equally to the destruction of proslavery men."[38]

This new feeling of defiance and opposition led many free-state settlers—most of whom also condemned the Pottawatomie murders—nevertheless to gather their weapons and take to the brush for out-and-out battle with the pro-Southern side. Leading the way was "Old Osawatomie Brown," whose legend was growing fast. He was now an outlaw with a price on his head and federal troops, vigilantes, and crowds of Missourians in near-constant pursuit. Brown's guerilla band initially hid out near Ottawa Creek and was the subject of a colorful passage by the Scottish-born reporter James Redpath, who described the material—and matériel—context for several Northern and antislavery newspapers: "A dozen horses were tied, all ready saddled for a ride for life, or a hunt after Southern invaders. A dozen rifles and sabers were stacked around the trees . . . and two fine-looking youths were standing, leaning on their arms, near by." Brown himself "stood near the fire, with his shirt-sleeves rolled up, and a large piece of pork in his hand. . . . He was poorly clad, and his toes protruded from his boots."[39]

The battles of Black Jack and Osawatomie in June and August of 1856 sealed John Brown's fame as a fearsome guerilla fighter and transformed him from a business failure and poor father into a full-scale warrior-prophet. Just ten days after Pottawatomie, Brown led a dawn strike on a much larger force of proslavery men headed by Henry Clay Pate, all veterans of the sack of Lawrence. After a five-hour firefight conducted in the wagon ruts on the Santa Fe Trail just outside of Palmyra, a confused Pate, who believed his side was outnumbered, surrendered to Brown. He later claimed, "I went to take Old Brown, and Old Brown took me." The battle was the first instance of organized white men battling over the future of slavery, nearly five full years before the firing on Fort Sumter.[40]

The summer of 1856 constituted the heart of "Bleeding Kansas," as fighters on both sides took to the brush to terrorize, rob, torch, and attack their enemies.[41] The conflicts culminated in August with the Battle of Osawatomie, when several hundred proslavery soldiers, armed with artillery, descended on the antislavery town where many of Brown's family members lived. With a ragtag group of forty men, Brown inflicted significant casualties on the invaders before retreating to watch the town burn. "God see it," the man now known as Osawatomie Brown told his son Jason as they took in the smoky view. "I have only a short time to live—only one death to die, and I will die fighting this cause. There will be no more peace in this land until slavery is done for. I will give them something else to do than to extend slave territory. I will carry the war into Africa." By Africa, Brown meant he would next attack slavery where it already existed: in the South. Once again a rapt readership in the east were told of a scrappy battle where an outnumbered Brown proved that antislavery men would fight, and fight well, for their cause.[42]

"Money, Sharps Rifles, Recruits," was the angry cry in antislavery newspapers as the word reached the East Coast. The *New York Tribune,* on the suggestion of one subscriber, announced it would collect $1 subscriptions for "Kansas relief," a war matériel fund that quickly raised $22,000. Aid committees sprang up across the north like mushrooms after a prairie thunderstorm, and these were consolidated into state committees that often raised sums in the tens of thousands of dollars.[43]

In fact, the story of two hundred of the Sharps rifles purchased by the Kansas State Committee of Massachusetts for $4,947.88 closes the circle of John Brown's antebellum attacks on the Slave Power. Instead of being shipped straight to Kansas, the carbines were transported to Tabor, Iowa. In the meantime, free-state leaders succeeded in enlisting territorial governor John W. Geary to broker a cease-fire of sorts, and many of the military bands that were not absorbed into the new state militia were disbanded. John Brown used his influence with the officers of the Kansas State Committee of Massachusetts to sway a skeptical national committee into awarding him the carbines for a new plan of attack on the Slave Power, this time in Harpers Ferry, Virginia. These firearms were ones captured by the Maryland State Militia after a raid had been foiled there in October 1859.[44]

The historian W. H. Isely wrote about the arming of the Kansas free staters in 1907, claiming the actions were "not an act of aggression, but purely a measure for protection and defense. The winning of Kansas was a great and important victory for Freedom. Here the slave power received its first stunning defeat," a defeat in which breech-loading firearms played a significant role alongside antiquated weapons used to great effect to inflict terror. But the escalation of tension and violence these well-intentioned men and women unleashed on the territory was also a portent of what sectional warfare would look like in the years to come, in nearby towns like Osceola, Missouri, and Lawrence, Kansas (again, in 1863), and in faraway places like Washington, Ohio, and the Shenandoah Valley.[45]

NOTES

1. In the Electoral College, Lincoln won 180 electoral votes out of a total of 303. John C. Breckinridge, who came in second in the Electoral College vote, won just 72.

2. Starr to unknown recipient, December 1, 1854, Starr Papers, Kansas State Historical Society, Topeka (hereafter KSHS).

3. U.S. Congress, "Report of the Special Committee Appointed to Investigate the Troubles in Kansas, with the Views of the Minority of Said Committee," 34th Cong., 1st sess., House Report no. 200 (Washington, DC: Cornelius Wendell, 1856), 9 (hereafter *Howard Report*). See also Russell K. Hickman, "The Reeder Administration Inaugurated: Part I—the Delegate Election of November, 1854," *Kansas History Quarterly* 36 (Autumn 1970): 322; Nicole Etcheson, *Bleeding Kansas* (Lawrence, KS: University Press of Kansas, 2004), 54. A census in the territory in February 1855 gave the total number of voters in the territory as 2,905.

4. D. R. Atchison to Col. O. Anderson, January 30, 1855, quoted in Etcheson, *Bleeding Kansas,* 55.

5. *Howard Report,* 30.

6. Robinson to Eli Thayer, April 2, 1855, New England Emigrant Aid Company Papers, KSHS.

7. This number does not include those Sharps rifles brought to the region by individuals. See W. H. Isely, "The Sharps Rifle Episode in Kansas History," *American Historical Review* 12, no. 3 (April 1907): 546–66. Isely traces many of the shipments of the newfangled weapons to Kansas Territory. See also Frank M. Sellers, *Sharps Firearms* (n.p.: Beinfeld, 1978), chap. 7. Sellers adds between one hundred and two hundred to Isely's numbers, citing "fragmentary records of the Sharps Rifle Manufacturing Company" (97n5).

8. *New York Tribune,* February 8, 1856. After this date, Sharps rifles were popularly known as "Beecher Bibles" or "Beecher's Bibles."

9. Jonathan Earle and Diane Mutti Burke, eds., *Bleeding Kansas, Bleeding Missouri: The Long Civil War on the Border* (Lawrence: University Press of Kansas, 2013).

10. Charles S. Gleed, ed., *The Kansas Memorial, a Report of the Old Settlers' Meeting Held at Bismarck Grove, Kansas, September 15th and 16th, 1879* (Kansas City, MO: Press of Ransey, Millett, and Hudson, 1880), 184–85.

11. Dale E. Watts, "How Bloody Was Bleeding Kansas? Political Killings in Kansas Territory, 1854–1861," *Kansas History* 18, no. 2 (Summer 1995): 116–29.

12. *New York Tribune,* June 15, 1855; Isely, "The Sharps Rifle Episode in Kansas History," 553. Lane, a recent immigrant from Indiana, quickly moved to the free-soil side, eventually challenging Robinson for leadership of the settler movement. See Etcheson, *Bleeding Kansas,* 71.

13. See, for example, Michael Fellman, *Inside War: The Guerilla Conflict in Missouri during the Civil War* (New York: Oxford University Press, 1990).

14. Most recently, the Sharps carbine features in the Coen brothers' 2010 film *True Grit,* where the carbine's accuracy becomes a source of debate between Jeff Bridges's character, "Rooster" Cogburn, and Matt Damon's character, LaBoeuf. The accuracy of the gun is validated at the end of the film.

15. *Howard Report,* 658–70.

16. George W. Martin, ed., *Transactions of the Kansas State Historical Society,* vols. 1 and 2 (Topeka: State Printing Office, 1881), 221–23.

17. William B. Parsons, "David Starr Hoyt," *Kansas Magazine* 2 (1872): 42–45. Sharps carbines relied on a metal breech lock that "slides" up and down in grooves cut into the breech, controlled by a small lever. Without the slides, they were inoperable.

18. Ibid., 45. The steamship *Arabia* hit a snag in the Missouri and sank near what today is Parksville, Missouri, on September 5, 1856. It was rediscovered in 1988 by a team of researchers,

and today artifacts recovered from the site are housed in the Arabia Steamboat Museum in Kansas City.

19. Statutes of the Territory of Kansas, 1855, pp. 715–17, KSHS.

20. Etcheson, *Bleeding Kansas*, 78.

21. Florella and Samuel, both graduates of progressive, biracial Oberlin College, did stay in Osawatomie, founding a Congregational church there and, later, the first insane asylum in Kansas. The Adair cabin is now the location of the John Brown Museum.

22. H. Craig Miner and William E. Unrau, *The End of Indian Kansas: A Study of Cultural Revolution, 1854–1871* (Lawrence: University Press of Kansas, 1978), 16–17.

23. John Brown to John Brown Jr., August 24, 1854, in Franklin B. Sanborn, *Life and Letters of John Brown* (Concord, MA: Roberts Brothers, 1885), 264.

24. John Brown Jr. to John Brown, May 20, 24, 1855, in Sanborn, *Life and Letters of John Brown*, 200–201. He also left behind numerous lawsuits and business entanglements in Ohio, Massachusetts, and Great Britain for a new life as a full-time soldier in the war against slavery, a new life that would stretch from his departure for Kansas to his descent from the gallows in Virginia four years later.

25. Sanborn, *Life and Letters of John Brown*, 264. The sword in the Autry's exhibit is, according to the museum collection curator at the Kansas Museum of History, one of the curved sabers Brown brought from Akron and later presented to Otis Potter, who hosted the Browns at his cabin after Brown's Station was burned following the Battle of Osawatomie.

26. Testimony of John M. Banks before the Howard Commission, *Howard Report*, 1057. See also Watts, "How Bloody Was Bleeding Kansas?" 116–29.

27. John Brown to Mary Brown, December 16, 1855, in Sanborn, *Life and Letters of John Brown*, 217–21.

28. *Kansas: A Cyclopedia of State History, Embracing Events, Institutions, Industries, Counties, Cities, Towns, Prominent Persons, Etc. . . . with a Supplementary Volume Devoted to Selected Personal History and Reminiscence* (Chicago: Standard Publishing, 1912), 2:617–18.

29. Jay Monaghan, *Civil War on the Western Border, 1854–1865* (Lincoln: University of Nebraska Press, 1984), 58.

30. Amid all the property damage, only one fatality was recorded during the sack of Lawrence—a proslavery resident killed by falling masonry.

31. Undated, "Old Sacramento" clippings folder, Douglas County Historical Society, Lawrence, KS. The cannon was severely damaged in 1896 when it was used in an attempt to raise drowned bodies from the Kansas River and overpacked with mud and explosives.

32. Interview with Owen Brown, February 27, 1880, Houghton Library, Harvard University, quoted in Tony Horwitz, *Midnight Rising* (New York: Henry Holt, 2011), 49.

33. John Brown's son Salmon later recounted that news of Sumner's caning reached the Browns the same night they set out for Pottawatomie, saying, "It seemed to be the finishing, decisive touch." But this is unlikely. The news could well have reached the nearest telegraph station in Weston, Missouri, but it's doubtful anyone would have known about it in the Kansas brush on the evening of May 23. See Tony R. Mullis, "The Information Infrastructure" (unpublished essay, 2003), in author's possession.

34. *Howard Report*, 1193–99; see also Jonathan Earle, *John Brown's Raid on Harper's Ferry: A Brief History with Documents* (Boston: Bedford/St. Martin's, 2008), 56–57.

35. Jason Brown, statement to F. G. Adams, April 2, 1884, Oswald Garrison Villard–John Brown Papers, Columbia Rare Book Library, Columbia University. See also Jason Brown, letter to the editor, *Lawrence Journal*, February 8, 1880, microfilm, Oswald Garrison Villard–John Brown Papers.

36. For two twenty-first-century interpretations, see David Reynolds, *John Brown, Abolitionist: The Man Who Killed Slavery, Sparked the Civil War, and Seeded Civil Rights* (New York: Random House, 2006), 163–66, and Tony Horwitz, *Midnight Rising* (New York: Henry Holt, 2011), 49–55.

37. *Westport (MO) Border Times,* May 27, 1856, quoted in Oswald Garrison Villard, *John Brown, 1800–1859: A Biography Fifty Years After* (New York: Houghton Mifflin, 1910), 189.

38. Quotation in James Hanway, Memorandum Book, entry about June 1, 1856, James Hanway Papers, KSHS. James Hanway Collection, no. 372, Manuscript Volume, 1856, pp. 6–7, KSHS. Also available online at Kansas Memory, www.kansasmemory.org/item/90225.

39. James Redpath, *Public Life of Captain John Brown* (Boston: Thayer and Eldridge, 1860), 112–14.

40. Henry Clay Pate, "John Brown as Viewed by H. Clay Pate," West Virginia Archives and History, July 9, 1856, www.wvculture.org/history/jbexhibit/pateonbrown.html.

41. Watts, "How Bloody was Bleeding Kansas?" 116–29.

42. Villard, *John Brown,* 248.

43. *New York Tribune,* January 23, 1857. The Kansas Committee of New York spent $643 on Sharps rifles for Kansas in one year; the Kansas State Committee of Massachusetts raised over $48,000, more than 10 percent of which was spent on Sharps rifles. See also Isely, "The Sharps Rifle Episode in Kansas History," 560–61, 116–29.

44. U.S. Senate, Mason Committee, *Report on the Invasion of Harper's Ferry,* 36th Cong., 1st sess., Senate Report 278 (Washington, DC, 1860), 245–47.

45. Osceola was sacked by invading "Jayhawkers" in September 1862; in August of 1863, Lawrence was destroyed, and most fighting-age men were killed, by the forces of William Clark Quantrill. Washington was raided by John Hunt Morgan's raiders that same year, and John Singleton Mosby formed a "partisan" unit that was effective in pinning down federal forces behind Union lines in northern Virginia after 1864.

4

LIBERTY, EMPIRE, AND CIVIL WAR IN THE AMERICAN WEST

Durwood Ball

During four years of the Civil War, Union conflicts with American Indians escalated to a violent pitch unseen since the War of 1812. The war to restore the Union and destroy slavery translated into a conflict to fulfill liberty and empire in the West. Western Union volunteers waged brutal, destructive, and lethal operations against Indian communities throughout the trans-Mississippi West. Their campaigns were so violent and indiscriminate that near the Civil War's end, Congress launched a wide-ranging inquiry into the nation's relations with the western Indians.

The Union war on the Indians was "destructive" or "hard."[1] Since 1815, the prosecution of liberty, both personal and national, had assumed a high measure of totality, though the federal army sometimes mediated and moderated the level of violence. From its beginning in 1789, the United States had intended to incorporate all lands under its legal sovereignty, and all Native inhabitants in the way of American progress were subjugated, dispersed, removed, incarcerated, assimilated, or destroyed. By mid-1863, the Union war had become an epic struggle to terminate the shameful social injustice of Southern slavery; that same war, when waged in the West, advanced the national program to subjugate, reduce, and concentrate those Native Americans still living freely. The western war inaugurated the final cataclysm that would, in the space of a quarter century, engulf, dispossess, and incarcerate all western Indians.

Found among the Autry's historical artifacts are three devices—a telegraph key, a trumpet or bugle, and a U.S. Model 1842 Percussion Pistol—that figured in ways large and small in the Union war on its internal enemies, white and Indian. All three aided the Union's retention of the Pacific Coast, especially California, and its prosecution of ferocious campaigns against American Indians, particularly the Sioux in 1862–65 and the Navajos in 1863–65. And all three demonstrate the extent to which modern technologies fueled the progress of liberty and empire in the West. Depending on who operated them, the pocket sounder, bugle, and 1842 pistol were the instruments of freedom or subjugation, civilization or barbarism.

THE WEST ON THE EVE OF CIVIL WAR

When Confederate artillerists bombarded Fort Sumter in Charleston Harbor on April 12, 1861, President Abraham Lincoln faced steep strategic and tactical challenges in the American West. He had to raise combat troops, supply and arm them, and maneuver them across rugged geography and vast distances. Complicating these missions were slow or unreliable communications, and independent, indifferent, or hostile white and Native peoples. Although expecting resistance from Indians, anxious Unionists also cast a suspicious eye on western whites—farmers, miners, merchants—who seemed inclined more to fulfill their own liberty than to save the Union. Modern technologies helped the Union bridge western distances, organize the region's human and material resources, coordinate federal troops in the western theater and on its battlefields, and punish and conquer rebellious peoples, particularly Indians.

United States territory west of the Mississippi River measured over two million square miles of woodlands, prairies, plains, mountains, mesas, and canyons. The trans-Missouri West was mostly arid or semiarid desert intersected by high mountain chains and a few rivers, creeks, and streams.[2] In 1861, the railroad went no farther west than Saint Joseph in far northwestern Missouri. Nearly all travelers crossed this rugged land the premodern way—by horse, mule, cart, or wagon, or on foot, along hundreds of miles of unimproved traces, trails, and roads. In the few places where it was possible, river navigation was slow, undependable, or treacherous. Communication with states or territories west of Missouri was accomplished by horse-borne or -drawn mail couriers traveling by overland roads such as the Oregon/California Trail (two thousand miles) to Sacramento or the Santa Fe/Chihuahua Trail to Santa Fe (nine hundred miles) or to Franklin (twelve hundred miles). Mail was also shipped through the Gulf of Mexico, ported over the Isthmus of Panama, and sailed up the Pacific Coast to California—a process that took about three weeks. The most rapid communication between California and Missouri was nine to twelve days by Pony Express, and army express riders covered the nine hundred miles between Santa Fe and Fort Leavenworth in about half that time.[3]

According to the federal census of 1860, the West was still sparsely settled, with a white population of about 1.4 million in a nation of about 31.4 million.[4] California, overrun by miners since 1849, boasted the largest number. Among the trans-Mississippi West states and territories, Arkansas, Louisiana, and Texas joined the Confederacy. All others extant in April 1861 remained loyal, and Dakota, Nevada, Montana, and Arizona, created almost as wartime measures, would join them as federal territories during the conflict. The citizens of Minnesota, Iowa, Nebraska, and Kansas—all free states or territories—were strongly pro-Union, but probably half the population of Missouri, a slave state, was pro-Confederate. Pockets of sympathizers declared for the South along the Missouri River in Iowa and Nebraska, in southern New Mexico, in southern California, and in Nevada.[5] Slow or unreliable communications hampered the Lincoln administration's efforts to measure the strength of pro-Southern feeling in the West, and the faintest rumor or smallest hint of treason among westerners panicked policy makers in the White House and Capitol.

In 1861, most westerners were occupied peoples. Ten thousand federal regulars garrisoned the American West, surveilling white frontiersmen as much as Indians, Mexicans, and Mormons. Presidential appointees controlled the executive and judicial branches of federal territories such as New Mexico and Nebraska. Union authorities worried that Hispanos in New Mexico and Mormons in Utah would either actively sympathize with the rebels or passively let them cut the overland trails to California and jeopardize the Union hold on the Pacific Coast. Nuevomexicanos had been United States citizens only for thirteen years, and the polygamous Mormons lived beyond the pale.[6] Despite their United States citizenship, Nuevomexicanos and Mormons were not considered "white" and were thus unstable, unreliable, and potentially disloyal in the minds of most Unionists.

And, of course, Native American peoples, "warlike" to federal authorities and the American public, also worried Washington, D.C. The disloyalty of slave-owning Cherokees in Indian Territory, for instance, cast the pall of treason over all Indians and suggested a Southern conspiracy to organize Native peoples against the Union. Numbering about 360,000 in 1860, Native Americans were dispersed widely across the West. Although some lived on federal reserves on the West Coast and in Indian Territory, Kansas, Iowa, and Minnesota, the vast majority, such as Comanches, Navajos, Bannocks, and Sioux, enjoyed autonomy with little federal scrutiny or interference.[7] Their independence stirred unease among Union leaders, especially civilian and western military officials tasked with keeping trails and roads safe and open and telegraph lines operational. William P. Dole, Lincoln's commissioner of Indian Affairs, advocated a "reform" solution: the end of treaties with Indians, the concentration of Indians on a few reservations, the application of severalty to Native homelands and reservations, and the assimilation of Indians into mainstream white society. The federal government had the right to punish or subjugate all Indians who resisted this purportedly humane policy. In wartime especially, Dole's concentration policy justified federal armed force against the Indians and intensified the militarization of U.S. Indian policy.[8]

During the Civil War, western governors and volunteers prosecuted campaigns against the Indians with little oversight from the preoccupied Union authorities in Washington, D.C. Raised from civilian populations in the trans-Mississippi West, federal volunteers in the region numbered fifteen thousand by late 1862 and nearly twenty thousand by 1865—double the number of regulars in the region four years earlier. In early to mid-1862, the Republican-controlled Thirty-Seventh Congress secured the western volunteers' investment in the war with passage of the Transcontinental Railroad Act, the Homestead Act, the Morrill Land-Grant College Act, and the act to establish a Department of Agriculture. The Republicans designed these measures to facilitate western emigration, economic development, and geopolitical expansion. Now, these Union volunteers simply had to deprive Native Americans of their freedom to advance their own liberty in the American West.

POCKET SOUNDER

The Lincoln administration faced three strategic problems in the West when the Civil War began: guaranteeing California's loyalty to the Union, checking any Confederate lunge to the Pacific Coast, and keeping the principal roads in the West open to commercial and emigrant traffic. The distance between the Pacific Coast and Washington, D.C.— about twenty-eight hundred miles—isolated California, Oregon, and Washington State and hampered the exchange of political intelligence and military instructions. Holding California, with its rich gold and silver deposits, was critical to the Union's fiscal security and to financing the war. The Lincoln administration believed that it had to keep the Pacific Coast in Union hands and contain the Confederacy in the South. A Southern empire on the Pacific, Lincoln feared, would scuttle United States continental destiny, freedom, and liberty and break the back of the embattled Union.

The Autry's telegraph key, or "pocket sounder," was a modern instrument that went a long way toward cinching the Pacific Coast to the Union. The Lincoln administration understood that continental power in North America flowed on currents of reliable communication between the East and West Coasts, secured and controlled by the federal government. By transmitting information in Morse code along a wire with electric current, the telegraph generally resolved the problem of slow and unreliable communications between Washington, D.C., and California.

This specific telegraph key was designed and produced in 1860 by the Caton Telegraph Instrument Shop headquartered in Ottawa, Illinois.[9] The instrument belonged to Dwight Byington, a telegrapher working in Saint Louis on the eve of the Civil War. After the conflict erupted, Byington joined the United States Military Telegraph Corps, a civilian unit created by the War Department in spring 1861. The corps's mission was to transmit and manage all military-related telegraphs between political centers and field armies, and between units of those armies. Like his peers in the corps, Byington strung and repaired telegraph lines and received and transmitted messages for the War Department and headquarters of Union field armies operating in the South and West.[10]

A combination of telegraphy and Pony Express brought news of Fort Sumter to California in the last week of April. Electrified by the report, tens of thousands of Californians rallied for the Union in cities, towns, and mining camps, and that summer thousands

FIGURE 4.1

Telegraph key, Caton Telegraph Instrument Shop, circa 1861. Telegraph operators were cutting-edge agents of modern communication during the Civil War. Each purchased and carried his own telegraph key, also known as a pocket sounder. Autry National Center, 88.25.4AB. For a color version of this image, see plate 5.

joined the California volunteers to replace the regulars departing for the East. By late summer, General Edwin V. Sumner, whom Lincoln had dispatched specifically to hold California, was so confident in the strength of the state's Unionism that he requested reassignment to a combat command in the eastern theater of the war. His brother-in-law, Colonel George Wright of the Ninth United States Infantry, replaced him in San Francisco and brought an iron fist down on all remaining Confederate sympathizers still active in Sumner's wake.[11] California gold was still Union gold.

On October 24, 1861, in the same month that Sumner returned to Washington, the Pacific Telegraph and the Overland Telegraph companies connected their transcontinental line in Salt Lake City, Utah. Two days later, the Pony Express ceased operations in the West. So long as the line was not compromised, the Lincoln administration and the Union now enjoyed rapid communication with federal and state authorities in California; departmental and district Union commanders could pass tactical information along the line, which followed the Oregon Trail westward from Omaha, Nebraska, to Salt Lake City and thence traced the central overland route to Carson City, Nevada, and on to California.[12] The transcontinental telegraph became a conduit of Union power and sover-

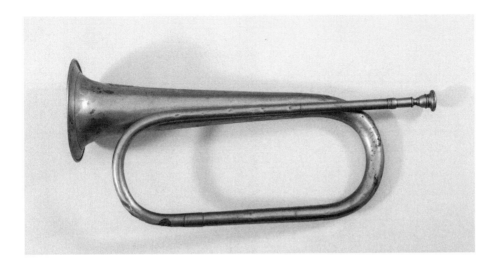

Seventh Iowa Cavalry bugle, mid-nineteenth century. Autry National Center, 89.76.8. For a color version of this image, see plate 6.

eignty and a hot wire of freedom and liberty in the American West. During the remainder of the rebellion, no power, Confederate or otherwise, threatened the Union grip on California and no movement or party seriously tested the loyalty of Californians.

BUGLE

The Autry collection's metal, silver-toned "trumpet," which was probably manufactured in the mid-nineteenth century, is a simple instrument, a single metal tube wrapped once into an oval. The tubing gradually enlarges from the stem to the bell, a design suggesting that it is a true bugle, not a "trumpet." The mouthpiece is removable and likewise silver. Stamped into the bell is a Grecian key design.[13] Thousands of these instruments were issued to buglers in Union and Confederate armies during the Civil War.

If rapid and reliable communication between disparate regions was strategically critical to solidifying the stressed Union, it was equally needed to coordinate the regimens and operations of military units on the ground before, during, and after battle. The bugle blown stoutly could project farther than the unaided human voice; and in the roar and thunder of battle, soldiers could hear its bright calls better than drum rolls, the traditional signals for infantry. Bugle calls, signaling the instructions of a commanding officer, lifted spirits and rallied men, deployed armies and retired the vanquished.[14]

The horn, or bugle, came to American forces through British and French armies in the late eighteenth century. Continental and U.S. dragoons and cavalry employed buglers from the American Revolution through the U.S.-Mexican War. *Cavalry Tactics* of 1841, the U.S. Army's first extensive cavalry manual, placed the chief bugler directly behind

the commanding officer.[15] In his *Rifle and Light Infantry Tactics* of 1855, Lt. Col. William J. Hardee urged that "every officer" be able to deploy "the Bugle signals" in parade drills and in battle. Buglers proved their tactical value in the early battles of the Civil War. The Union Army standardized bugle calls and ordered all combat arms to adopt them.[16] From corps to company units, the mass armies of western European and American nation-states marched, deployed, and maneuvered in complex lines, columns, and rectangles; the buglers' signals choreographed those formations of military power in the field and unleashed their destruction against enemies foreign and internal.

Buglers served with Union volunteers in the western theater during the Civil War. In summer 1863, Brigadier General Alfred Sully led twelve hundred Iowa and Nebraska cavalry onto the northern plains to punish the Sioux and expand the Union footprint. His report of the Battle of Whitestone Hill demonstrates the critical role of the bugler's tactical communications on the nineteenth-century battlefield, even in the smaller operations or actions against Native Americans.

On September 3, an army scout burst into Sully's camp near a small lake to the east of the James River. The man raised the alarm that a large Sioux force had surrounded Major Albert H. House's battalion at Whitestone Hill. Sully probably ordered his bugler to sound "boots and saddles." He later reported, "At the sound of the bugle, the men rushed with a cheer, and in a very few minutes saddled up and were in line." Responding to Sully's commands, the bugler may have blown the signals—"walk," "canter," "trot," and "gallop"—to set his command in motion. With four companies left behind to pack and

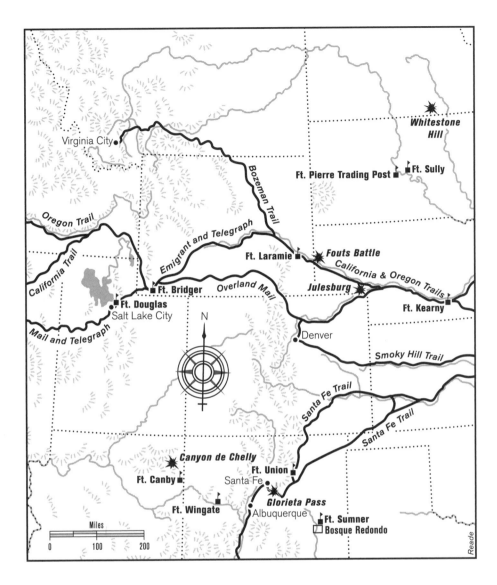

MAP 4.1

Map detail of the Civil War West. Map prepared by Deborah Reade Design, Santa Fe, New Mexico, for the Autry National Center.

move the camp, Sully led the Second Nebraska and Sixth Iowa Cavalries, and one company of the Seventh Iowa, along with the howitzers, in three columns "at a full gallop" toward House's position, covering "ten miles" in less than an hour.

On approaching the village site at Whitestone Hill, the chief bugler likely sounded "charge," the call repeated by regimental and company buglers down the line. Sully sent one wing to the "left" and another to the "right," and, with the center platoon, he sliced through the village. Again, likely to signals from Sully's bugler, the volunteers

dismounted, deployed as skirmishers, and "fought afoot." They took position on "hillocks" overlooking ravines in which hundreds of Sioux warriors had taken cover. Armed with repeating carbines, the volunteers poured a "murderous fire" on the Sioux combatants, who responded with muskets, bows and arrows, lances, and "all manner of projectiles." Their courageous delaying action bought precious time for their families to escape. As darkness settled over the dusty, smoky battlefield, the general "ordered all the buglers to sound the 'rally,'" which called them back to the abandoned village.

Sully's assault, partly orchestrated through buglers' signals, was a bloody and destructive affair. The Sioux suffered some three hundred dead, a catastrophic human loss, and abandoned "400,000 to 500,000 pounds of dried buffalo meat" and "300" lodges with "property of great value." Sully ordered all this plunder "burned up." He reported his "killed number" at twenty, with thirty-eight men wounded. After his men scouted the area, Sully countermarched his command to Fort Pierre on the Missouri River.[17] In the explosive political climate of the American Civil War, the general had delivered destructive, or hard, war to the Plains Sioux and demonstrated that the empty spaces and scarce resources of the northern plains would not protect them from the punishment of the U.S. Army.

The owner of the Autry's bugle served in a different wing of the Union's war against the Sioux. Born in Indiana, Private Barclay J. Charles was resident in Pleasant Plain, Iowa, when, at the age of nineteen, he enlisted in the Seventh Iowa Cavalry on February 15, 1863. Upon the reorganization of the Seventh two months later, he transferred to Company D. An inscription on the horn states that the instrument was a gift from "his friends" in that company. His service, devotion, or courage must have won him the esteem and affection of his comrades.[18]

A skilled bugler was worth his weight in silver in a campaign or on a battlefield. His tactical calls, correctly blown, maneuvered men into formation to skirmish, advance, or defend or extracted them from untenable positions and certain defeat. During the Union suppression of the Sioux Rebellion in late summer and early fall 1862, for instance, an errant bugle call threw the Third Minnesota into confusion at the Battle of Wood Lake. Taking fire from three directions, the survivors fled in disorder to a hastily assembled skirmish line.[19] By all accounts, Charles was a skilled and reliable bugler who knew his calls and confidently blew his horn in the stress of battle and in the quiet of the garrison.

Union authorities organized the Seventh Iowa Cavalry in response to a Sioux uprising in Minnesota and Dakota Territory in 1862 and to ongoing unrest among the Sioux, Blackfeet, and other Plains tribes in 1863. The regiment's charge was to contain the Indians, protect overland mails and travelers, and defend white settlers and friendly Indians. Assigned to the District of Nebraska, the twelve companies of the Seventh Iowa Cavalry rendezvoused at Omaha. Colonel Samuel W. Summers, the Seventh's command-ing officer, assigned two or three companies to Cottonwood Springs, Fort Kearny, Omaha, and Dakota City and to positions farther north along the Missouri River. Company D, with Private Charles, went to Fort Kearny, a post critical to the security of the vital Oregon Trail on the plains of Nebraska.[20]

Soon transferred northwest to Fort Laramie on the Oregon road, Company D missed the large operations launched from Fort Kearny to the east in summer 1864. Iowa and Nebraska volunteers campaigned against Sioux, Cheyenne, and Arapaho warriors, who were attacking stagecoaches, stage stations, emigrant caravans, and other travelers along the Oregon Trail and destroying ranches and farms in the Central Plains region that summer. However, Private Charles was likely present with Company D as it escorted some fifteen hundred friendly Sioux over the Oregon Trail from Fort Laramie east to Fort Kearny in June 1865.

Responding to pressure from independent Sioux and Cheyennes, the Sioux refugees rose up near sunrise at Horse Creek on June 14. While supervising the Sioux camp, Captain William D. Fouts of Company D was shot dead. Private Charles likely blew signals as the men of Company D mounted their horses and raced east to the command's corralled wag-ons two miles away. Taking over the seventy troopers, Lieutenant John Wilcox galloped Company D after the "criminal fugitives," rode by fleeing Sioux women and children, bumped into a long skirmish line of Native troops, and deployed his men on foot. However, the "more than 500 warriors equally armed" overlapped both flanks and forced the Iowans to flee. Charles probably blew "mount up," "front into line," and "retreat." Company D skir-mished with Natives in front and rear, likely in response to Charles's signals. In a short time, the Iowans reached the wagon corral, whose defenders drove off the Native pursuers.[21]

Units of the Seventh Iowa, Company D among them, later participated in Brigadier General Patrick Connor's Powder River Expedition in late summer and fall of 1865, although Charles's company was not in the force that assaulted the Arapaho village along the Tongue River in late July. After spending another winter on the Central Plains, the Seventh Iowa Cavalry was mustered out on May 17, 1866, at Fort Leavenworth, Kansas. Charles went home to Iowa.[22]

The summer campaigns in 1863–64, followed by volunteer operations to protect vital roads in 1865, served notice to the Sioux, Cheyennes, Arapahos, and other Plains Indians that the United States would use all available means to extend federal power over their homelands west of the James River and southwest of the Missouri. General Sully gave the Union a firm toehold in western Sioux country along the Missouri from Fort Rice to Fort Union. If they resisted or harassed emigrant and commercial traffic on the overland trails and the Missouri River, the Sioux, Cheyennes, and Arapahos would become the target of brutal punitive operations designed to inflict maximum violence, mayhem, and destruction on their communities. White Americans would enjoy their liberty in the West, making sure that the Indians had none.

NAVAJO-DECORATED PISTOL

The Autry's Navajo-decorated pistol, a U.S. Model 1842 Percussion Pistol, was the U.S. Army's standard pistol through the war with Mexico and into the early 1850s. A sturdy, reliable, and lethal short arm, the 1842 pistol was caliber .545 and fourteen inches long (with an eight-and-a-half-inch barrel), and it weighed two pounds and twelve ounces. The basic materials were wood, brass, and steel. The stock was black walnut "smoothly finished" and stopped "short of the swivel ramrod." This sidearm was a beautiful product of artisan craftsmanship and a distinguished entry in the vibrant history of American gun design and manufacturing.[23]

Percussion-cap ignition represented a technological advance over the old flintlock system that had dominated musket ignition for nearly two centuries. The regular service armed its dragoons and mounted riflemen with the 1842 pistol. Although these horse regiments generally skirmished with musketoons on foot, the troopers favored the pistol in combat on horseback. Once it began production in 1845, the 1842 pistol soon earned a reputation as the finest martial pistol issued to an army of the Western world, and it held that distinction for a quarter century. Posted to New Mexico in the early 1850s, Sergeant Frank Clarke of the First Dragoons reported to his father that he and his men still carried "a heavy single barreled Dragoon pistol" in addition to "one of Colt's Revolving Pistols (6 shooters)." Likewise, dragoons and cavalrymen in other United States regiments, and later in Union and Confederate forces, often carried the 1842 pistol as an extra short arm, reliable and lethal.[24]

United States regulars and volunteers carried a combination of old flintlock and new percussion-cap firearms when the Army of the West occupied New Mexico in 1846. Almost immediately, they began campaigning against the Navajos, whom the Americans had labeled the "Lords of the Southwest" and considered the largest and most dangerous

FIGURE 4.5

A Navajo artist augmented the simple, elegant design of this U.S. Model 1842 Percussion Pistol (manufactured by H. Aston & Company) with brass tacks hammered into the grip and arrayed in graceful lines. The General Charles McC. Reeve Collection, Southwest Museum of the American Indian Collection, Autry National Center, 491.G.2480A. For a color version of this image, see plate 7.

Native tribe in the region. To demonstrate its power, the United States intended to stop Navajo raiding of New Mexican settlements for livestock and captives. From 1846 to 1861, the U.S. Army campaigned intermittently but inconclusively against the Navajos. In 1858, however, regular troops operated more frequently to destroy villages and crops in Dinétah, the Navajo homeland. Indeed, the Navajos felt the pressure and negotiated with American authorities, but the frequency of their raids still increased from 1860 to 1861.[25]

This 1842 pistol came into the possession of a Diné, or Navajo, although precisely how is unclear.[26] If the approximate date of 1860 for the Navajo-decorated pistol is reasonably accurate, the firearm was likely acquired sometime during this violent and tumultuous era in Navajo history. The Diné individual who carried the pistol might have traded for it or scavenged it from a dead soldier or a vacated army camp. If he was among the Navajos who scouted for the army, he might have received an old or unused 1842 pistol from the service. The pistol was well adapted to equestrian tactical warfare, the kind generally practiced by the Navajos and most other Native peoples who lived between the Sierra Nevada and the Missouri River in the nineteenth century. This pistol likely endured hard and punishing service in the Navajo conflicts with the federal army, Nuevomexicanos, and Indian enemies.

How or when this weapon was used by its Navajo owner(s) is unknown, but the decoration of the grip subverted two ideological pillars, standardization and conformity, that lay at or near the heart of the modern nation-state, particularly its armed forces. Defying army regulations, the state, and modernity, the Navajo owner of this 1842 pistol drove brass tacks into the black walnut grip in three graceful lines paralleling both sides of the

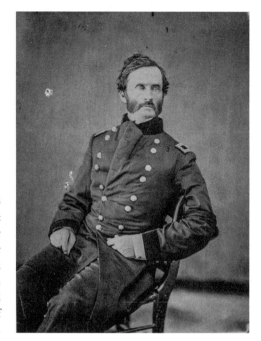

FIGURE 4.6
Colonel James H. Carleton, photograph, First California Infantry. The California, New Mexico, and Colorado volunteers under Brigadier General Carleton's command in New Mexico delivered the militant power of a modernizing nation-state to the Apaches and Navajos between 1862 and 1865. Library of Congress, Prints and Photographs Division.

brass back strap. A Navajo combatant was no cog in the military machine of a nation-state but an individual with personal power and unique vision. His primary allegiance was to the clan into which he was born and to the land or place where he grew up and resided. There is a better than even chance that this 1842 pistol was used by the Navajos to resist the violent invasion and destruction of Dinétah by the armies of the United States at some point between 1846 and 1865.

With the outbreak of the Civil War in spring 1861, Union military authorities in New Mexico expected a Confederate invasion of the Southwest from Texas. Indeed, Texas forces expelled United States troops from garrisons in southern New Mexico. In late winter and early spring 1862, the Confederate Army of New Mexico campaigned from Texas north along the Rio Grande to Santa Fe, but Colorado volunteers defeated Sibley's force at the Battle of Glorieta, forcing the Texans to evacuate the territory.[27] When the two thousand California volunteers arrived in New Mexico from the Pacific Coast during the summer, there were no Confederates to fight. When their commanding officer, Colonel James H. Carleton, took over the Department of New Mexico in September, he turned his troops loose on the Apaches and Navajos in the Southwest. His object was to attack both in their homelands, terrify and impoverish them, concentrate them on reservations, and open the Southwest to economic development, particularly mining, in which he was personally invested.[28]

After Carleton's Union volunteers—New Mexicans, Californians, and Coloradans—under Colonel Christopher "Kit" Carson crushed the Mescalero Apaches in fall 1862, Carleton unfolded his Navajo campaign in two stages. From July to December, five hun-

FIGURE 4.7

Christopher "Kit" Carson, photograph, circa 1865, colonel of New Mexico volunteers during the Civil War. He commanded destructive campaigns against the Mescalero Apaches, Navajos, Comanches, and Kiowas. Library of Congress, Prints and Photographs Division.

dred New Mexico volunteers, augmented by Zuni Pueblos, Jemez Pueblos, Utes, and civilian Nuevomexicanos, scoured Dinétah west to Hopi. Carson personally commanded a field battalion. All units torched crops, villages, and food stores; the Native and civilian auxiliaries also took captives. By December, the Navajos had reportedly lost "78 killed, 40 wounded, and 196 captured." The many raiders also carried off about five thousand head of livestock. Despite the deaths and mayhem, the Navajos still retaliated against settlements in the Rio Grande Valley.[29]

Carleton intended the second stage, a winter campaign, to finish the Navajos. He ordered the exhausted Carson to wage a destructive war in Canyon de Chelly, the sacred sanctuary of the Diné. In early January 1864, two Union forces campaigned through and around the canyon. The Navajos hurled rocks, lances, and curses, and shot arrows from canyon rims. Two volunteer companies returned through the canyon to destroy hogans, food stores, and fruit orchards. Carson's second operation had taken twenty-three Navajo lives, but the sustained penetration of Canyon de Chelly shattered most Navajos' will to fight or resist. No place in Dinétah was "safe" from Carson's pillagers—troops or auxiliaries. On January 23, Carson explained, "When they become convinced that destruction will follow on resistance, they will gladly avail themselves . . . of peace and plenty under the fostering care of the Government." During the fall, a few hundred Navajos had come into Forts Wingate and Canby (formerly Defiance) for transfer to Bosque Redondo; in only three weeks after Carson's foray, several thousand were encamped around the two posts. Terror, impoverishment, starvation, and destruction—the hard hand of the Civil War—had pounded the Diné into submission.[30]

Carleton's solution for the Navajos was their concentration at Bosque Redondo, a forty-square-mile reservation on the Pecos River in eastern New Mexico. From early 1864 to mid-1865, eight thousand Navajos, or two-thirds of the people, endured the Long Walk (over three hundred miles) from Forts Canby and Wingate to Bosque Redondo in the arid valley. Their enemies plundered and sometimes kidnapped them along the treacherous routes. Another four thousand Navajos moved westward into the Colorado Plateau beyond the reach of New Mexicans and the army.[31] Carson had been an ambivalent warrior in Union wars against the Indians; but with Carleton's unqualified recommendation, he received a brevet promotion to brigadier general of Union volunteers in 1865. Old, battered, and ailing, he finally mustered out of the volunteer service in 1867.[32]

Carleton would hunt, harass, and kill to coerce Indian submission, but Bosque Redondo would be his great reservation experiment. His long-term vision was to create Navajo and Mescalero pueblos on the Pecos River and transform these "wild" Indians into orderly, obedient Christians, farmers, and stockmen. If left on their own in the wilderness, he believed, the Navajos and Mescaleros would return to plunder and murder and ultimately suffer extermination by vengeful whites. Concentrating Indians on federal reservations—a humane reform policy in the minds of Carleton and other Union authorities—would be their best hope for long-term survival.[33]

The general's dream, although applied and enforced with bullets and fire, was high-minded in his time, but an avalanche of problems scuttled his utopian Indian experiment at Bosque Redondo. Crops perished from insects, drought, and floods, forcing Carleton's department to sustain his Indian wards. Corruption, incompetence, or scarcity in his commissary and quartermaster bureaus led to inadequate food rations, blankets, clothing, and other supplies at Bosque Redondo. By late 1864, the Navajos began succumbing to exposure, famine, and disease. They desperately wanted to return to Diné-tah, which, in Carleton's eyes, no longer existed.[34]

Now the most powerful man in the Southwest, Carleton argued bitterly with his federal Indian Service counterpart, Superintendent Michael Steck. Early on, Steck had opposed Bosque Redondo as foolhardy. In no way, Steck declared, could the Pecos Valley support thousands of uprooted Navajos. Ignoring Carleton's pleas and protests, the superintendent refused to apply any portion of his department's funds to Bosque Redondo or to request of the commissioner of Indian affairs an appropriation to support the reservation. As Carson had forewarned, the Navajos and Mescaleros—traditional enemies—quarreled and brawled. Fed up with their captivity, the Mescaleros fled back to southeast New Mexico and west Texas in December 1865.[35]

Cost overruns, human disaster, and critical reports caught Congress's eye and doomed Carleton. Outrage over the unspeakable massacre of peaceful Southern Cheyennes by Colorado volunteers at Sand Creek in southern Colorado during winter 1864 drove Congress to form the Special Joint Committee to investigate the condition of the Indians generally in the West. (The Sand Creek atrocity was instigated and commanded by Colonel John Chivington, the hero of the Battle of Glorieta in 1862.) A subcommittee led by

Senator James R. Doolittle of Wisconsin was charged with scrutinizing Indian affairs in New Mexico. Arriving in late summer 1865, the committee closely examined Bosque Redondo. The appalling conditions profoundly affected Doolittle and his colleagues, who recommended that the commissioner of Indian affairs launch a special investigation into the catastrophe.[36] Another round of failed crops in 1866 sealed the fate of Bosque Redondo. Two years later, in late May 1868, Navajo leaders, desperate to leave Bosque Redondo and return to their homeland, eagerly treated with a federal commission headed by humanitarian Samuel F. Tappan and Union Civil War hero William T. Sherman. A month later the Navajos retraced their Long Walk to Dinétah; they returned with "1,550 horses, 20 mules, 950 sheep and 1,025 goats"—a shocking level of attrition and destitution for this once-wealthy tribe.[37]

In April 1866, Carleton had been mustered out of the volunteer service and returned to the regular army at the rank of lieutenant colonel, one grade above his pre–Civil War majority. His grasp for military glory through Indian wars and the reservation experiment had failed to surpass the eastern battlefield victories of Union generals such as Phil Sheridan, William T. Sherman, George Thomas, and a host of other officers. By this time, Hispanos and Anglos had joined Natives in their hatred of Carleton, the recent master of the Southwest, and roundly condemned his inability to protect them from Indian raids. Five months later, the War Department relieved him of departmental command in New Mexico and ordered him to join his new regiment, the Fourth Cavalry, in Texas.[38] Despite the failure of Bosque Redondo, the federal government would adopt Carleton's model—reduction, concentration, assimilation—for its post–Civil War Indian policy.

IN THE END

The Civil War did not stop at the western borders of Missouri, Arkansas, and Iowa. The Republican Party, seconded by the Lincoln administration, advanced the cause of American liberty on the western frontier with the Homestead Act of 1862 and the transcontinental railroad acts of 1862 and 1864. Those laws and other Republican policies offered a vision of the future West developed with farms, ranches, businesses, and towns. Those policies motivated western volunteers to enlist in the Union armies and to prosecute their hard and destructive war on the western Indians. In this way, the Republican Party and President Lincoln gave the western war a strategy, albeit a simple framework, a full six to eight months before Lincoln's official application of the Emancipation Proclamation in January 1863.

The pocket sounder, the trumpet or bugle, and the 1842 pistol were modern technologies incorporated into the western war. The Union applied the electricity and wire of the telegraph to bridge the continent and coordinate its empire. Its armies used metal and sound to maneuver armies and units on the battlefield. In the mid-nineteenth century, modernity reached into the remotest places of the West. Indians armed themselves with firearms such as the 1842 pistol to defend their homelands from invasion by the

people and government of the United States, a modern nation-state. They also compre-
hended the imperial power of the telegraph. So they cut the wires that carried strategic
and tactical communications east and west across the plains, mountains, and deserts.
They adopted every firearm old and new to fend off the expanding United States. Union
volunteers used modern logistical networks, telegraphic communications, and repeating
rifles and pistols to operate in distant western frontiers and vanquish their Native enemies. In lines and columns, coordinated by signals blown through a metal horn, they
delivered the imperial power of their nation with fire, lead, and steel. In a quarter century,
their liberty would completely overrun and displace that of the American Indians in the
West.

NOTES

1. These terms come from two works: Charles Royster, *The Destructive War: William Te-
cumseh Sherman, Stonewall Jackson, and the Americans* (New York: Knopf, 1991); and Mark
Grimsley, *The Hard Hand of War: Union Military Policy toward Southern Civilians, 1861–1865*
(New York: Cambridge University Press, 1995).

2. The western military frontier is described in Durwood Ball, *Army Regulars on the Western Frontier, 1848–1861* (Norman: University of Oklahoma Press, 2001), xxi–xxxi; Averam B.
Bender, *The March of Empire: Frontier Defense in the Southwest, 1848–1860* (Lawrence: University of Kansas Press, 1952), chap. 1; and Robert M. Utley, *Frontiersmen in Blue: The United States
Army and the Indian, 1848–1865* (1967; reprint, Lincoln: University of Nebraska Press, 1981),
3–6.

3. For a map of railroads in 1860, see James M. McPherson, *Battle Cry of Freedom: The
Civil War Era*, vol. 6 of *The Oxford History of the United States*, ed. C. Vann Woodward (New
York: Oxford University Press, 1988), 101. The time for the Pony Express rider comes from
the website of the Pony Express National Museum in Saint Joseph, Missouri. See the website's
"About" section, http://ponyexpress.org/history/, accessed June 15, 2014.

4. This census figure for the West comes from Robert M. Utley, *The Indian Frontier,
1846–1890*, rev. ed., Histories of the American Frontier, ed. Ray Allen Billington et al. (Albuquerque: University of New Mexico Press, 2003), 4. See also United States, Census Bureau,
8th Census, 1860, *Population of the United States in 1860*, comp. Joseph C. G. Kennedy (Washington, DC: Government Printing Office, 1864).

5. Ray C. Colton, *The Civil War in the Western Territories* (Norman: University of Oklahoma
Press, 1959), is a classic work on the western war. Other valuable histories of the West during
the Civil War are Alvin M. Josephy Jr., *The Civil War in the American West* (New York: Alfred
A. Knopf, 1991); Howard R. Lamar, *The Far Southwest, 1846–1912: A Territorial History*, rev. ed.
(Albuquerque: University of New Mexico Press, 2000), chaps. 5, 9, 14, 16–17; Howard R. La-
mar, *Dakota Territory, 1861–1889: A Study of Frontier Politics* (New Haven, CT: Yale University
Press, 1956); Richard W. Etulain, *Lincoln and Oregon Country Politics in the Civil War Era*
(Corvallis: Oregon State University Press, 2013), chap. 4.

6. Ball, *Army Regulars on the Western Frontier*, xxi; Utley, *Frontiersmen in Blue*, 12–13. All
historical works on the frontier army tell the history of this occupation, but see Ball, *Army*

Regulars on the Western Frontier, chaps. 6, 8–9; Utley, Frontiersmen in Blue, chaps. 4–6; and Michael L. Tate, The Frontier Army in the Settlement of the West (Norman: University of Oklahoma Press, 1999), chap. 4. Two works treat specific army occupations: Ralph Emerson Twitchell, The History of the Military Occupation of the Territory of New Mexico from 1846 to 1851 by the Government of the United States, together with Biographical Sketches of Men Prominent in the Conduct of the Government during that Period (Denver: Smith-Brooks, 1909); and Will Bagley, The Mormon Rebellion: America's First Civil War, 1857–1858 (Norman: University of Oklahoma Press, 2012).

7. Utley, The Indian Frontier, 4.

8. David A. Nichols, Lincoln and the Indians: Civil War Policy and Politics (Urbana: University of Illinois Press, 1978), 161–64.

9. Accession data for telegraph key, ID no. 88.25.4, Tools and Utensils, Autry National Center, Los Angeles (hereafter Autry National Center); Robert Ferguson, A Biographical Sketch of John Dean Caton, Ex-Chief-Justice of Illinois (Chicago: Fergus Printing, 1882), 9–10. J. Caton enjoyed a wide-ranging intellectual life. See his Miscellanies (Boston: Houghton, Osgood; Cambridge: Riverside Press, 1880); J. Casale, "The Telegraph Instrument Factory of John Dean Caton," Telegraph History website, n.d., www.telegraph-history.org/caton-ottawa/index.html, accessed June 15, 2014.

10. William R. Plum, The Military Telegraph during the Civil War in the United States . . . (Chicago: Jansen, McClurg, 1882), 1:336. Byington is also mentioned in an extract of a letter written by General Samuel Curtis, commanding the Department of Kansas, Headquarters, Fort Leavenworth, in 1864. See ibid., 2:215. Major Geo[rge] H. Smith offers a thumbnail sketch of Byington's career in Leavenworth following the war in "The Military Telegraph in the West," Midland War Sketches, no. 23, Midland Monthly Magazine, July 1896, 51.

11. Robert J. Chandler, "The Velvet Glove: The Army during the Secession Crisis in California, 1860–1861," Journal of the West 20 (October 1981): 35–42; Josephy, Civil War in the American West, 236; Carl P. Schlicke, General George Wright: Guardian of the Pacific Coast (Norman: University of Oklahoma Press, 1988), 218–21; Ball, Army Regulars on the Western Frontier, 195–96.

12. David Hochfelder, The Telegraph in America, 1832–1920, Johns Hopkins Studies in the History of Technology (Baltimore: Johns Hopkins University Press, 2012), 183. See chap. 2 for Hochfelder's discussion of the telegraph's impact on politics, strategy, and tactics, particularly on the Union side, in the Civil War. The telegraph system was underdeveloped in the Confederacy.

13. The "trumpet" description is taken from accession data on trumpet, ID number 89.76.8, Autry National Center. Allan J. Ferguson discusses the evolution of horns, bugles, and trumpets in British and French armies and their adoption by the U.S. Army in "Trumpets, Bugles and Horns in North America, 1750–1815," Military Collector and Historian 36 (Spring 1984): 2–7. Ferguson also describes the bugle's shape in the caption to fig. 5 on p. 5.

14. William Carter White devotes a brief chapter to the military bugle or trumpet in A History of Military Music in America (New York: Exposition Press, 1944), chap. 22. See also Ferguson, "Trumpets, Bugles and Horns in North America," 2–7, and David L. Woods, A History of Tactical Communication Techniques, Telecommunications series, ed. Christopher H. Sterling et al. (New York: Arno Press, 1974), 135–36.

15. U.S. War Department, *Cavalry Tactics* (Washington, DC: J. and G. S. Gideon, Printers, 1841), 1:4, 12. The War Department reissued this manual in 1855, when Congress legislated the creation of two new mounted regiments, the First and Second Cavalry.

16. Army infantry manuals worked drums into instruction, drills, and maneuvers. See U.S. War Department, *Rules and Regulations for the Field Exercise and Manoeuvres of Infantry, Compiled and Adapted to the Organization of the United States . . .* (New York: Printed by T. & W. Mercein, 1815). This infantry manual, compiled by Brigadier General Winfield Scott, was reissued in 1824, 1840, and 1861. In 1834, the U.S. War Department issued *A System of Tactics for the Exercise and Manoeuvres of the Cavalry and Light Infantry and Riflemen of the United States* (Washington, DC: F. P. Blair, 1834). A single paragraph, no. 1440 on p. 202, notes a bugler. Hardee's system is *Rifle and Light Infantry Tactics; for the Exercise and Manoeuvres of Troops When Acting as Light Infantry or Riflemen* (Washington, DC: U.S. War Department, 1855; reprint, Philadelphia: J. B. Lippincott, 1860). His declaration on the bugle is on p. 7, par. 55. Hardee wrote his manual under the commission of Secretary of War Jefferson Davis; Hardee's *Tactics* became the basic infantry manual in the Confederate States Army during the Civil War.

17. Sully's official report is Brig. Gen. Alfr[ed] Sully to Maj. J. F. Meline, September 11, 1863, Camp at the mouth of the Little Cheyenne River, in *War of the Rebellion: A Compilation of the Official Records of the Union and Confederate Armies* [hereafter O.R.] (Washington, DC: Government Printing Office, 1880–1901), series 1, vol. 22, pt. 1, pp. 555–61.

18. Barclay J. Charles, Company D, Seventh Iowa Cavalry, "Roster and Record of Iowa Soldiers in the War of the Rebellion, together with Historical Sketches of Volunteer Organizations 1861–1866," vol. 4, in Iowa in the Civil War, n.d., a project of the IAGenWeb, http://iagenweb.org/civilwar/regiment/cavalry/07th/coD.html, accessed June 15, 2014; Accession date, trumpet, ID no. 89.76.8, Autry National Center.

19. The official report of the Battle of Wood Lake is Brig. Gen. Henry H. Sibley to [Gov.] Alexander Ramsey, September 23, 1862, Camp at Wood Lake near Yellow Medicine, Minnesota, in *O.R.*, series 1, vol. 13, pp. 278–81; Utley, *Frontiersmen in Blue*, 268–69.

20. David P. Robrock, "The Seventh Iowa Cavalry and the Plains Indian Wars," *Montana: The Magazine of Western History* 39 (Spring 1989): 2–17; Robert W. Frazier, "Kearny II," in *Forts of the West: Military Forts and Presidios and Posts Commonly Called Forts West of the Mississippi River to 1898* (Norman: University of Oklahoma Press, 1965), 87.

21. Capt. John Wilcox to Capt. George F. Price, June 21, 1865, Camp near Julesburg, Colorado, in *O.R.*, series 1, vol. 48, pt. 1, pp. 322–24; Robrock, "The Seventh Iowa Cavalry and the Plains Indian Wars," 15–17.

22. See also Brigham D. Madsen, *Glory Hunter: A Biography of Patrick Edward Connor* (Salt Lake City: University of Utah Press, 1990), chap. 10.

23. Colonel George Bomford of the Ordnance Bureau spelled out the specifications for the new percussion arms, including the pistol, in his letter to Major J. W. Ripley, Springfield Armory, November 23, 1841. Lieutenant Colonel George Talcott of the Ordnance Bureau placed the order for twelve models of the pistol with Ripley, June 10, 1842. Both letters are transcribed and published in Major James E. Hicks, *U.S. Military Arms, 1776–1956* (La Cañada, CA: James E. Hicks & Son, 1962), 70–71. Detailed descriptions of the 1842 pistol are found in Charles Winthrop Sawyer, *United States Single Shot Martial Pistols* (Boston: Arms Company, 1913), 29–32; and Carl P. Russell, *Guns on the Early Frontiers: A History of Firearms from Colonial Times through*

the Years of the Western Fur Trade (Berkeley: University California Press, 1957), 211–13. My description also draws on the following sources: Major Arcadi Gluckman, *United States Martial Pistols and Revolvers* (Buffalo, NY: Otto Ulbrich, 1939), 78–79; Louis A. Garavaglia, *Firearms of the American West, 1803–1865* (Albuquerque: University of New Mexico Press, 1984), 140.

24. Berkeley R. Lewis, *Small Arms and Ammunition in the United States Service* (Washington, DC: Smithsonian Institution, 1956), 52; Randy Steffen, *Horse Soldier, 1776–1943: The United States Cavalryman, His Uniforms, Arms, Accoutrements, and Equipments* (Norman: University of Oklahoma Press, 1978), 1:21; Martin Pegler, *Firearms in the American West, 1700–1900* (Rainsbury, Marlborough, Wiltshire, England: Crowood Press, 2002), 158; Clarke to Father, September 29, 1852, in Darlis A. Miller, *Above a Common Soldier: The West of Frank and Mary Clarke in the American West and Civil War, 1847–1872*, rev. ed. (Albuquerque: University of New Mexico Press, 1997), 42–43.

25. Two standard works on wars with the Navajos are Frank McNitt, *Navajo Wars: Military Campaigns, Slave Raids, and Reprisals* (1972; reprint, with a new introduction by Robert M. Utley, Albuquerque: University of New Mexico Press, 1990); and Lynn R. Bailey, *The Long Walk: A History of the Navajo Wars, 1846–68* (Tucson, AZ: Westernlore Press, 1988). On Navajo raids in the Rio Grande Valley and army responses to them, see Durwood Ball, "Fort Craig, New Mexico, and the Southwest Indian Wars, 1854–1884," *New Mexico Historical Review* 73 (April 1998): 153–73. On the expeditions led by Lt. Col. Dixon S. Miles against the Navajos in 1858 and those of Maj. Edward R. S. Canby in 1860–61, see Ball, "The U.S. Army in New Mexico, 1848–1886," in *Telling New Mexico: A New History*, ed. Marta Weigle with Frances Levine and Louise Stiver (Santa Fe: Museum of New Mexico Press, 2009), 173–90.

26. U.S. Model 1842 Percussion Pistol, accession data, ID no. 491.G.2480A, Southwest Museum of the American Indian Collection, Autry National Center.

27. Two general histories of the Civil War in the regional West are Colton, *The Civil War in the Western Territories;* and Josephy, *The Civil War in the American West.* The standard works on the Texas invasion of New Mexico are Martin Hardwick Hall, *Sibley's New Mexico Campaign* (Austin: University of Texas Press, 1960); and Donald Frazier, *Blood and Treasure: Confederate Empire in the Southwest* (College Station: Texas A&M University Press, 1996).

28. Aurora Hunt, *Major General James Henry Carleton: Western Frontier Dragoon*, Frontier Military Series no. 2 (Glendale, CA: Arthur H. Clark, 1958), 274–75; Adam Kane, "James H. Carleton," in *Soldiers West: Biographies from the Military Frontier*, 2nd ed., ed. Paul Andrew Hutton and Durwood Ball (Norman: University of Oklahoma Press, 2009), 134–35.

29. See Carson reports on July 24, August 19, August 31, October 5, and December 6, 1863, in *O.R.*, series 1, vol. 26, pt. 1, pp. 234–38, 250–57. On Carson's Mescalero campaign, see Ball, "Fort Craig, New Mexico," 161–62.

30. Col. Carson to Capt. Benjamin C. Cutler, January 23, 1864, Fort Canby, in *O.R.*, series 1, vol. 34, pt. 1, pp. 72–75; Tom Dunlay, *Kit Carson and the Indians* (Lincoln: University of Nebraska Press, 2000), 292–300; David Remley, *Kit Carson: The Life of an American Border Man* (Norman: University of Oklahoma Press, 2011), 228–29.

31. Bailey, *Long Walk*, 166–72; Utley, *Frontiersmen in Blue*, 143–44.

32. Francis B. Heitman, *Historical Register and Dictionary of the United States Army, from Its Organization, September 29, 1789, to March 2, 1903* (Washington, DC: Government Printing Office), vol. 1, s.v. "Christopher Carson."

33. For Carleton's vision, see Ball, "Fort Craig, New Mexico," 163; Kane, "James H. Carleton," 137–38; Hunt, *Major General James Henry Carleton*, 274–75; Utley, *Indian Frontier,* 84–85.

34. Bailey, *Long Walk,* chap. 9; Utley, *Indian Frontier,* 86.

35. Kane, "James H. Carleton," 139–40; Nichols, *Lincoln and the Indians,* 166–67; Lamar, *Far Southwest,* 110.

36. Bailey, *Long Walk,* 220–21; Kane, "James H. Carleton," 141–42. Carleton's Bosque Redondo policy was the great political divide in New Mexico by 1865. See Lamar, *Far Southwest,* 110–12.

37. Bailey, *Long Walk,* 234–35; Peter Iverson, *Diné: A History of the Navajos,* photographs by Monty Roessel (Albuquerque: University of New Mexico Press, 2002), 63–67.

38. Heitman, *Historical Register and Dictionary of the United States Army,* vol. 1, s.v. "James Henry Carlton"; Hunt, *Major General James Henry Carleton,* 344–45.

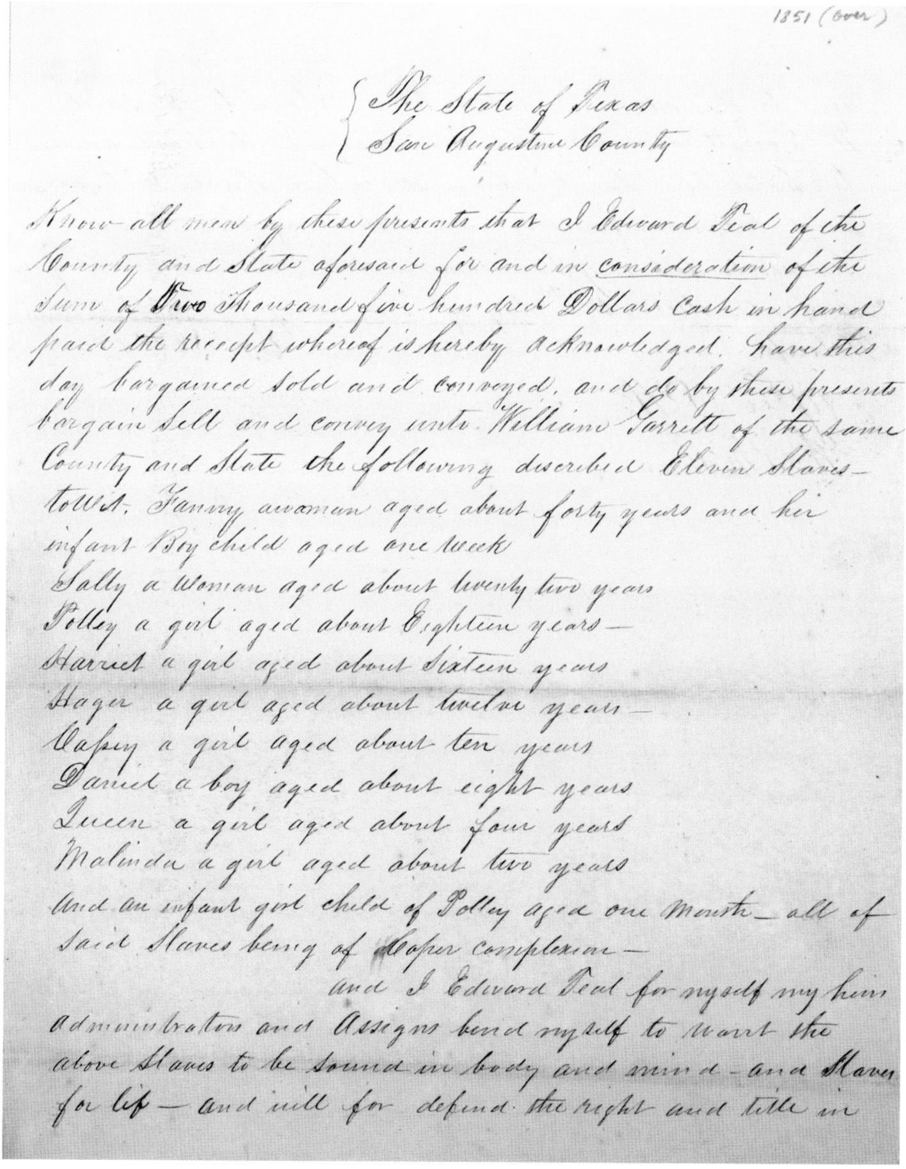

The State of Texas
San Augustine County

Know all men by these presents that I Edward Peal of the
County and State aforesaid for and in consideration of the
Sum of Two Thousand five hundred Dollars Cash in hand
paid the receipt whereof is hereby acknowledged, have this
day bargained sold and conveyed, and do by these presents
bargain Sell and convey unto William Garrett of the same
County and State the following described Eleven Slaves—
to wit. Fanny a woman aged about forty years and her
infant Boy child aged one week
Sally a Woman aged about twenty two years
Polley a girl aged about Eighteen years—
Harriet a girl aged about Sixteen years
Hagar a girl aged about twelve years—
Cassey a girl aged about ten years
Daniel a boy aged about eight years
Queen a girl aged about four years
Malinda a girl aged about two years
And an infant girl child of Polley aged one Month—all of
said Slaves being of proper complexion—
                    And I Edward Peal for myself my heirs
administrators and Assigns bind myself to warrant the
above Slaves to be Sound in body and mind—and Slaves
for life—and will for defend the right and title in

PLATE 1

William Garrett bill of sale for eleven slave men, women and children, 1851. Rosenstock Collection,
Autry Library Collection, Autry National Center; 90.253.4100.32

PLATE 2

Frémont expedition flag, circa 1841–1842. Gift of Elizabeth Benton Fremont. Southwest Museum of the American Indian Collection, Autry National Center; 81.G.5A

PLATE 3

One of the Sharps Model 1853 carbines purchased by the New England Emigrant Aid Society and shipped to Kansas, 1854–1857. Donated by Mr. R. L. Wilson. Autry National Center, 87.104.1

PLATE 4

Saber brought by John Brown to Kansas in 1855. Kansas State Historical Society

PLATE 5

Telegraph key, Caton Telegraph Instrument Shop, circa 1861. Telegraph operators were cutting-edge agents of modern communication during the Civil War. Each purchased and carried his own telegraph key, also known as a pocket sounder. This one was used in the Civil War by Dwight Byington, chief electrician at Leavenworth, Kansas. Autry National Center, 88.25.4AB

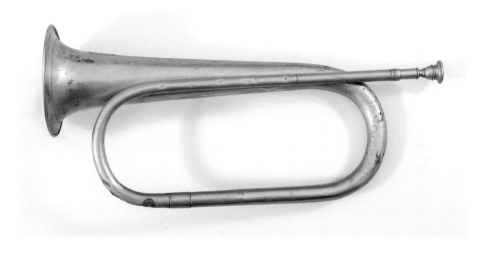

PLATE 6
Seventh Iowa Cavalry bugle, mid-nineteenth century. Autry National Center, 89.76.8

A Navajo artist augmented the simple, elegant design of this U.S. Model 1842 Percussion Pistol (manufactured by H. Aston & Co.) with brass tacks hammered into the grip and arrayed in graceful lines. The General Charles McC. Reeve Collection, Southwest Museum of the American Indian Collection, Autry National Center, 491.G.2480A

Bowie knife given to Stand Watie on his becoming a Confederate general circa 1862. Cherokee History Museum

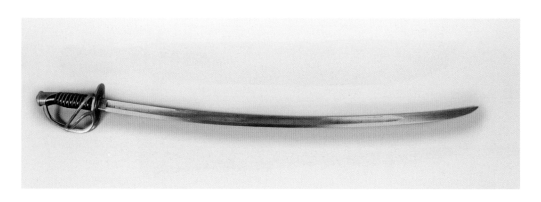

PLATE 9
The 1860-model cavalry sword of Juan de la Guerra, 1862. History Collections, Los Angeles County Museum of Natural History

PLATE 10

John Gast, *American Progress*, 1872. Autry National Center, 92.126.1

PLATE 11

Hand-stitched wedding dress made by Janet McOmie for her wedding to Richard Sherlock, circa 1860. Donated in memory of Janet S. Payne. Autry National Center, 98.142.1–.3

PLATE 12

Hand-stitched wedding dress made by Janet Sherlock for her wedding to James Smith, 1875.
Donated in memory of Janet S. Payne. Autry National Center, 98.142.4

PLATE 13
Ernest Blumenschein, *New Mexico Peon*, 1930–1942. James R. Parks Collection.
Autry National Center, LT2011-43-1

PLATE 14

Mian Situ, *The Powder Monkeys, Transcontinental Railroad, Cape Horn, 1865*, 2001–2, oil on canvas.
Autry National Center, 2002.3.1

Electrical lamp with carved steer horns, circa 1891. Acquisition made possible by Mr. James H. Hoiby. Autry National Center, 91.2.1

Biil eh' (woven dress) worn by Asdząą́ Tłʼógi (Lady Weaver), also known as Juanita
Manuelito, circa 1868. The George Wharton James Collection. Southwest Museum
of the American Indian Collection, Autry National Center, 421.G.1115

PLATE 17

Dahaastłoo (saddle blanket) woven by Asdzáá Tłʼógi, 1895–1905. The George Wharton James Collection. Southwest Museum of the American Indian Collection, Autry National Center, 421.G.1108

5

WHEN THE STARS FELL FROM THE SKY

The Cherokee Nation and Autonomy in the Civil War

Kent Blansett

In March of 1862, Cherokee leader Degataga—also known by his English name Stand Watie—received a bowie knife in honor of his official appointment as a military colonel in the army of the Confederate States of America. The knife was personally inscribed to "Col. Stand Watie from F. A. [Frank Armstrong] Rector." Colonel Rector, who commanded the Seventeenth (and later the Thirty-Fifth) Arkansas Infantry for the Confederacy, had survived the carnage of the Battle of Pea Ridge alongside Colonel Watie. After this battle in northern Arkansas, Rector presented the knife to Watie as a public gesture of camaraderie and high regard for Watie's military service to the Confederacy.[1]

Watie's bowie knife represents more than just a gift from one soldier to another; it is emblematic of the Cherokee Nation's pivotal role in the fighting of the Civil War. But viewed as a chapter of Cherokee history, the fight was more than the battles between the North and South over slavery and emancipation. As a Cherokee leader, Col. Stand Watie also fought to preserve his own vision of Cherokee independence. Watie was not the only Cherokee political leader to fight for sovereignty, however. Principal Chief John Ross (Koowisguwi), too, envisioned an independent future for the Cherokees, including the treaty right to continue the practice of chattel slavery. Ross and Watie maintained opposing views about Cherokee involvement in the U.S. Civil War.

Like the United States, the Cherokee Nation was deeply divided during the 1860s. Watie's knife, a relic of war, symbolizes the double-edged violence that connects the Civil War with United States expansion. The knife's wooden handle, brass accents, large

FIGURE 5.1
Bowie knife given to Stand Watie on his
becoming a Confederate general, circa 1862.
Cherokee History Museum. For a color
version of this image, see plate 8.

FIGURE 5.2
Carte-de-Visite, Stand Watie, date unknown,
WICR 31445, in the collection of Wilson's
Creek National Battlefield. Image courtesy the
National Park Service.

tempered-steel blade, and leather sheath marked it as both a tool of conquest and a weapon of liberty. Today it remains an important artifact that recalls the national debate over slavery and emancipation. At the same time, it is a material reminder that the Cherokee Nation was entrenched in vicious debates over Indian Removal, treaties, and issues of citizenship, sovereignty, and survival.[2]

During the nineteenth century, Cherokee citizens endured shifting patterns of land loss, political alliances and betrayals, and overwhelming incidents of brutal violence and death. Stand Watie's bowie knife represents the tangled and vicious stories of how Cherokee leaders dealt with dispossession and citizenship, debated the institution of slavery, and struggled to protect their sovereignty in the face of western expansion and the competing imperial desires of both the Union and the Confederacy. The significance of the Cherokee Nation in the Civil War can be understood through the struggles of two Cherokee leaders, Watie and Ross. Each leader waged a legal, political, and military war to protect Cherokee independence against the onslaught of Indian Removal and the Civil War. For both the Union and Confederacy, Indian Territory represented a key strategic borderland that tipped the direction of the Indian Wars and American Civil War in the West.[3]

The following story transcends Civil War narratives that are typically entrenched in debates over slavery and freedom and North versus South. While these debates are vital forces that have shaped the foundations of Civil War history, they do not account for other conflicts that emerged simultaneously among Indigenous populations through-out the United States. The majority of scholarly interpretations of the Civil War fail to address the thousands of Native peoples who valiantly served both the Union and Confederacy, and the ways that Native nations, as a result of this service, paid the ultimate price. Throughout the Civil War, Native nations increasingly became the targets of a *second* removal campaign led by a reconstructed military that included both Confederate and Union war veterans. After the American abolition of slavery and the Union victory, the war against Indigenous peoples in the American West rapidly intensified.

In the early 1800s, before their removal, the Cherokee Nation numbered between seventeen thousand and twenty thousand people and owned more than fifteen hundred African slaves. Cherokee territorial land-base spanned millions of acres across the present-day southeastern states of Alabama, Georgia, Tennessee, and North Carolina. By the 1820s, Cherokee families were well situated in plantation agriculture while maintaining traditional governance in upper and lower towns. Having experienced tremendous economic growth in this period, the Cherokee Nation gained national recognition for their success in the enterprise of cotton farming, which the largest Cherokee planters grew, as did other Southerners, using slave labor. This meant, of course, that such a lucrative enterprise controlled by Native nations and entrepreneurs threatened the long-term viability of colonial Southern plantations.[4] Several key Supreme Court decisions, known collectively as the Marshall Decisions, blocked Southern states from terminating Indian competition and removal from their lands. The first, *Johnson v. M'Intosh* (1823), recognized Tribal ownership of lands, protected exclusive rights to such lands, and acknowledged shared title of these lands with the federal government. This last protection is noteworthy in that Native nations could sell their lands only to the United States. By the 1830s, American settler interests sought to supplant Indigenous nations that controlled access to some of the richest cotton-growing lands in the South. The economic strength of the Cherokee Nation emerged as one of many reasons that President Andrew Jackson lobbied for the passage of the Indian Removal Act in 1830.[5]

The Indian Removal Act, which narrowly passed Congress, authorized the president to exchange Native lands in the East with new lands west of the Mississippi, stipulating that any exchange of lands depended on the proper consent of the Tribe. In the 1831 Supreme Court decision *Cherokee Nation v. State of Georgia,* Chief Justice John Marshall declared the Native nations to be domestic, dependent nations as opposed to foreign states. One year later in the 1832 *Worcester v. Georgia* decision, Marshall asserted that the "Cherokee nation . . . is a distinct community occupying its own territory . . . in which the laws of Georgia can have no force, and which the citizens of Georgia have no right to enter." This final decision defined Native nations as independent political communities and as treaty nations that reside outside the authority of state law.[6] Based on the Supreme Court's decision, states lacked the right to forcibly remove or force their laws upon Native nations. Indian Removal therefore depended on the consent of both the Tribe and the federal government.

Cherokee people confronted instability and uncertainty about their status in the Southeast in the years following *Worcester v. Georgia.* While supporters lobbied on their behalf in Congress, some Cherokee believed that no matter how hard they fought against the Indian Removal Act, the U.S. military would remove them from their homelands. Cherokee leaders such as Major Ridge, John Ridge, Elias Boudinot, John Ross, and Stand Watie confronted this horrific possibility. This prompted them to engage in conversations that concluded with the idea to sign a treaty with the U.S. government consenting to removal.[7]

Stand Watie's family (including the Ridges and Watie's brother Boudinot) played a central role in support of the Treaty or Removal party. As the leaders of the treaty initiative, this Cherokee political party (without John Ross) had negotiated and signed the 1835 Treaty of New Echota. This controversial treaty, which supposedly provided consent for removal, sold all the remaining ancestral Cherokee lands in Georgia in exchange for lands in Indian Territory (present-day Oklahoma). The treaty signers believed that no matter how hard they negotiated or fought, Cherokees would inevitably face removal. From the perspective of the Treaty party, they were acting in the best interests of their people and ensuring the prolonged survival of the Cherokee Nation.[8]

But not all Cherokee citizens agreed with this course of action, and from 1839 to 1846 nearly all members of the Treaty party, except for Watie, met violent deaths. John Ross, Principal Chief of the Cherokee Nation, initially backed the Treaty party's actions. But he later branded them as traitors and unofficial representatives of the Cherokee Nation. Their deaths occurred at the hands of Ross supporters, including the brutal death of Boudinot, whose assailants stabbed him in the back with a bowie knife and then bludgeoned him with a tomahawk. Hundreds of assassinations ensued in the months following removal, during a period known as the Cherokee Civil War between the Treaty and Antitreaty parties. This bloody episode produced two rival political parties led by families who remained at odds throughout the nineteenth century.[9]

The Cherokee Nation continued to struggle to maintain sovereignty during the removal process and after their arrival in a completely new homeland. The removal of Cherokee people from the South began in 1835 and concluded in 1839. The excruciating process caused the deaths of thousands of Cherokee men, women, and children (estimates range between four thousand and ten thousand deaths). Despite the loss of nearly half their total population, the Cherokee Nation survived this most dismal chapter in American history. Once in Indian Territory, the families and supporters of Watie and Ross remained bitter enemies. Even though thousands of Cherokees perished, the deep divisions and political rivalries survived.[10]

Despite the hatred between Watie and Ross, the two leaders shared many similarities. Both Cherokee leaders maintained large plantations and profited from large-scale slave labor. While less than 10 percent of the Cherokee owned slaves, this same minority struggled for control over Cherokee politics. Most Cherokee remained skeptical about adopting the colonial practice of slavery, especially because the idea of individual property rights clashed with the idea of communal property rights. Older Cherokee slave practices, more fluid and complex than the chattel slavery of the colonist, often provided for the adoption of non-Cherokee slaves into a clan, bestowing all the rights and privileges of Cherokee citizenship. The adoption of the Cherokee Constitution had usurped clan law, disenfranchised Cherokee women, and placed political authority in the hands of an exclusive few. Watie and Ross remained at opposite ends of the Cherokee political spectrum. Yet before, and following, the decades of Cherokee removal to Indian Territory, each of these two leaders maintained large slave plantations, and each was a member of the Cherokee elite, a wealthy class that clamored for a controlling interest in Cherokee governance. Given consensus among otherwise bitterly opposed slaveholding Cherokee leaders, the slavery question sat uncomfortably in the background rather than commanding the forefront of Cherokee political debate.[11]

As early as the 1850s, threats of violence over slavery, coupled with settler expansion in surrounding states, tore at the Cherokee Nation. The Kansas-Nebraska Act of 1854 opened Kansas to a flood of proslavery and abolitionist emigrants. The federal government, however, had already promised some of these lands to Native nations. Indigenous populations in these states faced another removal and moved to tracts of land in Indian Territory. Indigenous land loss and forced relocation set the stage for "Bleeding Kansas" and the Kansas and Missouri border wars, and this violence spread to Native peoples in Indian Territory and Arkansas. Cherokee citizens watched as waves of squatters invaded the Cherokee Neutral Lands in Kansas.[12] Slaveholding Cherokee leaders found themselves in the middle of an expanding conflict. In Chief John Ross's annual message to the Cherokee National Council on October 5, 1857, he spoke about the threat of widespread violence in northern Cherokee lands. Ross feared a second removal, alluding to the fate of Native peoples in Kansas and Nebraska and to continued efforts by the U.S. government to relocate them. His message also highlighted the treaty responsibilities of the federal government to protect Cherokee sovereignty, but he projected an uncertain and unstable future. How much longer would it be before the people in Indian Territory faced a fate similar to that of other Native nations in the region?[13]

Ross hoped to unify the Cherokee around the issue of treaty rights. Cherokee citizens, he claimed, should have faith in the treaties and the pledged protection of the United States. But the United States would not prove to be a reliable protector. By 1858, federal forces abandoned their forts and installations in Indian Territory.[14] The United States would not evict squatters from Cherokee Neutral Lands in Kansas. In 1859, squatters took valuable resources—such as timber, game, mineral deposits, and water—from Cherokee Neutral Lands without any compensation. Meanwhile, proslavery settlers in Arkansas feared that a Cherokee Nation alliance with Kansas abolitionists might push the war against slavery into Arkansas.[15] In such a fear-ridden climate, the editors of *The Arkansian* asked, in 1859, what would be the fate of Arkansas if the Cherokee Nation, too, declared war on the institution of slavery?[16]

With the establishment of the Confederacy in 1861, proslavery forces believed that a victory in the American West was contingent upon maintaining an alliance with the Native nations of Indian Territory. Union forces also sought to ally with, and often to control, Indigenous nations in Oklahoma. Indian Territory served as a key buffer zone between Union Kansas and the surrounding Confederate states of Missouri, Arkansas, and Texas. While neither side could really depend on the loyalty of the Indian Territory population early on, this place remained the "western wildcard": both the North and the South actively sought to claim it in the ultimate war for the American West.

The U.S. Army swore to protect the Cherokee Nation. But at the outbreak of the war, the U.S. Army had already abandoned posts throughout Indian Territory in flagrant disregard for treaty obligations, leaving the Western Cherokee Nation vulnerable to a Confederate invasion. Cherokee citizens were divided over how to confront this immediate threat. Should they ally with the Union or the Confederates or attempt to remain neutral?[17]

Slavery shaped the debate between Stand Watie, John Ross, and other Cherokee slave owners. Like most slaveholding Southerners, they all argued for the preservation of slaveholding. As much as they disagreed, Watie and Ross agreed on the protection of Cherokee slavery as an exclusive *treaty* right, a property right protected by the federal government.

Ross and Watie mostly disagreed on the different strategies for protecting Cherokee sovereignty.[18] Before the Civil War, Ross campaigned for Cherokee loyalty to the United States through a policy of neutrality as a way to protect their current land base and treaty rights. He argued that the institution of slavery by law remained a protected Cherokee treaty right. Furthermore, Ross believed that a Cherokee alliance with the Union had absolutely nothing to do with the abolitionist cause, insisting, "We are not dogs to be hissed on by abolitionists."[19] But Watie, who had served as Speaker for the Cherokee National Council from 1853 to 1859, supported an alliance with the Confederacy to thwart a "northern invasion." Like Ross, Watie fought to maintain the institution of slavery in the Cherokee Nation, but he hoped to negotiate greater Cherokee independence through an alliance with the Confederacy. Both men gambled on their differing strategies to uphold Cherokee sovereignty. These two competing visions, dating back to the period of removal, fractured the Cherokee Nation in the midst of American desires for western expansion, a process that preceded, traversed, and succeeded the years of the Civil War.[20]

Cherokee citizens formed associations that represented the views of either Ross or Watie. Organized around 1855, the Keetoowah Society was supported by Ross and his followers. Keetoowah members (also known as the "Pins") wore crossed feathers underneath their lapels and swore allegiance exclusively to the Cherokee Nation and the United States. Members of this fraternal society petitioned to end the practice of slavery.[21] In stark opposition stood the Knights of the Golden Circle, or Southern Rights Party, which was supported by Watie. The Knights organized shortly before the Keetoowah and were linked to the proslavery "Blue Lodges" in Kansas. Blue Lodges emerged as secret societies that advocated and supported slavery in abolitionist Kansas. As historian William McLoughlin suggests, the Knights were not necessarily slave owners but they supported their Southern economic ties and neighbors.[22]

By 1861, Chief Ross struggled to establish some semblance of unity and neutrality in the Cherokee Nation. This became especially challenging after the Cherokee Southern Rights Party attempted to raise a Confederate flag at Webber Falls in June of 1861. Although the Keetoowah Society quickly removed the Confederate flag, the Cherokee Nation made the lines of division clear on that day. In an article published in the *Washington Post,* Ross stressed the importance of Cherokee neutrality: "We do not wish our soil to become the battle ground between the States, and our homes to be rendered desolate and miserable by the horrors of a civil war." But the escalation of events in the country (such as the Battle of Carthage in southwest Missouri and the Battle of Bull Run) prevented the seventy-one-year-old leader from containing the spread of violence into the Cherokee Nation. Watie joined the Confederacy early, participating in strategic raids against Kansas and, by July 12, 1861, becoming a colonel in the army of the Confederate States of America.[23]

In August of 1861, Cherokee soldiers, not including Stand Watie, had participated in the Battle of Wilson's Creek near Springfield, Missouri. The battle resulted in over twenty-five hundred casualties and included the death of Union general Nathanial Lyon.[24] The Cherokee Southern Rights Party continued to lobby the Cherokee Nation to join the Confederacy. It became clear to Chief Ross that if he wanted to remain in power and avoid a military coup led by Watie, he had little choice but to follow the course embraced by all the other Indigenous nations in Indian Territory and endorse an alliance with the Confederacy. On August 20, 1861, Ross surrendered to overwhelming political pressures, and the Cherokee Nation ceased to claim its title as the last neutral Nation in Indian Territory.

After a long struggle to keep the Cherokee people out of the Civil War, Chief Ross yielded to Watie's influence.[25] When, in August 1861, a Confederate flag was hoisted over the Cherokee Council House in Tahlequah, Ross's wife, Mary, tried to contain her feelings of betrayal. Mary Ross, who had been raised a Quaker, ordered a halt to the

Confederate flag raising and instructed her six-year-old son to climb up the flagpole and tear it down. Her vocal protest and direct action resonated with many Cherokees, who gathered at the council house on that infamous day. Mary Ross soon fled the Cherokee Nation to live out the duration of the war in her hometown of Philadelphia, embracing the Union cause.[26]

Her husband, meanwhile, played a dangerous political game. On March 3, 1862, John Ross rode to the Arkansas border with his close associate Colonel John Drew and Drew's regiment of Cherokee Mounted Rifles. Stand Watie's regiment traveled a different path to the Confederate front, but they combined their forces for the first day of fighting at the Battle of Pea Ridge. Ross turned back for Indian Territory before reaching the Arkansas border; it was Chief Ross's single combat experience in the Civil War.[27]

As Cherokee troops marched to war, most lacked formal military training. Although familiar with violence, most of this generation had not witnessed war. Once they joined the Confederate encampment, Cherokee soldiers began to paint their faces and took the necessary time to prepare themselves for battle and for death. Other soldiers understood that the Cherokee regiments fought not only for the Confederacy but also, more vitally, for the Cherokee Nation. Some Cherokee soldiers dressed in traditional hunting jackets that covered loose-fitting calico shirts that hung slightly over deerskin leggings and moccasins. Many more carried Cherokee war clubs, tomahawks, knives, and their own firearms into battle. Their fellow soldiers flinched when they heard the Cherokee war calls alongside the Rebel yells.[28]

On their first charge toward Union lines, Cherokee forces moved swiftly past every Union obstacle. The combined regiments overwhelmed a Union battery. Cherokee forces lost only two soldiers in their initial charge yet took the lives of thirty to forty Union

FIGURE 5.4
Cherokee flag captured at Locust Grove, Cherokee Nation, Indian Territory, on July 3, 1862. Battle Flag of 1st Cherokee Mounted Rifles Regiment, CSA, WICR 30118, in the collection of Wilson's Creek National Battlefield. Image Courtesy of the National Park Service.

soldiers and captured several cannons. Victory proved short-lived as they met more Union cannon fire. Shells exploded around them while shrapnel shot through the surrounding trees. The loud popping of cracked branches mixed sharply with gunpowder in the air. From a distance, a line of Union infantry approached, and the Cherokee troops fell back and found concealment behind a nearby tree line. With their positions hidden in the timber, Colonels Watie and Drew divided their forces to outflank the approaching Union lines.[29]

When Confederate general Albert Pike took over after General Benjamin McCulloch's death during the battle, the Union quickly captured the main supply lines for the Confederacy. Under Pike's command the Cherokee soldiers lacked proper supplies and ammunition to sustain their fight against Union forces. The Confederate loss at the Battle of Pea Ridge changed the direction of the war. Two days of fighting had resulted in over three thousand casualties.[30]

Northern newspapers claimed that Confederate Cherokee soldiers had scalped and mutilated the bodies of Union troops. After a thorough investigation, evidence surfaced that only one Union soldier might have been scalped. As the reports spread, however, more Union and some Confederate troops feared any future encounter with Confederate Cherokees. Eleven members of Watie's unit were captured and detained by Union forces.

The prisoners were sent to Rolla, Missouri, for incarceration. They never lived to see the inside of a prison cell. According to scholar Frank Cunningham, who wrote one of the first biographies of Stand Watie, Cherokee prisoners feared torture and were shot and killed by Union troops while trying to escape. Speculation surrounded their deaths as rumors surfaced that all Cherokee prisoners had been executed in retaliation for the reports of scalping and mutilation.[31]

The Civil War brought violence to Cherokee soldiers and civilians. Smaller battles and skirmishes continued throughout the summer of 1862. At Cowskin Prairie, Watie's forces were vastly outnumbered by Union troops. Cherokee families became refugees, fleeing to Kansas, Arkansas, or Texas, seeking to evade Union vengeance or Confederate looting. Overnight, once-prosperous Cherokee communities became ghost towns. Confederate Cherokee faced similar danger on July 3, 1862, when Colonel William Weer's newly organized Union Indian Brigade led an offensive push into Indian Territory. Colonel Weer's surprise attack claimed the lives of one hundred Confederate soldiers and almost killed Colonel Watie on his property near Spavinaw Creek in Arkansas.[32]

In so many ways, the violence of the Civil War represented continuity for Indigenous peoples throughout Indian Territory. In 1861, the year before Pea Ridge, thousands of Cherokee and Creek civilians had become refugees in the Union-controlled camp of Fort Roe in southeastern Kansas. Many of them were survivors of the 1830s removal and relived the nightmare of another forced march. By the time they had reached Fort Roe their clothes were little more than rags that hung from their emaciated bodies. Refugees lost fingers and toes to frostbite, while others battled with pneumonia and the flu. Fort Roe was rapidly overrun with Union loyalist refugees from all across Indian Territory. Bad water and the scarcity of rations claimed countless lives. A fort meant to serve and protect became a tomb for hundreds of Native peoples. Women, men, and children died horrific deaths within the confines of Fort Roe, a place the early-twentieth-century historian Annie Heloise Abel labeled a "concentration camp."[33]

Although Ross and Watie both signed on to support the Confederacy, their political views remained at odds. Chief Ross and Colonel Drew surrendered to Union forces in Tahlequah, and Ross, with his family, fled into Union territory, where he joined his wife. Ross thereby vacated the office of Principal Chief, which Watie swiftly claimed. In his first official act as Principal Chief, Watie ordered the conscription of every male Cherokee between the ages of sixteen and thirty-five into military service for the Confederacy. Any Cherokee who refused enlistment faced imprisonment. Cherokee women, such as Margaret Brackett, also served as spies and collected bounty rewards for their families. In the meantime, Watie also confiscated precious rations and supplies from Cherokee civilians. Thousands of Cherokee women and children who had lost their husbands, fathers, uncles, brothers, and sons to the war were forced to scavenge for roots or to raid for subsistence.[34]

Whatever Watie's authority, much of Indian Territory had been brought under the control of Union forces, responding to the pressures of national politics. By February of

1863, in the wake of Lincoln's Emancipation Proclamation, the Cherokee National Council, now reorganized behind Union lines in Tahlequah, passed a resolution emancipating all slaves within the Cherokee Nation. This proclamation called for compensation to be paid by the federal government to loyal Cherokees who had emancipated their slaves in accordance with its terms. Watie responded to the Cherokee Emancipation Proclamation by issuing a death sentence to any Keetoowah member found carrying a weapon. For his part, Ross left Philadelphia for Washington, D.C., to lobby President Lincoln to honor Cherokee treaties that guaranteed their protection from demands for excessive reparations leveled against Indian Territory.[35]

But worse was yet to come. The July 17, 1863, Battle of Honey Springs was one of the largest Civil War battles ever fought in Indian Territory. Beyond Northern and the Southern regiments, this diverse battle included the First Regiment of Kansas Colored Infantry, as well as a gory fight among several Indian nations, including the Choctaw, Chickasaw, Creek, and Cherokee Nations. Although the Confederate regiments put forth a strong effort, they were not victorious. Two hundred soldiers lost their lives, and over four hundred were wounded; the Confederacy's days in Indian Territory were numbered.[36]

The Union victory at Honey Springs took place shortly after the defeat of General Robert E. Lee at Gettysburg, where over forty-six thousand soldiers lost their lives. Confederate leaders, all too aware of their dire situation, looked to supplies and provisions from the West to ensure future victories. Watie fought furiously to capture precious Union supplies from steamboats and forts to sustain Confederate campaigns.

In the midst of the military fighting, Colonel Watie also led a political fight. He resorted to guerrilla tactics and intimidation of Cherokee citizens to keep them loyal to the Confederacy. But by August of 1863, 80 percent of the Cherokee Nation had fled into Kansas to seek Union protection. Whole communities in the Cherokee Nation had been abandoned, and hundreds of miles of war-torn lands separated Union and Confederate Cherokee families. In response, Watie ordered the burning of the Cherokee capitol in Tahlequah and reduced John Ross's elaborate Rose Cottage plantation to ashes. As the war hurtled to its bloody conclusion, Confederate president Jefferson Davis promoted Watie from colonel to brigadier general.[37]

Even so fierce and unyielding a Confederate partisan as Watie experienced ambivalence and regret. In a letter to his wife, Sarah, he mentioned his fear of being remembered forever as the "Cherokee Quantrill," a reference to the Confederate guerrilla fighter William Quantrill, who destroyed civilian towns and lives. Watie's letter highlights the struggle that most soldiers confronted in their attempts to justify to their loved ones the cruel, violent, and unnatural state of war. On April 9, 1865, the Confederacy surrendered at Appomattox Court House. Despite the stars and bars falling from the sky, General Watie continued to fight the war in the West. He was the last Confederate general to surrender.[38]

One month after Watie's surrender, John Ross lost his beloved wife, Mary, on July 20, 1865. During the next year Ross worked to negotiate a settlement with the federal government to make amends for the Cherokee alliance with the Confederacy. The "Reconstruction Treaty" compelled the Cherokee Nation to open its lands to settlement and to provide Cherokee citizenship to the Delaware, the Shawnee, and all former Cherokee slaves. Finally, the Cherokee were required to cede all the Cherokee Neutral Lands in the state of Kansas. In comparison, Southern states lost very little territory to the North and escaped direct and excessive financial penalties. Veterans of the Confederate military joined the U.S. Army for a renewed military campaign of Indian Removal in the American West. As vigorous as the military assault on the Cherokee Nation had been, they faced further economic challenges. For the rest of the nineteenth century, the Cherokee Nation struggled to protect its territorial base against railroad interests and land allotment policy. The Cherokee Reconstruction Treaty also produced one of the most controversial legacies for the Cherokee Nation—that of citizenship. During the next one hundred years the Western Cherokee Nation faced its greatest debates over the battle lines of citizenship, racialization, and sovereignty. For decades to come the Cherokee Nation would deal with the legacy of their slaveholding past. The leader of the treaty negotiations, John Ross, died a year after his wife, on July 31, 1866, in Washington, D.C. Given the complexities of his own life as a Cherokee leader, he might not have been surprised at the challenges faced by his own successors.[39]

General Stand Watie refused to attend the treaty negotiations in Washington. He retired his weapons forever and lived out his remaining years as a farmer in the Choctaw Nation. His choice might be interpreted as a self-prescribed banishment and a way for him to avoid coming face-to-face with all the lives destroyed or lost under his command. He died on September 9, 1871, at his former home at Honey Creek within the Cherokee Nation. His wife, Sarah, followed him in death nine years later.[40]

At the conclusion of the Civil War, the Western Cherokee Nation had experienced yet another period of great violence and loss among their people. Federal military strength and tactics utilized to gain victory over the South morphed into a campaign against Indian Country in the West. A successful U.S. reconstruction depended primarily on a renewed campaign of Indian Removal and containment, known popularly as the "Indian Wars."[41]

At the beginning of the Civil War, Native people represented 87 percent of the population in Indian Territory. By 1890, this percentage dropped to less than 40 percent. Much of this population shift is attributed to land-rush and allotment policies that accompanied assimilation. But it also attests to the tremendous loss of life during the Civil War and Reconstruction.[42] Thousands of Native people fought and died under multiple flags. The Cherokee Nation lost over one-quarter of its population and over half of its land base through the infamous "reconstruction treaties." More than "one-third of adult Cherokee women were widows at the close of the Civil War, and one-quarter of Cherokee children (1,200) were orphans. . . . Husbands who did return from the war were disabled or seriously wounded."[43]

As a result the Western Cherokee people faced a highly uncertain future. Families picked up the shattered pieces of their lives and migrated back to their former homes, now

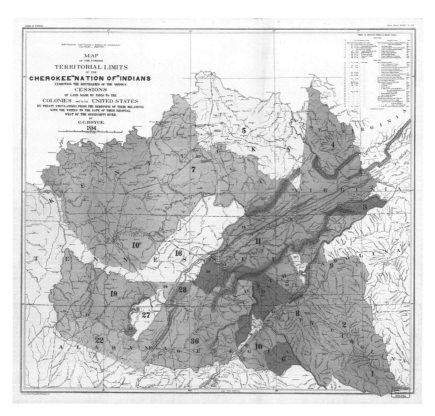

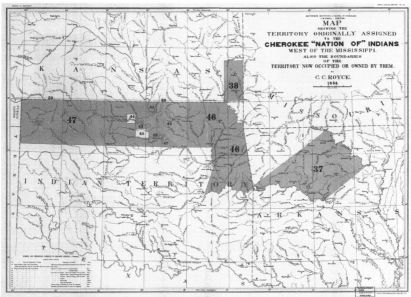

FIGURE 5.5

Above: C.C. Royce, *Map of the former territorial limits of the Cherokee "Nation of" Indians,*
Department of the Interior, 1884. Library of Congress, Geography and Map Division. *Below:*
C.C. Royce, *Map showing the territory originally assigned to the Cherokee "Nation of" Indians,*
Department of the Interior, 1884. Library of Congress, Geography and Map Division.

desolate lands that appeared foreign to them. As survivors of war, they saw that their nation's landholdings had been reduced to the charred remains of stone chimneys, resembling tombstones in a graveyard that memorialized a nation that had experienced decades of removal, war, and annihilation. Their first task was to dig through the rubble to recover any valuables or memories that remained buried in the scorched earth. This recovery process was part of the Cherokee Nation's strategy for survival, in which they continued to struggle to persevere despite the scars of war. Cherokee citizens would have to overcome seemingly insurmountable odds to guarantee their future and their survival.[44]

Today, hundreds of spectators stroll past General Stand Watie's knife at the Cherokee Heritage Museum in Tahlequah, Oklahoma, and view only a small part of the Cherokee Nation's involvement in the American Civil War. The bowie knife is certainly a symbol of the violence of war, but it is also a poignant reminder that the Cherokee Nation survived this horrific chapter and persisted in protecting their sovereign status.

NOTES

Editor's note: Per the author's direction, this essay follows current practice in scholarship on Native American history regarding capitalization and the use of singular and plural constructions. The other essays in this volume follow standard conventions of capitalization and the use of singular and plural constructions.

1. For a description of Watie's knife, see Deborah L. Duvall, *Tahlequah and the Cherokee Nation* (Chicago: Arcadia, 2000), 39. The knife is on display at the Cherokee Heritage Museum in Tahlequah and represents one of the few Cherokee material items that survived the Civil War.

2. For more information, see Arrell Morgan Gibson, "Native Americans and the Civil War," *American Indian Quarterly* 9, no. 4 (Autumn 1985): 386; Alvin M. Josephy Jr., *The Civil War in the American West* (New York: Random House, 1991), xiii; Elliot West, *The Last Indian War: The Nez Perce Story* (New York: Oxford University Press, 2009), xix–xxii.

3. Owing to space limitations and for the sake of cohesion, I cannot, in this essay, begin to tell the entire story of the Cherokee Nation in the Civil War. This work represents only a small part of a larger manuscript that explores the pivotal role that both Indian Territory and the Cherokee Nation played in determining the outcome of the Civil War in the American West. While I desire to write the entire story, for the purposes of this essay many of the key events and battles have been omitted or condensed to maintain balance with the other essays and overall theme of this anthology.

4. For more on the importance of cotton to the Southern economy, see David G. Surdam, "King Cotton: Monarch or Pretender? The State of the Market for Raw Cotton on the Eve of the American Civil War," *Economic History Review* 51, no. 1 (February 1998): 113–32.

5. The population statistic for the Cherokee Nation before removal is a little tricky since one-quarter (thirty-five hundred to four thousand) of the "Old Settler" Cherokee already lived west of the Mississippi River. Back east, the Cherokee population remained at between fourteen thousand and fifteen thousand people before removal. Russell Thornton, "Nineteenth-Century Cherokee History," *American Sociological Review* 50, no. 1 (February 1985): 125. For

more information on Native economic competition and removal, see Kent Blansett, "Intertribalism in the Ozarks, 1800–1860," *American Indian Quarterly* 34, no. 4 (Fall 2010): 475–97. After removal the Cherokee Nation was composed of three different political entities: the Eastern Cherokee (Tsali holdouts in North Carolina), Old Settler or Western Cherokee, and Constitutional Cherokee (Treaty and Antitreaty parties). For more on Cherokee history before and during removal, see also William G. McLoughlin, *Cherokee Renascence in the New Republic* (Princeton, NJ: Princeton University Press, 1986); Thurman Wilkins, *Cherokee Tragedy: The Ridge Family and the Decimation of a People* (Norman: University of Oklahoma Press, 1986); and Grant Foreman, *Indian Removal: The Emigration of the Five Civilized Tribes of Indians* (Norman: University of Oklahoma Press, 1972).

6. Robert T. Anderson, Bethany Berger, Philip P. Frickey, and Sarah Krakoff, *American Indian Law Cases and Commentary* (Saint Paul, MN: Thomson/West, 2008), 52, 70; John R. Wunder, *"Retained by the People": A History of American Indians and the Bill of Rights* (New York: Oxford University Press, 1994), 24–29.

7. For more information on the Marshall decisions, see also Frank Pommersheim, *Broken Landscape: Indians, Indian Tribes, and the Constitution* (New York: Oxford University Press, 2009), 87–124; and Robert N. Clinton, Nell Jessup Newton, and Monroe E. Price, *American Indian Law: Cases and Materials* (Charlottesville, VA: Michie, 1991), 2–27.

8. Edward Everett Dale and Gaston Litton, *Cherokee Cavaliers: Forty Years of Cherokee History as Told in the Correspondence of the Ridge-Watie-Boudinot Family* (Norman: University of Oklahoma Press, 1939), 10–17; see also William G. McLoughlin, *After the Trail of Tears: The Cherokees' Struggle for Sovereignty, 1839–1880* (Chapel Hill: University of North Carolina Press, 1993), 1–58.

9. McLoughlin, *After the Trail of Tears*, 23–59; Dale and Litton, *Cherokee Cavaliers*, 3–55.

10. The years following removal and the reconstruction of the Cherokee Nation in the West are often referred to as the "golden years" in Cherokee history. The Cherokee land base, by the 1850s, extended from the northeastern corner of Indian Territory to the Cherokee Strip (a wide swath of land that ran the entire northern length of the modern state of Oklahoma) and included a section of land known as the Neutral Lands, situated in the southeastern corner of Kansas. For demographics of Cherokee removal, see also James Mooney, *Myths of the Cherokee* (Mineola, NY: Dover, 1995), 123–50; Russell Thornton, "Cherokee Population Loss during the Trail of Tears: A New Perspective," *Ethnohistory* 31, no. 4 (Autumn 1984): 289–300.

11. McLoughlin, *After the Trail of Tears*, 123–25. For more information on slavery among Native peoples in the Southeast, see also Tiya Miles, *Ties That Bind: The Story of an Afro-Cherokee Family in Slavery and Freedom* (Berkeley: University of California Press, 2005); Fay A. Yarbrough, *Race and the Cherokee Nation: Sovereignty in the Nineteenth Century* (Philadelphia: University of Pennsylvania Press, 2008); Claudio Saunt, *A New Order of Things: Property, Power, and the Transformation of the Creek Indians, 1733–1816* (New York: Cambridge University Press, 1999). The once "king" cotton in Indian Territory that had so dominated Tribal economies in the past was quickly being replaced by cattle ranching, which depended on skilled free labor, rather than slave labor. The writing was on the wall: the days of plantation slavery in Indian Territory were numbered.

12. For more information, consult McLoughlin, *After the Trail of Tears*, 110–20.

13. "If our political rights are of any value, they should be zealously maintained, and no violation of them be permitted to pass without invoking redress from the United States

government, which is pledged for our protection. . . . You cannot fail to be seriously impressed with the change in policy shown by the United States government in her dealing with the Indian tribes of Kansas and Nebraska. As an evidence of the danger with which we ourselves are threatened[,] . . . the renewal may be at hand of those measures of agitation which but so recently forced us from the homes of our fathers." From the unsigned newspaper articles "The Cherokee Nation-Message of John Ross," *Milwaukee Daily Sentinel,* November 19, 1857, and "Condition of the Cherokee Nation," *Kansas City Herald of Freedom,* November 21, 1857.

14. Craig Gaines, *The Confederate Cherokees* (Baton Rouge: Louisiana State University Press, 1989), 25.

15. "A Black Spot in the Cherokee Nation," *Charlestown Mercury,* December 28, 1859. Civilians throughout Indian Territory, Arkansas, Missouri, and Texas became the exclusive target for abolitionist vigilantes desperate to terminate the seeds of slavery through a campaign of terror. A growing fear among Arkansas slaveholders was that a "free" Indian Territory might inspire slave revolts or increase the number of runaways from both Arkansas and Texas.

16. Arkansas newspapers also targeted the work of the Northern Baptist minister Evan Jones, whom reporters nicknamed the "John Brown of the Cherokee Nation." One newspaper reported, "If Jones is not routed from this country, Old John Brown scenes will be again enacted on a large scale. . . . If Jones was out of the way . . . they would be good Southern men." Later reporters even called for the assassination of Jones. "Another John Brown Raid in Perspective," *New York Herald,* June 14, 1860.

17. "Stark News from Southern Kansas: The Settlers on the Cherokee Indian Land Driven Away by U.S. Troops—Seventy-Five Houses Burned—One Hundred Families Turned Out on the Prairie," *Cleveland Daily Herald,* November 6, 1860.

18. Cherokee Nationalism can easily be defined as a Tribal assertion or defense of sovereignty, the right to self-governance over an exclusive territory as defined and protected by treaty rights. While rooted in the defense of this and other sovereign powers, Native Nationalism counters popular definitions of ethnonationalism, which link such nationalism exclusively to the overthrow of a nation-state. In difference, Cherokee or Native Nationalism honors a political alliance and bond with a colonial power for the preservation of treaty rights. Both Ross and Watie were nationalists, but each leader advocated a different diplomatic strategy to protect Cherokee rights to self-government.

19. McLoughlin, *After the Trail of Tears,* 169.

20. Dale and Litton, *Cherokee Cavaliers,* 99–102; Wilfred Knight, *Red Fox: Stand Watie and the Confederate Indian Nations during the Civil War Years in Indian Territory* (Glendale, CA: Arthur H. Clark, 1988), 50–51; McLoughlin, *After the Trail of Tears,* 162–79.

21. The Keetoowah Society was established under the auspices of the Northern Baptist Circuit Rider Evan Jones. Members practiced an Indigenized form of Christianity, which combined both Cherokee and Christian beliefs, while continuing to practice sacred Cherokee traditions and ceremonies. Theda Perdue, *Slavery and the Evolution of Cherokee Society, 1540–1866* (Knoxville: University of Tennessee Press, 1979), 132 and 172. Historian Theda Perdue argues on page 127 that the Cherokee Nation politically did not divide loyalties simply on the basis of pro- or antislavery; this split over whether to ally with the Union or the Confederacy centered on protecting treaty rights. The rights to property as outlined in previous treaties, Perdue asserts, included slaves as property. Therefore any act of emancipation by the

U.S. president or Congress would have no bearing on the continuation of slavery within the Cherokee Nation. In other words, as a dividing line within the Cherokee Nation, treaty rights were more important than protecting the institution of slavery.

22. McLoughlin, *After the Trail of Tears*, 153–75; Gaines, *Confederate Cherokees*, 21–22.

23. McLoughlin, *After the Trail of Tears*, 180–81; Stanley W. Hoig, *The Cherokees and Their Chiefs: In the Wake of Empire* (Fayetteville: University of Arkansas Press, 1998), 221–22; "Disloyalty of the Cherokee Indians," *Washington Post*, October 7, 1861.

24. Knight, *Red Fox*, 66; McLoughlin, *After the Trail of Tears*, 181–82. Watie did not fight in the Battle of Wilson's Creek as Frank Cunningham's 1959 biography suggests. Cunningham, *General Stand Watie's Confederate Indians* (Norman: University of Oklahoma Press, 1998), 40–41.

25. Gaines, *Confederate Cherokees*, 11–13. The Cherokee Nation officially joined the Confederacy on August 21, 1861.

26. "Disloyalty of the Cherokee Indians"; Hoig, *Cherokees and Their Chiefs*, 222. Other acts of Union support occurred throughout Indian Territory. Creek leader Opothle Yahola, a friend of John Ross, led an intertribal exodus of thousands of Native peoples out of Indian Territory and into Union-controlled Kansas. Along the way his confederacy survived winter storms, starvation, and major battles against Confederate Cherokee and Creek regiments. Many of the survivors ended up at Fort Roe and later formed the first Union Indian Brigade. For a firsthand account, see Wiley Britton, *The Union Indian Brigade in the Civil War* (Kansas City, MO: Franklin Hudson, 1922).

27. Gaines, *Confederate Cherokees*, 77–78.

28. Clarrisa W. Confer, *The Cherokee Nation in the Civil War* (Norman: University of Oklahoma Press, 2007), 98–99; Gaines, *Confederate Cherokees*, 80.

29. Gaines, *Confederate Cherokees*, 81–91; Cunningham, *General Stand Watie's Confederate Indians*, 57–65; and Knight, *Red Fox*, 89–106.

30. Gaines, *Confederate Cherokees*, 87.

31. Cunningham, *General Stand Watie's Confederate Indians*, 63.

32. Ibid., 68–70; Knight, *Red Fox*, 113–14. President Lincoln authorized the enlistment of four thousand refugee Indians, many from Opothle Yahola's original confederacy, to form the Union Indian Brigade. Members of the Union Indian Brigade saw themselves as the true representatives of their Nations and believed that their loyal dedication to the Union would be recognized by the Union at the conclusion of the war. See also Britton, *Union Indian Brigade in the Civil War*, 11; McLoughlin, *After the Trail of Tears*, 203.

33. Annie Heloise Abel, *The American Indian in the Civil War, 1862–1865* (Lincoln: University of Nebraska Press, 1992), 85. Abel published a total of three books on the Cherokee Nation in the Civil War, including *The American Indian as Slaveholder and Secessionist* (1915), the aforementioned *American Indian in the Civil War* in 1919, and *The American Indian and the End of the Confederacy, 1863–1866* (1925).

34. McLoughlin, *After the Trail of Tears*, 206–7; Carolyn Ross Johnston, *Cherokee Women in Crisis: Trail of Tears, Civil War, and Allotment, 1838–1907* (Tuscaloosa: University of Alabama Press, 2003), 86–90.

35. McLoughlin, *After the Trail of Tears*, 207–8.

36. For more on the Battle of Honey Springs, see also Cunningham, *General Stand Watie's Confederate Indians*, 101–3; Gaines, *Confederate Cherokees*, 120; Knight, *Red Fox*, 166–74.

37. Johnston, *Cherokee Women in Crisis*, 89.

38. Dale and Litton, *Cherokee Cavaliers*, 155–57.

39. Johnston, *Cherokee Women in Crisis*, 101; McLoughlin, *After the Trail of Tears*, 222–30; Knight, *Red Fox*, 274–75.

40. Knight, *Red Fox*, 286–87; Confer, *Cherokee Nation in the Civil War*, 158; Cunningham, *General Stand Watie's Confederate Indians*, 212.

41. See also McLoughlin, *After the Trail of Tears*, 225–88; and for a general overview on the Indian Wars, consult Dee Brown, *Bury My Heart at Wounded Knee* (New York: Bantam, 1972); Robert M. Utley, *The Indian Frontier of the American West, 1846–1890* (Albuquerque: University of New Mexico Press, 1984).

42. Donald A. Grinde Jr. and Quintard Taylor, "Red vs. Black: Conflict and Accommodation in the Post Civil War Indian Territory, 1865–1907," *American Indian Quarterly* 8, no. 3 (Summer 1984): 213–18.

43. Johnston, *Cherokee Women in Crisis*, 104.

44. Mooney, *Myths of the Cherokee*, 149.

6

ON THE EDGE OF EMPIRES, REPUBLICS, AND IDENTITIES

De la Guerra's Sword of the War and the
California Native Cavalry

Daniel Lynch

In fall of 1865, Juan de la Guerra and the other men of the California Native Cavalry Battalion arrived at Fort Mason, located south of Tucson near the U.S.-Mexico border. There, the Native Cavalrymen would engage the Apaches as well as forces supporting the French puppet, Emperor Maximilian of Mexico. They had enlisted to fight Confederate expansionists in the Southwest, but the U.S. Civil War was over. They were still needed in Arizona, however, because Native American raiding for livestock and human captives had increased amid the turmoil of the war years, and another ongoing civil war threatened to spill over the border. The chance to face down the French, or the Mexican allies of the French, would have appealed to most of the Native Cavalrymen born in Mexico: native-born Californios (such as Juan), for whom the unit was named, as well as Mexican immigrants. Many of these men felt an attachment to the Republic of Mexico and saw enlisting in the army of an allied sister republic, also struggling for survival, as a way to help secure liberty on both sides of the border. In retrospect, it's striking that Mexican Americans would have served in the American military so soon after the Mexican-American War (1846–48). Juan was born in 1847, in the midst of that conflict. Eighteen years later, the five-hundred-mile journey he took with the battalion, from Southern California to Fort Mason, roughly paralleled the new U.S.-Mexico border.

Juan rode along that far southwestern edge of the American empire with an 1860-model saber hanging by his side. This state-of-the-art cavalry sword was the only reliable weapon issued to all members of the Native Cavalry. An industrial-age version of an ancient weapon, it was a finely tuned instrument for fighting Indians and consolidating

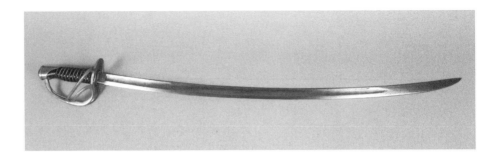

FIGURE **6.1**

The 1860-model cavalry sword of Juan de la Guerra, 1862. History Collections, Los Angeles County Museum of Natural History. For a color version of this image, see plate 9.

U.S. power in the Civil War–era West. But men of the Native Cavalry also used this imperial tool and the other trappings of military service for their own purposes: to advance a distinctly Mexican-American dual nationalism and to stake a claim to full citizenship in a more perfect Union.

CALIFORNIOS AND THE CALIFORNIA NATIVE CAVALRY

Juan de la Guerra came from a long line of warriors who used military service to build and maintain social status. His surname originated with an ancestor in medieval Cantabria, a region on the northern coast of the Iberian Peninsula. That ancestor was known as El Conde don Pedro el de la Guerra—Count Pedro, "the One of the War." He earned this appellation for valorous deeds in battle. Juan's grandfather, José de la Guerra y Noriega, was born in Cantabria in 1779 to noble parents. Although he did not receive an inheritance in terms of property, he was able to cash in on his lineage to gain wealth and power on the Spanish-American frontier, where noble blood was particularly scarce. José arrived in Alta California as a young military officer, and in 1804 he married into an upwardly mobile mestizo family of mixed European and Native American ancestry. His father-in-law was the commander of the Santa Barbara presidio, an important military installation on the coast of Southern California. José eventually took over command of the presidio and also established himself as the patriarch of a large family and a pillar of Californio society. The de la Guerras became one of the most powerful families in California, and their influence survived both Mexican independence from Spain, achieved in 1821, and the 1848 U.S. takeover.[1]

This influence was rooted in military service, and de la Guerra's participation in the Native Cavalry can be seen as an attempt to bolster the family's social standing, which by the 1860s was in decline. Based in Santa Barbara, Company C of the Native Cavalry Battalion was essentially a de la Guerra operation, with Juan's uncle Antonio Maria de la Guerra serving as captain and most of the other high-ranking positions filled by either relatives or Anglo-Americans. Juan was promoted by his uncle to the highest enlisted rank in the company—first sergeant. Considering that he was only seventeen at the time, this high rank probably had more to do with kinship than leadership qualifications. Under the more racially conscious American regime, Juan may have also benefited from his relative whiteness compared to the other enlisted men. As recorded in a Company C muster roll, Juan's "grey" eyes, "auburn" hair, and "light" complexion stood out, since the most common characteristics recorded were "black" eyes, "black" hair, and "dark" complexion.[2]

Although participation by the de la Guerras in the Native Cavalry represented the continuation of a long tradition of military service, it also represented a break from local precedents of resisting U.S. imperialism and allying politically with Anglo-Americans from the U.S. South. During the Mexican-American War, an insurgency that began in Los Angeles recaptured most of Southern California from American forces. At the high point of this insurgency—the Battle of San Pasqual, near San Diego—a small group of lance-wielding Californio horsemen led by Andrés Pico defeated the Americans, whose industrial edge in firepower had been neutralized by wet gunpowder. This was one of the most embarrassing setbacks for the United States in the entire war. After negotiating the terms of a surrender agreement that ended the insurgency, Pico was well respected by Californios and Anglo-Americans alike and, therefore, well positioned to launch a post-war political career. He served in the state legislature and as the commander of the southern section of the state militia. Like many Californios in the southern counties, Pico joined forces with migrants from U.S. slave states in the proslavery "Chivalry" faction of the state Democratic Party. A Southern and Californio alliance in Southern California made sense on a practical level, since both groups were relatively large and influential in the southern counties. But there was more to this alliance than a marriage of convenience. It was also held together by similar values regarding male honor, the need for clear social hierarchies, and the importance of land ownership.[3]

This alliance between Southerners and Californios fell apart against the backdrop of the Civil War. Perhaps fearing that nothing threatened their property or status more than risky schemes for secession, several leading Californio elites, including Pico, broke with the Chivalry and joined the minority of Californio Republicans in supporting the Union. One such Californio Republican was state senator Romualdo Pacheco, a former Mexican Army officer who would later briefly serve as California's first and, thus far, only Mexican American governor. In 1862, Pacheco proposed a unit of "native cavalry" made up of Spanish-speaking horsemen from the ranchos of the southern and central coast.[4]

Pacheco's idea caught on with California Latinos in part because it tapped into a widespread hatred of Texans—the enemy the Native Cavalry was supposed to fight. Following two vicious wars and decades of racial violence, there was a good deal of bad blood between Texans and U.S. Latinos. When Texas joined the Confederacy in 1861, this encouraged Latino support for the Union, especially in New Mexico. Texan expansionists had a history of threatening New Mexico; and in 1861, Texan Confederates moved into the New Mexico Territory in order to support a secessionist uprising already under way in the recently proclaimed Confederate Territory of Arizona. This was the first political entity that went by the name *Arizona*, but it did not have the same shape as the modern state. The territory roughly coincided with the narrow strip of land between Texas and California that had recently been acquired from Mexico through the Gadsden Purchase. As U.S. secretary of war in the 1850s, Jefferson Davis was instrumental in the acquisition of this land, and he promoted the idea that a transcontinental railroad line should pass through it—a dream he may have held on to as Confederate president. During the war, Davis assigned Texans the task of pushing the Confederacy west. He hoped they might seize, or at least interrupt the flow of, precious metals from western mines. Leaving the campaign to the Texans spared Confederate resources sorely needed elsewhere, but it also ensured that Latino support for the South would be extremely limited. With the conquest of the Southwest still fresh in the minds of Latinos, their loyalty to the United States was not strong at the start of the Civil War. But the war would prove to be a galvanizing moment for Mexican American identity.[5]

Before the Native Cavalry could begin to take shape, elite Californios would have to get behind the idea. Although in published newspaper announcements Andrés Pico offered his "sword" for the cause of the Union, he turned down an appointment to lead the Native Cavalry Battalion, citing health issues. Command was then given to Salvador Vallejo of Northern California, another owner of vast ranch lands. Vallejo had developed a strong hatred of Anglo-American squatters, particularly those from the South. Not harmed nearly as much by gold rush era squatters as the northern Californio families, such as the Vallejos, the de la Guerras and other southern Californio ranching families had actually benefited from a gold rush spike in beef prices. But an increasingly competitive western cattle market, as well as a combination of flooding and drought in the early 1860s, devastated the ranchos of Southern California. In the midst of this downturn, the Native Cavalry offered the de la Guerras and other ranchero families the opportunity to bolster their declining status while providing their relatives and ranch hands with employment as U.S. servicemen. Antonio de la Guerra took it upon himself to raise a cavalry company in Santa Barbara, and he supported the group with his own resources until it was retroactively authorized by the California governor.[6]

Aside from the concerns of elite Californio rancheros and a long-standing resentment of Texans, there was another critical factor that helped rally Latino support for the Union. In 1862, the French emperor Napoleon III had taken advantage of America's distraction with the Civil War to invade Mexico, without regard for the Monroe Doctrine—the U.S. policy of resisting further European expansion in the Western Hemisphere. Napoleon III sent the Austrian archduke Maximilian to Mexico to rule as emperor with the support of French troops. Of course, Mexico already had a president, Benito Juarez, and had been independent of Spain since 1821. As a consequence of the French intervention, Mexico became embroiled in a civil war between those supporting Maximilian's empire and those loyal to the republic. It was no secret that Washington wanted a Juarez victory, or that supporters of the Confederacy and those of Maximilian shared a desire to see the Union crumble.

For their part, U.S. Latinos generally wanted to see the sister republics of Mexico and the United States triumph. Historian David E. Hayes-Bautista emphasizes this in his 2012 study of the origins of the Cinco de Mayo holiday.[7] He argues that a network of *juntas patrióticas,* or "patriotic assemblies," deliberately created this tradition in California during the 1860s. These groups included a diverse array of Latinos but were dominated by working-class Mexican immigrants. Sprouting up across the state in the wake of the French intervention, their primary purpose was to raise funds and other forms of support for the Mexican Republic, but they also encouraged Latinos to back the Union. On May 5, 1862, Mexican forces won a stunning victory by repelling a French attack on the city of Puebla. In the spring of 1863, the French launched another, much larger assault in the hope of taking the city before the anniversary of their May 5 defeat. California Latinos were riveted as news trickled in from the siege of Puebla, and tensions heightened further when news arrived of a crushing Union defeat at the Battle of Chancellorsville in Virginia. In their linked struggles for survival, both republics appeared to be on the ropes. But when word arrived that Mexican forces had held Puebla through the May 5 anniversary, this was cause for celebration. In Los Angeles, the largest *junta patriótica* organized the first public celebration of Cinco de Mayo and thereby kick-started an annual tradition that is still with us. The celebration was a decidedly Mexican American affair. A U.S. flag was raised alongside a Mexican one, and banners for the respective founding fathers, Washington and Hidalgo, were paraded through the streets. Addressing the crowd in Spanish, the Californio Republican Francisco Ramirez blended American and Mexican patriotisms and urged those present to support both embattled republics.

Ramirez also made a plea to non-Mexican Latinos in the audience, calling on the citizens of other Latin American republics to defend Mexico in her hour of need. Additionally, he expressed a hope that all these nations would one day "come together to form a great Hispanic American Union!"[8] Although predominantly Mexican American, the Native Cavalry recruited members born elsewhere in Latin America. Companies A and B of the battalion, raised in Northern California, were especially diverse owing to the gold-rush inflow of migrants from all over the world. A good number of the men in these two companies came from South America as well as countries in Latin Europe, such as Spain, France, and Sardinia. In this respect, the vaguely Latino identity of the Native Cavalry resonated with an idea promoted by supporters of Maximilian, that Mexicans should embrace the French as allies because of underlying cultural commonalities—namely, the use of romance languages and adherence to the Roman Catholic faith. The Native Cavalry, however, was far from solidly Latino, even according to this broad conception. There were a significant number of German immigrants and Yaqui Indians in companies A and B, and all the companies also had a few Anglo-Americans, usually in positions of leadership. Companies C and D came closest to Pacheco's Californio-

FIGURE 6.2

Soldier's bounty paid to José Dionisio Torrez upon enrollment in the Native Cavalry Battalion, dated December 31, 1864. Wayne and Pamela Sherman Collection.

centered vision. Drawing on the cow counties of Santa Barbara and Los Angeles, they were dominated by the Californio ranchers as well as by their ranch hands and others in the local laboring class, many of whom had migrated from the bordering Mexican state of Sonora.[9]

In addition to having ranching skills, many of the cow-county recruits were also familiar with using weapons from horseback. The traditional weapon of choice for the Californios was the horseman's spear—the lance—which typically consisted of a long wood shaft with a double-edged, pointed metal blade for a tip. Brought to Mesoamerica by conquistadors in the sixteenth century, the lance had been taken north into Alta California by Spanish colonial soldiers in the late eighteenth century. These frontier soldiers continued the conquest on the northern frontier by guarding Catholic missionaries and disciplining Indians who worked and worshipped at the missions. As shown by Pico's men at San Pasqual, the lance was a highly effective weapon in the hands of skilled Californios. The mounted lancer could puncture with precision from a distance and in rapid succession. Most of the dead and wounded Americans at San Pasqual had multiple lance wounds.[10]

The California state militia manufactured new lances for the Native Cavalry Battalion, a unit that was also known as the California Lancers. Before parading through California towns, the Native Cavalrymen would adorn their lances with colorful flags. The image presented in these parades was both ironic and romantic. The legendary *lanceros* of Alta California had returned in full medieval splendor, now proudly wearing the uniform of the nation that had conquered them. Juan participated in at least one such parade through the German settlement of Anaheim, a moment that was remembered seven

FIGURE 6.3
Spanish or Mexican lance point, seventeenth to nineteenth century. Autry National Center, 88.127.111.

decades later when he was made an honorary member of the city's German cultural club at the advanced age of eighty-five.[11]

Although central to the unit's image, there was one major problem with the lances provided by the state militia. They were lousy weapons. Once the Native Battalion arrived in Arizona, the lances were described in official unit paperwork as unfit for service. No such complaints were made regarding the sabers, however. Though not as clearly associated with the Spanish-American warrior tradition as the lance, the saber evoked a more general European-American notion of a gentleman warrior on horseback that complemented the Californio image. Functionally, the 1860-model saber was in some respects very similar to a lance. For a sword, it was long, thin and lightweight. With its double-edged tip, it could produce devastating puncture wounds when thrust. But the saber had an added function, its main function: it served as an incredibly deadly hatchetlike hacking tool. This key difference between lance and saber tells us a great deal about the type of Indian fighting traditionally conducted by Californios compared to that of American cavalry. The Spanish-Mexican soldiers of Alta California had a grisly record of mistreating California Indians that included mutilation and murder as well as rape and kidnapping. Ranchero-led expeditions to track down Indian horse thieves also often ended with violence. But the scale of massacre that occurred at the hands of Union forces in the West during the Civil War era—most notably at Sand Creek, Colorado, in 1864—was unheard of in the history of Alta California. The 1860 saber was a finely made precision instrument of combat, but it could also be an effective tool for wholesale slaughter.[12]

THE SABER

For over a thousand years, the saber served warriors on horseback as a highly effective killing tool. Raiding horsemen carried the saber from Central Asia into Europe in the ninth century. The English word *saber* comes from the French *sabre*. This term traces back to the Hungarian term *szablya*, which means "a tool to cut with." The key distinguishing feature of the weapon is its curved blade. The curvature reduces the area of impact, focusing the force of the blow and increasing the likelihood that the blade will break skin. Sabers are particularly useful when wielded from horseback. Holding the reins with one hand, a mounted warrior can wield the weapon with the other. A horse's speed can greatly enhance the saber's slicing power; but even when the horse is still, a mounted warrior can take advantage of his elevated position to strike downward at those on foot, hacking as if with a hatchet.[13]

The 1860 model was designed by the Ames Manufacturing Company in Massachusetts. An important player in the industrialization of the United States, Ames was central to the development of what has been called the "American system" of manufacturing. Actually modeled on military-industrial complexes in Britain and France, this production system took hold in the United States when the Army Ordnance Department reformed weapons manufacturing following the War of 1812, a conflict that exposed many shortcomings in the young nation's military readiness. Ordnance officers presided over the standardization and mass production of interchangeable weapons parts—blades, handles, and handguards, for example—which sped up repair times, minimized waste, and controlled quality. This system of arms manufacture, and the industrialization of the Northeast that it helped spur, provided the United States with critical advantages for making war against Mexico, the Confederacy, and resistant Native American groups in the West.[14]

As a private company whose major customer was the U.S. Army, Ames was responsive to the complaints of American cavalrymen. Based on feedback that the 1840 model was too heavy for use in the West, Ames built a lighter saber that would not be as much of a burden on long treks across the rugged landscape or in pursuit of (or escape from) fast-moving Native Americans. Compared to the three-and-a-half-pound 1840 version— "old wrist breaker," as it was known to cavalrymen—the redesigned 1860 model weighed a little over two pounds. Much of the weight was taken out of the blade, moving the center of gravity back toward the handle and making the sword easier to wield. Reducing the saber's mass decreased the potential force of its blows, but this was an acceptable loss considering that western Indians did not typically have the thick uniforms of European or Euro-American soldiers.[15]

Although designed for the West, the 1860 saber was issued to eastern units as well and became the standard saber of Civil War cavalrymen, North and South. But escalating firepower on eastern battlefields quickly altered the nature of cavalry combat. Charges with sabers drawn became increasingly suicidal and increasingly rare. The new normal was to dismount before fighting. Still taking advantage of their superior mobility, cavalry units would ride to a key position on the battlefield. Then, leaving one of every four men behind to hold the horses, the rest would advance on foot with rifles in hand and assume a firing formation. They could still use their sabers as backup weapons, but shotguns and revolvers were better on that score, especially while the user was dismounted. Sabers retained their importance as status symbols, however. The cavalry saber was a beautiful weapon reserved only for the trooper, a semielite category of soldier.[16]

Juan de la Guerra's sword is a work of art, but it's not an original Ames (see figure 6.1). This is made clear by the inscription on one side of the ricasso, the dull section of the blade directly above the hilt, which reads "D. J. MILLARD/CLAYVILLE NY." When Ames could not satisfy wartime demand, other manufacturers were contracted to produce sabers on the Ames pattern; David J. Millard was the smallest of six such manufacturers. A second-generation scythe manufacturer in Upstate New York, Millard predicted in 1860 that swords would be a growth industry in the event of a war between the states. With this in mind, he traveled to Germany and brought back Georg Scheuch, a trained swordsmith. Scheuch, who eventually married one of Millard's daughters, showed Millard how to retool his factory for swords. The plan paid off in 1861, when Millard received a U.S. government contract for ten thousand sabers. On the opposite side of Juan's blade, another inscription reads "U.S. / C.E.W. / 1862." The initials are those of a Charles E. Wilson of Clayville, who in 1862 inspected the sword that would be issued to Juan. This was the American system at work. As long as the pattern was followed under the supervision of a skilled craftsman, and an effective inspection process was in place, multiple manufacturers could produce the same weapons with interchangeable parts. Although Millard ran a small operation, there's no indication that his product was in any way substandard. In fact, Millard blades were good enough for Tiffany & Company of New York City, which bought them to make unique silver-mounted presentation swords for special Union officers.[17]

The Native Cavalrymen did not receive any presents from Tiffany. Stationed in a remote outpost on the West Coast, more than a thousand miles from the major battles of the Civil War, they were lucky to get high-quality weapons of any kind. Although a state since 1850, California in some ways operated as an overseas colony of the United States until the completion of the transcontinental railroad in 1869. Most manufactured goods, including most weapons destined for the military post named Drum Barracks, found their way to California by steamship. Three years after its inspection in Millard's factory, and after a journey of roughly six thousand miles from New York to Panama to California—about twenty-three hundred miles as the crow flies—this 1860-model saber found its way to Drum Barracks and into Sergeant Juan de la Guerra's hands. He was probably delighted to receive it, especially after enduring almost a year of discomfort, hard labor, and boredom at Drum Barracks. Imagine yourself in the shoes of the young de la Guerra, holding the saber for the first time. Right away, you're struck by how the long, yet lightweight, sword seems almost to float in your hand. Gently swinging the saber, you feel its inertia most keenly where the twisted copper wire wrapping the handle meets your skin. This grip wire is intended to prevent the sword from slipping away when it's forcefully swung. As you tighten your imaginary hold, you realize that the wire could easily draw blood. But we generally have soft, twenty-first-century hands that are not accustomed to ranch work or the kind of hard labor that was demanded of the men at Drum Barracks.[18]

DRUM BARRACKS DRUDGERY

Drum Barracks was named for Lieutenant Colonel Richard Drum, an officer whose assistance was critical to the founding of this military post and supply depot. Located on the

Southern California coast near the modern Port of Los Angeles, this facility was built during the early years of the Civil War for two main reasons: to establish a strong military presence in Southern California, a region of questionable loyalty; and to provide a training ground and staging area for the 1862 invasion of Confederate Arizona by a force known as the California Column. For the better part of a year, from fall 1864 through spring 1865, most of the Native Cavalry waited at Drum Barracks for orders to go to Arizona as a relief force for the Column. Before being sent to Arizona, some in the Native Cavalry were deployed throughout California to campaign against resistant Native Americans, pursue pro-Confederate bandits, and clamp down on the activities of other copperheads (Southern-sympathizers). Most of the Native Cavalry's service in the state, however, consisted of dull labor in and around Drum Barracks. Among other projects, the men dug an enormous aqueduct that brought fresh water to the barracks and the surrounding area.[19]

For many in the Native Cavalry, being put on ditchdigging detail would have been humiliating. After months of delay at Drum Barracks, Commander Salvador Vallejo resigned, saying that his duty had been "devoid of interest."[20] The work would have been an abrupt and unwelcome change for Juan, who grew up in an elite Californio society that valued leisure time and saw hard labor as suited for Indians or perhaps lower-status Latinos. There were, of course, perks to being a well-connected de la Guerra, even if the duty was miserable. This is revealed in the following excerpt from a letter that Juan wrote from Drum Barracks to his aunt: "Tell my mother that I wrote her and I have [had] no response[;] also that the sweet that I received was very good, they ate of it, my uncle [Antonio de la Guerra], Capitan Bale, Lieutenant Cox, and Lieutenant Streeter."[21] In addition to the comfort he received from his mother's treat, sharing it probably didn't hurt his standing with the officers. Elite Californios and high-ranking Anglos likely enjoyed many such perks that were not available to Native Cavalrymen of more humble backgrounds.

Major John C. Cremony, an Anglo-American, was appointed to replace Vallejo as the battalion commander. Cremony embraced this opportunity with relish, even going so far as to adopt certain flamboyant elements of Californio dress. He was in some ways perfect for the job. He spoke Spanish fluently, had previously fought the Apaches, and had even participated in the binational effort to demarcate the new U.S.-Mexico border.[22] Immediately upon taking control, Cremony moved the unit toward fighting readiness by drilling the battalion hard. Years later, he would claim that he taught the men "a lesson or two, which they have not forgotten to this day." When orders finally came to ride to Fort Mason, the companies left one at a time so as not to overtax scarce water resources along the arid route. Luckily for Juan, Company C brought up the rear, which meant they left in the early fall of 1865 and not in the heat of summer.[23]

PATROLLING THE BORDERLANDS

When the Native Cavalry arrived at Fort Mason in Arizona in the fall of 1865, the Texans were long gone and the Confederacy was no more. Still unresolved, however, was the civil war south of the border, which would continue until 1867, when Maximilian was captured and executed. Also far from settled was the relationship between the United States and the Native Americans of the borderlands. Showing little regard for the poorly defended border or claims of sovereignty by governments on either side, several Indian groups continued raiding for livestock and human captives. Cross-border Indian raids did not stop in the region until Geronimo and his band of Apaches surrendered to the United States in the mid-1880s.[24]

Although assigned to watch and, to the extent that was possible, secure the border, the Native Cavalry themselves crossed into Mexico in at least two official operations. Companies A and B arrived at Fort Mason in September. Shortly thereafter, an astounding twenty-six Native Cavalrymen—approximately 13 percent of the men in those companies—fled to Mexico. Captain José Ramón Pico, the nephew of Andrés Pico, and Captain Porfirio Jimeno, the cousin of Juan de la Guerra, led a detachment of thirty men in pursuit of the deserters. When they arrived in Magdalena, Sonora, Captain Pico had a tense standoff with the pro-Maximilian prefect in charge of the city's garrison. Pico marched into the prefect's office and stated that he was looking for the deserters. The prefect objected to him making demands on Mexican soil, but Pico responded by brazenly proclaiming that he did not recognize the government of Maximilian, only that of the Mexican Republic, with which the United States had an extradition treaty. He left the office, and tensions rose as both sides readied their men for a fight. Pico then called out to the prefect, telling him that he had better kill Pico and all his men, since they would not be taken prisoner. At that point, an old man in the crowd that had gathered called out, *"¡Vivan los Americanos!"* This salute to the Spanish-speaking U.S. cavalrymen may have shaken the prefect's confidence, since he offered to sit down and negotiate with Pico. This dramatic episode reveals the Native Cavalry's problem with desertion—the missing men were never captured or extradited—but it also shows the zeal with which some in the unit embraced their status as U.S. servicemen and allies of the Mexican Republic.[25]

Juan's Company C arrived at Fort Mason in November, in time for another cross-border mission—the pursuit of Refugio Tánori, an Opata Indian chief and colonel in Maximilian's imperial army. Having already been defeated by Tánori in battle, Republican general Garcia Morales avoided another confrontation by crossing over into the United States and taking shelter in the small town of San Gabriel, Arizona. Tánori followed and fired on San Gabriel, wounding one civilian. Major Cremony, the commander of the Native Cavalry, responded to this raid on American soil by hastily organizing a response force of 150 of his "best troopers," perhaps including Juan.[26]

The Native Cavalry detachment never caught Tánori, but Cremony later claimed that this incursion had important consequences nevertheless. Imperial forces had vacated nearby Santa Cruz, in Sonora, Mexico, ahead of the Native Cavalry, and Cremony decided to seize the town. As he later explained, he took Santa Cruz in order to give his troopers a place to lay low for a few days with the hope that Tánori, "thinking the coast was clear," might return. After a few days, Cremony led the detachment back to Fort Mason. Although

FIGURE 6.4
Photograph of Major José Ramón Pico, Union
Army, Civil War, 1860s. Seaver Center for
Western History Research, Los Angeles
County Museum of Natural History.

he failed in his mission to catch Tánori, Cremony claimed that he had helped pave the way for a Republican comeback in the region. Tánori did not lead his men into battle again, and his absence allowed Republican forces to reassert their authority in Sonora.[27]

The Apaches had a long history of raiding settlements throughout the region for livestock and human captives. These practices only intensified amid the turmoil and escalating violence of the Civil War era. The Apaches began steering clear of Fort Mason around the time of the Native Cavalry's arrival, however, probably owing to their awareness of a military buildup. Patrols would sometimes see large groups of Apaches in the distance. Captain Jimeno reported killing an Apache he came across once while on patrol. In a later incident, a detachment of Native Cavalrymen commanded by Jimeno ambushed a group of Apaches. They killed one Apache and wounded two others before the rest got away. Generally though, Apache raiders focused their attention south of the border during this time and stayed out of the Native Cavalry's way. Although not responsible for vanquishing any band of hostile Indians, the battalion did appear to have influenced the actions of the Apaches as well as the Opatas.[28]

These Native American groups may have been intimidated by the Native Cavalry's sabers in particular. The men also received common rifles upon their arrival at Fort Mason, but these were second-rate firearms, issued only because the superior Sharps carbines were worn out from overuse. California Column commander James Carleton remarked that the common rifles were "worthless as weapons for mounted men."[29] Some of the higher-ranking troopers carried effective sidearms, but the sabers were the only high-quality weapon issued to all the Native Cavalrymen. In addition to their utility as killing tools, the psychological effect of so many sabers could be overwhelming. As remembered by a U.S. cavalry veteran of a war against the Cheyennes in 1857: "Our three hundred bright blades flashed out of their scabbards, [and] the Cheyennes, who were coming on at a lope, checked up. The sight of so much cold steel seemed to cool their ardor."[30] It wasn't that groups like the Cheyennes, Opatas, or Apaches had never seen glistening sabers. One way or another, Native American warriors in the West got hold of all sorts of European- and American-made weapons; but seeing scores of identical, shining steel blades would have been an unusual and potentially terrifying sight.

The Native Cavalrymen were probably frightened at times by their Native American adversaries, but the most fearsome foe they faced was disease. Unusually heavy rains produced pools of stagnant water around Fort Mason, and a mosquito-borne illness ravaged the battalion. At the height of the epidemic nearly half the men were sick, and seven eventually died of the disease. Not all illnesses could be linked to environmental causes, however. Juan's uncle, Captain Antonio de la Guerra, apparently contracted a sexually transmitted disease during his time in the Native Cavalry. When orders came in January of 1866 for the battalion to return to Drum Barracks to be mustered out, Captain de la Guerra's worsening condition caused Company C to take a less onerous route. They rode only as far as the Gulf of California before traveling by steamship to San Francisco for discharge.[31]

VETERAN OF THE WAR

Juan de la Guerra did not move back to Santa Barbara after leaving the Native Cavalry. In the afterglow of Union victory, Republican free-labor ideology reigned triumphant in California, and nowhere more so than in the Unionist stronghold of San Francisco. Juan may have come to embrace this ideology, which held that if he worked hard, saved, and charted his own destiny, he could build a prosperous new life for himself away from his family and their declining fortunes. His veteran status probably opened doors for him that would have otherwise been closed to a Mexican American. Also, his military experience may have given him the confidence that he could operate effectively in an Anglo-dominated society. Making use of his fluency in English and Spanish, he worked as a court translator in San Francisco before obtaining a more prestigious position in Sacramento as a clerk in the state legislature, in charge of translating documents. Apparently finding time to study on the side, he soon passed the bar and began practicing law throughout Northern California.[32]

Emulating his Spanish-immigrant grandfather, Juan secured high social standing by marrying into a prominent Californio family. Based in what is now Orange County in Southern California, the Yorbas were one of the last Californio families to hold on to a good portion of their once vast ranch lands. After his marriage to Ramona Yorba, Juan moved onto a portion of this land and, among other things, supervised the production of oranges—a cash crop that boosted Southern California real estate values and helped make the region famous worldwide. Not only was he connected to the booming Southern California economy, but he was also enmeshed in the region's expanding Anglo-American male social world.

FIGURE 6.5

The eighty-three-year-old Juan de la Guerra *(center)* was photographed with other distinguished members of the Southern California Historical Society during their 1930 tour of the Los Angeles Plaza and the new Olvera Street, a historically themed Spanish-Mexican marketplace. On the left are two Civil War veterans who had also been recruited in California: Charles M. Jenkins *(far left)* and Emanuel A. Speegle. On the right are two prominent, longtime Southern California residents: Judge J. E. Pleasants and businessman James H. Dodson *(far right)*. Los Angeles Public Library Photo Collection.

Among other organizations dominated by Anglo-Americans, Juan joined the Fullerton post of the nation's largest veterans group, the Grand Army of the Republic. Following the Civil War and the arrival of the railroad in 1876, Southern California, the onetime secessionist hotbed, was flooded with Union veterans, mostly migrants from the Midwest. Juan and these vets from the East would have had very different war stories, but some of the artifacts of their service would have spoken to a common experience. Perhaps Juan compared his saber side by side with those of other Union cavalrymen. After noting the different inscriptions and other distinctive touches of the various manufacturers, they would have realized that the swords were essentially the same. Despite coming from a different background, Juan bonded with his fellow veterans. He remained active in his Grand Army of the Republic post until he was one of the last surviving members.[33]

Juan de la Guerra died in 1940, at the age of ninety-three, at the Union Veterans Home west of Los Angeles. At the time, he was one of the last remaining Civil War veterans in Southern California and one of the last Californios born before the end of the Mexican-American War. He was also, almost certainly, the last Native Cavalryman. In the final decade of his life, Juan was the subject of several articles in the *Los Angeles Times*. Southern California elites, including writers for the *Times*, had a long-standing practice of celebrating a fantasy version of the region's Spanish past while marginalizing its Mexican present. Claiming that they were a burden on taxpayers, Los Angeles County officials deported thousands of Latinos—including American-born citizens—to Mexico during the Great Depression.[34] In stark contrast to these scapegoated working-class Latinos, Juan was frequently depicted in the pages of the *Times* as a charming relic of a whitewashed Spanish past. In his column The Lancer, Harry Carr even turned the gray eyes of "Don Juan" into "old blue eyes."[35]

One 1935 *Times* piece painted a fanciful picture of an 1865 dance held in honor of the Native Cavalry in Los Angeles. The accompanying photograph shows an eighty-eight-year-old Juan de la Guerra examining himself in the same mirror in the United States Hotel that he had looked into seventy years before to see "a dashing cavalry sergeant." As Juan recalled, "We were cavalrymen and we were terribly excited. We thought we had the finest cavalry outfit in the whole country. Probably it was. Such horses we all had! That night we went to a dance. A couple of days later the war was over. We never even started."[36]

But the Native Cavalry did start. The battalion rode to Arizona, where it was too late to engage Confederates but not too late to confront resistant Native Americans or influence a civil war still raging south of the border. Following family tradition, Juan bettered his own prospects through military service. He also contributed to a five-hundred-year project of Euro-American conquest in North America, as well as a thousand-year legacy of human conquest by horse and saber. More specifically, he assisted in the consolidation of U.S. power in the Civil War–era West and did so equipped with a cutting-edge piece of technology, the 1860-model cavalry saber.

Juan and the other Native Cavalrymen also started in another sense. They helped launch a long tradition of Mexican-American military service and staked a powerful claim to the full rights of U.S. citizenship. Looking back from the dark days of deportation in the 1930s, it may have seemed all for naught. In light of a recent Arizona law that invites the police to racially profile Latinos, equality may still seem a distant goal.[37] For this reason, it is incumbent on us to tell and retell the story of the Native Cavalry. Many of the men in this unit answered the call of a nation that had defeated and mistreated them. In doing so, they took a bold stand in favor of a strong Union, an independent Republic of Mexico, and their own place in a more equal society. De la Guerra's sword of the war remains a powerful symbol of that service.

NOTES

1. Alberto García Carraffa, *Diccionario Heráldico y Genealógico de Apellidos Españoles y Americanos* (Madrid: Impr. de Antonio Marzo, 1920), 193–218; Louise Pubols, *The Father of All: The de la Guerra Family, Power, and Patriarchy in Mexican California* (Berkeley: University of California Press; San Marino, CA: Huntington Library, 2009), 14–27.

2. Tom Prezelski, "Lives of the California Lancers: The First Battalion of Native Cavalry, 1863–1866," *Journal of Arizona History* 40, no. 1 (Spring 1999): 33–34; Richard H. Orton, *Records of California Men in the War of the Rebellion 1861 to 1867* (Sacramento, CA: State Office, 1890), 315–17; "Muster and Descriptive Roll of a Detachment of United States, Capt Antonio Ma. de la Guerra, forwarded by Company 'C' for the First Battalion Regiment of Native Cavalry, California Volunteers Stationed at Santa Barbara, Cal . . . ," manuscript, 1864, Drum Barracks Museum, Los Angeles.

3. Paul B. Gray, *Forster vs. Pico: The Struggle for the Rancho Santa Margarita* (Spokane, WA: Arthur H. Clark, 1998), 46–74.

4. Ibid., 91–93; Prezelski, "Lives of the California Lancers," 30.

5. Rafael Chacón, *Legacy of Honor: The Life of Rafael Chacón, a Nineteenth-Century New Mexican,* 1st ed. (Albuquerque: University of New Mexico Press, 1986); Alvin Josephy, *The Civil War in the American West,* 1st ed. (New York: A. A. Knopf, 1991), 3–94.

6. Prezelski, "Lives of the California Lancers," 29–34.

7. David E. Hayes-Bautista, *El Cinco de Mayo: An American Tradition* (Los Angeles: University of California Press, 2012), 51–74.

8. Ibid., 96–100.

9. Prezelski, "Lives of the California Lancers," 31–34; Hayes-Bautista, *El Cinco de Mayo,* 136.

10. George C. Stone, *A Glossary of the Construction, Decoration and Use of Arms and Armor in All Countries and in All Times* (Portland, ME: Southworth Press, 1934), 407–9; Robert W. Cherny et al., *Competing Visions: A History of California* (Boston: Houghton Mifflin, 2005), 37–49; John S. Griffin, *A Doctor Comes to California: The Diary of John S. Griffin, Assistant Surgeon with Kearny's Dragoons, 1846–1847* (San Francisco: California Historical Society, 1943), 43–54.

11. John S. McGroarty, "News of Southern Counties: Anaheim Fete Goes German," *Los Angeles Times,* September 17, 1932.

12. Prezelski, "Lives of the California Lancers," 46; Douglas Monroy, *Thrown among Strangers: The Making of Mexican Culture in Frontier California* (Berkeley: University of California Press, 1990), 3–98.

13. Leonid Tarassuk and Claude Blair, *The Complete Encyclopedia of Arms & Weapons* (New York: Simon and Schuster, 1982), 408; Stone, *Glossary of the Construction,* 530; *The Concise Oxford Dictionary of English Etymology* (New York: Oxford University Press, 1991), s.v., "saber."

14. Merritt R. Smith, "Army Ordnance and the 'American System' of Manufacturing, 1815–1861," in *Military Enterprise and Technological Change: Perspectives on the American Experience,* ed. Smith (Cambridge, MA: MIT Press, 1985), 39–86.

15. Randy Steffen, *The Horse Soldier, 1776–1943: The United States Cavalryman—His Uniforms, Arms, Accoutrements, and Equipments* (Norman: University of Oklahoma Press, 1977), 2:76; John H. Thillmann, *Civil War Cavalry & Artillery Sabers: A Study of United States Cavalry and Artillery Sabers, 1833–1865* (Lincoln, RI: A. Mowbray, 2001), 315–17.

16. Ian Drury and Tony Gibbons, *The Civil War Military Machine: Weapons and Tactics of the Union and Confederate Armed Forces* (New York: Smithmark, 1993), 27.

17. Richard H. Bezdek, *American Swords and Sword Makers* (Boulder, CO: Paladin Press, 1994), 59, 161–63, 208–9.

18. Don McDowell, *The Beat of the Drum: The History, Events, and People of Drum Barracks, Wilmington, California* (Santa Ana, CA: Graphic Publishers, 1993), 29–52; Tarassuk and Blair, *Complete Encyclopedia of Arms & Weapons*, 200–216.

19. McDowell, *Beat of the Drum*, 29–37; Tom Sitton, *Grand Ventures: The Banning Family and the Shaping of Southern California* (San Marino, CA: Huntington Library, 2010), 77–98; Prezelski, "Lives of the California Lancers," 33–36.

20. Prezelski, "Lives of the California Lancers," 36.

21. Juan José de la Guerra, "Letter to Joséfa (Moreno) de la Guerra," Wilmington, CA, October 4 1864, De la Guerra Family Collection Facsimile, 667 (391), Huntington Library, San Marino.

22. Prezelski, "Lives of the California Lancers," 36.

23. John C. Cremony, "How and Why We Took Santa Cruz," *Overland Monthly* 6 (April 1871): 336; Prezelski, "Lives of the California Lancers," 36–37.

24. James Brooks, *Captives & Cousins: Slavery, Kinship, and Community in the Southwest Borderlands* (Chapel Hill: University of North Carolina Press, 2002), 349–55; Brian DeLay, *War of a Thousand Deserts: Indian Raids and the U.S.-Mexican War* (New Haven, CT: Yale University Press, 2008), 306–9.

25. Hayes-Bautista, *El Cinco de Mayo*, 138–40.

26. Cremony, "How and Why We Took Santa Cruz," 335–40; Prezelski, "Lives of the California Lancers," 29–52.

27. Cremony, "How and Why We Took Santa Cruz," 335–40; Prezelski, "Lives of the California Lancers," 45–46.

28. Prezelski, "Lives of the California Lancers," 45–48.

29. Andrew Masich, *The Civil War in Arizona: The Story of the California Volunteers, 1861–1865* (Norman: University of Oklahoma Press, 2006), 69.

30. Thillmann, *Civil War Cavalry*, 315–17; Robert M. Peck, "Recollections of Early Times in Kansas," *Transactions of the Kansas State Historical Society* 8 (1904): 497.

31. Prezelski, "Lives of the California Lancers," 41–48.

32. "Death Calls Juan de la Guerra of Early California Family," *Los Angeles Times*, December 20, 1940.

33. "Remnant of Our Vanishing Army," *Los Angeles Times*, January 8, 1930; "Death Calls Juan de La Guerra of Early California Family."

34. George J. Sanchez, *Becoming Mexican American: Ethnicity, Culture, and Identity in Chicano Los Angeles, 1900–1945* (New York: Oxford University Press, 1993), 123.

35. Harry Carr, The Lancer, *Los Angeles Times*, September 30, 1935. For a thorough treatment of Southern California's constructed "Spanish fantasy past," see Phoebe S. Kropp, *California Vieja: Culture and Memory in a Modern American Place* (Berkeley: University of California Press, 2006).

36. "Glass Reflects Time's Toll," *Los Angeles Times*, June 17, 1935.

37. Lisa Magaña, "SB 1070 and Negative Social Constructions of Latino Immigrants in Arizona," *Aztlán: A Journal of Chicano Studies* 38, no. 2 (September 1, 2013): 151–62.

7

JOHN GAST'S *AMERICAN PROGRESS*
Using Manifest Destiny to Forget the Civil War and Reconstruction

Adam Arenson

Just before noon on May 10, 1869, Thomas Durant, vice president of the Union Pacific Railroad, took aim with a silver sledge. After a ceremonial tap, he handed it off to Leland Stanford, president of the Central Pacific Railroad, who took his turn hammering down the golden spike at Promontory Summit, in the Utah Territory.[1]

At the first blow, the telegraph operator had sent the signal "DONE." Cannons were fired in New York and San Francisco, and the bells were rung at Independence Hall. The festive mood stretched from Chicago to Washington and Maine to New Orleans. "We live in a wonderful era," declared the *Little Rock Daily Arkansas Gazette,* reflecting on the news, while a Washington correspondent wrote that "the completion of the Pacific Railroad has monopolized the public attention here to-day." In Philadelphia, the newspapers observed that the only similar scene in memory had derived from the news of Lee's surrender, at Appomattox Courthouse, four years earlier.[2]

The golden spike they tapped into place was engraved with the names of railroad officials and the wish "May God continue the unity of our Country as this Railroad unites the two great oceans of the world." Locomotives from the East and West were carefully rolled toward each other until they stood nose to nose, and hundreds of laborers, officials, and onlookers crowded into the celebratory photographs. One could now ride in a single railroad car from Sacramento to Omaha—cities not on the Pacific and Atlantic. But these termini were well enough connected to make the full transcontinental trip dramatically shorter and more direct, via one long connection across the Great Plains and through the Rockies and the Sierra.[3]

FIGURE 7.1

Lithograph after Thomas Hill, *Stanford Driving of the Last Spike (Gold) at the Joining of the Central and Union Pacific Lines—Promontory, Utah, May 10, 1869,* circa 1881. Gift of Clifford Park Baldwin. Braun Research Library Collection, Autry National Center, 14.C.1202.

"Accept this as the way to India," declared Grenville Dodge, a Union Pacific engineer speaking that day at Promontory Summit, invoking the memory of the late Missouri Senator Thomas Hart Benton. Standing at the center of the Saint Louis courthouse in October 1849, Benton had told a rapt audience that, in establishing a quick route to the Pacific Ocean and on to Asia, the American republic would complete the work that Christopher Columbus had not, when he first sailed west from Europe. When the railroad was completed, Benton said, they should carve the figure of Columbus into the Rockies, "pointing with outstretched arm to the western horizon, and saying to the flying passenger, there is the East! There is India!"[4]

In 1849, in the Saint Louis courthouse, Benton had argued that the transcontinental railroad would be "a band of Iron, hooping and binding the States together east and west[,] . . . a cement of union north and south." In June 1869, a month after the railroads were linked, a Colorado newspaper found that promise fulfilled: "It is this bringing of distant points together that renders the existence of a nation, spread over so vast a territory, possible, and . . . will render separation impossible."[5]

And so, you ask, the dream of decades, even centuries, was fulfilled in 1869? Maybe. And the transcontinental railroad solved all of the nation's problems? Hardly.

But such was the romance of sectional reconciliation, relying heavily on myths about the American West.[6] Images of a railroad crossing the plains were called upon to erase

FIGURE 7.2

John Gast, *American Progress*, 1872. Autry National Center, 92.126.1. For a color version of this image, see plate 10.

the traumatic experience of slavery and the Civil War, and to chase away the Reconstruction struggles for freedom and equal rights that were reaching a crisis point in 1869.

The Liberal Republican Party, organized in the 1870s and opposed to President Grant, argued for a willful amnesia about the Civil War and civil rights. Liberal Republicans saw in the myths of the West and in the railroad a more appealing history of the United States, a story with a specific vision of who belonged as an American, and who did not. Despite the party's short life, it transformed the debates over equality and civil rights. It led a new political coalition that rehabilitated the Democratic Party and set in motion changes that brought national Reconstruction to an end.

American Progress, the painting created in 1872 by artist John Gast for George Crofutt, publisher of a popular series of travel guides, embraces the vision of Liberal Republicanism. Painted less than four years after the completion of the transcontinental railroad, *American Progress* displays the mythic past, present, and future of the American West in an effort to use Manifest Destiny to save Reconstruction from itself.

For all its iconic power, the painting is at once alluring and somewhat puzzling. What did this encyclopedic image mean to its creators? How are we to understand this painting from the point of view of those who embraced its spirit? We can tease out the answer to the riddle of *American Progress* by going back to Promontory Summit and finding George Crofutt in the crowd that day in 1869.[7] The power of its imagery originates in events that occurred decades before, in the life experience of Crofutt's commissioned artist, John Gast.

Gast is often referred to in descriptions of *American Progress* as a "Brooklyn engraver" or a "German artist." He was both. But more important, he was the scion of a Saint Louis dynasty of German-American lithographers. Born on December 21, 1842, in Berlin, Prussia, Gast came to the United States as a child, when his family joined thousands fleeing the tumult of the "springtime of the peoples," the nationalist revolutions that had swept Europe in 1848. Gast's family moved from Germany to Saint Louis, a city growing rapidly and rising in stature as the "Gateway to the West."[8]

When John Gast was young, his father, Leopold, found commercial success with an engraving of Saint Louis's Great Fire of 1849. The blaze, which began with an errant spark from a steamboat and raged through the levee district, consumed twenty-three steamboats, 430 houses, and at least 310 businesses on fifteen downtown blocks. Leopold Gast's image captured both the drama of the conflagration and the confidence in Saint Louis's refounding. The hand-colored broadside displayed the fire in progress as seen from the Illinois shore. Gast's image pictured the tower of flames and the smoke billowing in perfect, beautiful spirals. But it also showcased the survivors: the thousands who came to profit from the disaster, via insurance payments, and the surviving cathedral, courthouse, and iron-framed city market buildings that figured prominently in the rebirth of the city. The level of detail allowed purchasers to point out exactly where they lived or worked and where the fire reached. Much like the tableau of western expansion his son would later create, Leopold Gast's engraving preserved the Great Fire as a moment of transformation.[9]

The aftermath of the Great Fire of 1849 cleared the way for new, western-focused development in Saint Louis. City leaders championed the political, economic, and cultural development of the West, declaring that the development of the transcontinental railroad could lead the nation out of the conflict over slavery and into prosperity—which *American Progress* would later celebrate.

After the Great Fire, Senator Thomas Hart Benton was not the only Saint Louis leader to put his faith in the transcontinental railroad plan as the source of the city's future prosperity. With "iron arms grasping two oceans," declared Josiah Dent, a founding officer of the Saint Louis Mercantile Library, in 1853, "we may say to the east and west, give up, and to the north and south, keep not back. And perhaps the contestants may compromise, by allowing King Commerce to fix his capital on the banks of the Mississippi," enriching Saint Louis with the bounty of the continent.[10]

Saint Louis was the largest city in the slave state of Missouri, but the city hosted a mix of antislavery and proslavery advocates. The adversaries agreed on one thing: that the westward construction of railroads—the boom industry of the 1850s—would threaten the future of slaveholding society. "Rail roads increase the facility of traveling so much that it will almost

FIGURE 7.3

Leopold and August Gast, *Saint Louis, MO. In 1855*, engraved panorama, 1855. Missouri History Museum, Saint Louis.

destroy the value of slave property on the frontier of the slaveholding states," one slaveholder wrote in 1854. "With the rapidity of the rail road[, slaves will] be in Canada before you are aware that they had started." The Kansas-Nebraska Act, passed that year, was intended to organize territories to facilitate the construction of the transcontinental railroad, but the inclusion of the popular sovereignty provisions championed by Illinois senator Stephen A. Douglas led to bloody, violent conflicts over slavery. The antislavery Massachusetts Emigrant Aid Society cheered the prospects that "the Missouri river, and the railroad across that State, [would] afford ready access" from Saint Louis to Kansas for their settlers. Meanwhile, U.S. secretary of war Jefferson Davis, future president of the Confederacy, worked to block the route by delaying approval of a right-of-way through the area's military installations.[11]

In 1855, Leopold and August Gast—John's father and uncle—engraved a panorama of Saint Louis together.[12] Depicted from nearly the same vantage point as the 1849 Great Fire image, the panorama highlights the rebuilt cityscape of Saint Louis. The foreground is filled with flatboats and wagons. A steamboat chugs past while more line the levee. Railroad engines enter from both edges of the image, seemingly on a course to meet, as the locomotives at Promontory Summit would meet two decades later. In the center foreground, a minuscule trio of figures sits upon a bluff, witnessing the tumult of activity. The Gasts worked on a grand scale, placing a variety of modes of transport on a wide field of vision to celebrate their city. These features also mark the younger Gast's work. The Gast family tradition of western boosterism shaped John Gast's worldview and imagery, a vision that became famous in *American Progress*.

The Gasts published their Saint Louis panorama in a critical year for the city's bid to become the central hub for a federally financed transcontinental railroad. After months of steady progress, the Missouri Pacific Railroad invited legislators, board members, investors, and well-wishers for the inaugural excursion to the state capital on November 1,

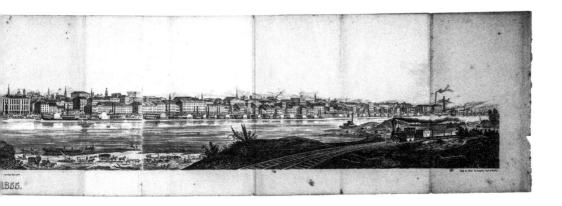

1855. That rainy afternoon ended in tragedy after a temporary bridge over the Gasconade River collapsed as the train was crossing, killing thirty-one and injuring hundreds. Five months later, a bridge over the Mississippi River at Rock Island, Illinois, was completed, providing direct access from New York through Chicago to the Platte River and the new city of Omaha. Saint Louis's railroad prospects faded as Chicago's rose—not because of slavery in Missouri or the growing conflict in Kansas, but because of Chicago's geographic advantages and better luck along the rails.[13]

In the 1850s, no one was exactly sure where the transcontinental railroad should cross the Rockies. White residents of Utah Territory, which then stretched from the eastern border of California to the western border of Kansas, were more likely to identify the territory as Deseret. They saw themselves less as Americans than as Latter-Day Saints, under the control not of Washington but of their prophet, Brigham Young. Joseph Smith, the first Mormon leader, had turned increasingly against slavery, but Young was more accommodating to Mormon slaveholders, tolerating slaveholding from Deseret's inception and legalizing slavery in the Utah Territory in 1852.[14]

In the first Republican Party platform, in 1856, advocates called on Congress "to prohibit in the Territories those twin relics of barbarism—Polygamy, and Slavery," with an eye on Utah, as well as on the rising violence in Kansas. Democratic president James Buchanan, with his Utah War of 1857–58, cynically tried to convince Northerners and Southerners to put aside their differences and fight against Mormon control of the territory.[15]

But what really transformed the Utah Territory was the discovery of gold and silver, first north of Pike's Peak and then in the Comstock Lode. Starting in 1858, prospectors rushed into these areas, at opposite ends of the territory. Like the earlier California gold rush, these mineral strikes highlighted the inaccessibility of the interior West—and the promise of how sudden wealth could sprout "instant cities" such as San Francisco and Denver. *New York Tribune* editor Horace Greeley came west to personally inspect the diggings. William Gilpin, an Army officer with extensive experience exploring the West, had once embraced Saint Louis as the nation's next capital—until he spent time in Denver and decided that that city was the true future metropolis of the American empire.[16]

In 1860, George Crofutt came west as well, to seek his fortune. Born in Connecticut in 1827, Crofutt was a miller's son who became a printer's apprentice. He worked for decades to open his own publishing venture in various eastern cities, only to see his fledgling newspaper bankrupted by the aftermath of the Panic of 1857. As Crofutt traveled overland to prospect around Pike's Peak, he passed through Saint Louis in 1860. In the midst of that year's presidential campaign, Kansas legislators debated whether to attempt to control the goldfields, or to petition to separate their settled communities from the emergent communities of the Front Range. In Congress, attempts to organize a new Colorado Territory were stymied by Southern congressmen, who feared the creation of yet another free state.[17]

By February 1861, President Lincoln's election had led to the secession of seven states and the empowerment of Republicans in Congress. Congress soon approved admission of Kansas as a free state and organized the territories of Colorado and Nevada, hemming in the Mormon presence in Utah Territory. Two months later, the new president, Abraham Lincoln, chose William Gilpin as Colorado's first territorial governor. Gilpin came west again from Missouri to accept the job.[18]

After the firing on Fort Sumter inaugurated all-out war between the United States and the newly created Confederate States of America, eastern railroads were essential for the movement of troops and supplies for both sides. Retreating regiments often blew up railroad bridges or bent the rails around trees in an effort to slow the enemy. In the newly organized territories, those troops that could be spared were sent to protect the mines from invasion, and the transcontinental telegraph line (completed in 1859) from disruption. In Congress, Republican leaders passed a number of bills that had been stalled by the conflict over the expansion of slavery, including the Homestead Act, the Morrill Land-Grant College Act, and the Pacific Railway Act, each of which strengthened government support for "free soil" settlement in the West and lessened the likelihood that slaveholding would survive the war.[19]

George Crofutt had been unsuccessful in the mines, but he found prosperity as a freight hauler based in Denver, working the trade from Kansas and Nebraska territories along the South Platte River. From his experience on the routes, he knew the people of the trails well, whether Cheyenne and Arapaho horsemen, Union soldiers during and after the Civil War, or old-time mountain men like Jim Bridger and Kit Carson. His familiarity with western landscapes and people gave Crofutt an advantage when it came to describing the sights to be encountered along the new transcontinental railroad.[20]

At the Golden Spike ceremony that May morning in 1869, Crofutt found before him railroad executives who had profited immensely from the changes the Civil War had wrought in the West. The Pacific Railway Act of 1862 granted land to the Central Pacific and Union Pacific railroads as an incentive for completing the transcontinental line. Leland Stanford served as founding president of the Central Pacific even as he served as governor of California, so he was perfectly positioned to advance railroad interests on every political, economic, and even military front. Thomas Durant organized financing for the Union Pacific—but he also developed a scheme to smuggle cotton out of the Confederacy, with the help of future transcontinental surveyor Grenville Dodge, who had commanded a Union brigade at the Battle of Pea Ridge and assisted in Sherman's Atlanta campaign before accepting command of the Department of the Missouri.[21]

After the Civil War, Dodge's department spearheaded the "Indian Wars," the renewed assault on Native American nations throughout the interior West, in part to create a corridor for the transcontinental railroad. By 1866, Dodge had discovered enough about the mountain passes—and the gilded opportunities in railroad finance and construction—to resign from the U.S. Army. He was then hired by Durant as the Union Pacific's chief engineer. Dodge's military knowledge served him well as they laid track heading west, on the road that led to Promontory Summit.[22]

But who laid those tracks? In 1865, the ratification of the Thirteenth Amendment had banned slavery and involuntary servitude throughout the United States. As ex-slaves and ex-slaveholders worked to remake their lives during Reconstruction, railroad companies were repeatedly accused of employing slave labor in the form of Chinese immigrant workers. The Central Pacific was the nation's largest employer of Chinese laborers, "heathen" migrant contract workers seen as impossible to assimilate into American society. That morning at Promontory Summit, Chinese workers had laid the last ties and rails, but then were pushed from the ceremonies and not visible in the final celebratory images. And the ceremony itself had been delayed by a labor dispute: two days before, Durant of the Union Pacific had been kidnapped by a group of his workers angry about not being paid their wages. It took a five-hundred-thousand-dollar payment wired from New York to free him and keep him moving west.[23]

After seeing the Golden Spike ceremony, Crofutt realized that the railroad had created an opportunity for him to return to publishing. Within weeks, he began producing the *Great Trans-Continental Tourist's Guide*. His publication joined a crowded field of overland guidebooks, but Crofutt drew on his firsthand knowledge of the West to provide engaging personal stories, along with itineraries made newly accessible by the latest extension of the railroad routes.[24]

It might have seemed like the completion of the transcontinental railroad was an event apart from the history of the Civil War, the fight over slavery that preceded it, and

FIGURE 7.4
Frontispiece to George A.
Crofutt, *Great Trans-Continental
Tourist's Guide* (New York: G. A.
Crofutt & Co., 1870), illustrated
by George Wilhelm Fasel.
Braun Research Library
Collection, Autry National
Center, 917.8 G74.

the debates over African American rights during Reconstruction, but the questions of
slavery and freedom, citizenship, and labor rights were not far removed from the minds
of those attending—if they wanted to see them. But, as George Crofutt, John Gast, and
the Liberal Republicans came to realize, most Americans looked for ways to ignore those
uncomfortable connections.

"The civil war, which once absorbed all our thoughts, is day after day receding into a
deeper past," declared Carl Schurz in June 1869, a month after the completion of the
transcontinental railroad line. "New wants, new problems, connected with the *future* of
the country, press irresistibly into the foreground." Schurz's background was much like
that of Leopold Gast: he had been a refugee of the German liberal revolution, and he
became enthusiastically involved with the politics of his adopted home, rising to be elected
to Benton's old seat as U.S. senator from Missouri.[25]

Like Benton, Schurz had dreams of transforming the nation, and in June 1869 he enumerated what would become the tenets of Liberal Republicanism. Schurz pledged allegiance to the Union but doubted the honesty of Grant's administration. He firmly believed in granting African Americans rights, but he felt the goals of Reconstruction had been achieved. Amnesty for ex-Confederates and national reconciliation were needed to heal the nation, Schurz argued, and the completion of the transcontinental railroad provided a new opportunity for radical realignment.[26]

In both Saint Louis and Denver, dreams of commanding the continent were reignited, and Horace Greeley came to feature in each. In Saint Louis, a failed schoolteacher and newspaper editor named Logan Uriah Reavis was obsessed with national transformation. Why should Washington, D.C.—that "distant place on the outskirts of the country," he wrote, "with little power or prestige"—remain the capital, when everything else was being transformed? After all, Pennsylvania's capital had moved from Philadelphia to Lancaster to Harrisburg, in the center of the state; Connecticut had moved its government from New Haven to Hartford; and South Carolina had transferred its government from Charleston to Columbia, among many other such examples in U.S. history. In pamphlets such as *A Change of National Empire* (1869), *St. Louis, the Future Great City of the World* (1870), and *The Capital Is Movable* (1871), Reavis made his case for relocation of the nation's capital from Washington to Saint Louis.[27]

In October 1869, Reavis arranged for a national convention in Saint Louis, drawing ninety delegates from seventeen states and territories. Predictably, support was greatest west of the Appalachian Mountains and included that of William Gilpin. Yet Reavis saw capital removal as a way to make Manifest Destiny and the agenda of the West work again for the benefit of the entire nation. Former president Andrew Johnson, from Tennessee, praised the effort, as did newspapers from Sacramento to Cincinnati. In his book *Democratic Vistas*, Walt Whitman, too, embraced the plan for an inland national capital in the Mississippi Valley, anchoring the continental nation.[28]

In January 1870, Representative John Logan of Illinois urged Congress to create a commission to study the practical and constitutional questions involved with capital removal, and some western legislators blocked further appropriations for D.C. construction until the removal question was resolved. In their glee, supporters even approved of Reavis's most radical suggestion, that the nation's public buildings—the White House, the newly completed Capitol, and the other government offices—be disassembled and freighted to Saint Louis.[29]

Horace Greeley wrote to Reavis in support of capital removal, stating that Saint Louis "advances steadily and surely to her predestined station of first inland city on the globe." But he hedged his bets: In 1870, a Greeley associate founded a "Union Colony" near Denver, which was advertised heavily in Greeley's *New York Tribune*. An agricultural settlement where residents had to sign a temperance pledge, it was soon renamed after Greeley. The settlement embodied the hope that the postwar West could effect a reunification built on the promise of the railroad, more than the aftermath of slavery.[30]

FIGURE 7.5

Cartoon of Carl Schurz pulling the capitol building westward. Keppler, "Verlor'ne Liebesmüh / Love's Labor Lost," *Die Vehme*, May 21, 1870. Missouri History Museum, Saint Louis.

While the capital removal effort eventually stalled and (obviously) did not come to fruition, it spun off one spectacular result when, in 1871, Reavis nominated Horace Greeley for president. President Grant had just begun his third year in office, and the election was eighteen months away, so this seemed like just another crackpot idea from Reavis. Greeley had strong reform credentials and was a champion of the West, and in 1867 he had joined those posting bond for former Confederate president Jefferson Davis, an act driven by his desire to see ex-Confederates treated less harshly. But Greeley had last served in political office in 1849, as a three-month vacancy replacement in the U.S. House of Representatives for the defunct Whig Party. This made for an unusual, and sparse, political résumé. And Greeley was on record opposing many of the Liberal Republicans' key platform pledges, including those on tariff elimination and civil-service reform. But the 1872 contest did not seem like a conventional election.[31]

In May 1872, Liberal Republicans gathered for their first and only national nominating convention, choosing Greeley for president and Missouri governor Benjamin Gratz Brown as the vice presidential nominee. Their chances increased when the newly invigorated Democratic Party ratified the Liberal Republicans' choices as their own that July. For a while the Greeley-Brown ticket drew large crowds, but soon their drawbacks, in policy and personal behavior, became evident. Carl Schurz, seeing the tide turn, moved from Missouri to New York and continued to transform himself, from a Republican Missouri senator to secretary of the interior under Rutherford B. Hayes, to New York Democratic political boss. Fellow German Americans in Saint Louis—including Joseph Keppler, publisher of the satirical magazine *Puck*; the newspaper editor Joseph Pulitzer; and the engraver John Gast—moved with him to the true capital of America's Gilded Age. On election day 1872, Greeley and Brown carried Missouri, Texas, Georgia,

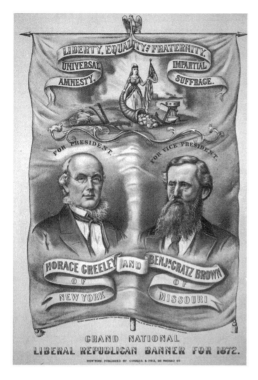

Kentucky, Tennessee, and Maryland. When Horace Greeley, exhausted and bereft, died a few weeks after the election, the Liberal Republican movement seemed to die with him.[32]

The ideas that had animated the Liberal Republican movement lived on in *American Progress*. In 1872, Crofutt dictated its design to Gast; and in 1873, Crofutt took pride in having the image "chromoed in *nineteen colors*" and announced it was to be "given *free* to each subscriber to CROFUTT'S WESTERN WORLD, $1.50 a year."[33]

Crofutt hastened to describe the picture in detail for his prospective customers. "At a glance," he wrote, *American Progress* depicted "the grand drama of Progress in the civilization, settlement and history of this country." An obvious place to start was "the 'Star of Empire'" on the forehead of "a beautiful and charming female." She carried a book, "the emblem of education," and "the slender wires of the telegraph, that are to flash intelligence throughout the land." Leaving the city for the West—where, in the painting, "the general tone . . . declares darkness, waste and confusion"—she guided "the three great continental lines of railway, passing the frontier settlers' rude cabin and tending toward the Western Ocean." A catalog of westering people and transportation—"wagons, overland stage, hunters, gold-seekers, pony-express, the pioneer emigrant"—moved across the page, while "the Indians, buffaloes, wild horses, bears, and other game . . . flee from, the presence of the wondrous vision."[34]

Equal parts patriot and salesman, Crofutt concluded by asking, "Is there a home, from the miner's humble cabin to the stately marble mansion of the capitalist, that can afford to be without this GREAT National picture, which illustrates in the most artistic manner all the gigantic results of American brains and hands?"[35] Such an image would be an ideal way to celebrate the future and forget about the past, including the all-too-recent Civil War.

Neither Crofutt nor Gast left us documents telling us whether they embraced the cause of Liberal Republicanism.[36] Still, Crofutt's connections to Denver, and Gast's experience in Saint Louis, link them to prime stages in the birth and growth of the Liberal Republican movement, to Greeley and Reavis, and to the efforts to replace memories of the Civil War and Reconstruction with the myth of Manifest Destiny in the West. And though Liberal Republicanism faded, in the following years the so-called "Redeemer" Democrats used Liberal Republican arguments to convince more voters to abandon progress toward equal rights for African Americans and other racial minorities, and to reorient the country toward reconciliation and economic advancement for whites only—often with a rosy view of the possibilities open in the West.[37]

American Progress is one of the most recognizable images of the American West, used as visual shorthand for Manifest Destiny and U.S. westward expansion in the 1840s in textbooks, on book covers, on posters, and as the subject of a recent iPad app from the Autry National Center.[38] The image yokes together past and present and future in the West, ignoring the legacies of slavery, the Civil War, and Reconstruction, and indeed, even obscuring the violence against native peoples and others perpetrated during the conquest of the continent—the kind of omissions that, after years of struggle and exhaustion, the Liberal Republicans desired. It depicts three railroad lines steaming west, and the Brooklyn Bridge complete—all of which were only realized about a decade later, in 1883.[39] *American Progress* elides its inconsistencies, lapses, and errors: What route are all these travelers taking? What happened to the Mississippi River and the eastern half of the continent? There seems to be just one large fertile plain, south of the Rockies. Are we in the snow-free deserts of the Southwest or, perhaps, even Mexico? If details seem hard to judge, we must remember it was designed for the cover of a pocket guide. Most of those viewing *American Progress*—now, and in its time, seen mostly in reproduction— do not know its actual size: 12 ¾ by 16 ¾ inches.[40] Realistic yet illusory, mesmerizing yet false, *American Progress* represents the passion of that vision and its convincing power, regardless of how far it was from reality.

As a seemingly encyclopedic image of the heroic story of American expansion, *American Progress* celebrated the marvels of transportation technology that were conquering the continent and banishing the Native Americans and taming the wilderness. It foreshadowed the most iconic word portrait of the American West, from Frederick Jackson Turner's influential essay "The Significance of the Frontier in American History": "Stand at Cumberland Gap and watch the procession of civilization, marching single file—the buffalo following the trail to the salt springs, the Indian, the fur trader and hunter, the cattle-raiser, the pioneer farmer—and the frontier has passed by. Stand at South Pass in the Rockies a century later and see the same procession with wider intervals between."[41]

But like Turner's essay,[42] *American Progress* is also a ghostly image, as we recall all those people and places that have been left out: no mixed-race fur-trading families, no coffles of chained slaves, no barges full of cotton, no fighting over slavery, no Civil War battlefields, no vaqueros on the cattle trail, no Ku Klux Klan violence, no "buffalo soldiers" or federal troops of any kind, and no African Americans.

If we regard it only as an image of the West, a palimpsest image of expansion divorced from the Civil War and Reconstruction, we pay tribute to the success of the Liberal Republican platform. We unknowingly affirm Crofutt's and Gast's determination to willfully forget about the struggle for slavery and freedom that occurred in the West and because of the West.

But if we can will ourselves to see what *American Progress* excludes as well as what it includes, and if we can stretch its story out to Promontory Summit and beyond, throughout the United States in the aftermath of the Civil War, it can encompass a far more complete story of the American West and its connections to the American Civil War and Reconstruction.

NOTES

Thanks to Virginia Scharff, Steve Aron, Sherry Smith, Carolyn Brucken, Amy Scott, Stephanie Narrow, Marni Sandweiss, Arielle Gorin, and John Mack Faragher.

1. Richard White, *Railroaded: The Transcontinentals and the Making of Modern America* (New York: W. W. Norton, 2011), 37; Robert V. Hine and John Mack Faragher, *The American West: A New Interpretive History* (New Haven, CT: Yale University Press, 2000), 274–75. For reasons to doubt the oft-told story that Durant and Stanford missed the spike, see David Haward Bain, *Empire Express: Building the First Transcontinental Railroad* (New York: Penguin, 2000), 666 and 756n31.

2. "Celebrations of the Completion of the Pacific Railroad," *Little Rock Daily Arkansas Gazette*, May 16, 1869, issue 149, col. A; the scene in Philadelphia is described in "Completion of the Pacific Railroad-Rejoicing over the Event in Eastern Cities," *San Francisco Daily Evening Bulletin*, May 21, 1869, issue 38, col. C. See also "Completion of the Pacific Railroad—How It Was Announced at Washington," *Milwaukee Daily Sentinel*, May 15, 1869, issue 114, col. D. All via the website 19th Century U.S. Newspapers, Gale Digital Collections, http://gdc.gale.com/products/19th-century-u.s.-newspapers/.

3. White, *Railroaded*, 37; J. N. Bowman, "Driving the Last Spike: At Promontory, 1869 (Concluded)," *California Historical Society Quarterly* 36, no. 3 (September 1957): 270, 266.

4. Speeches about the golden spike reprinted in "Completion of the Pacific Railroad," *Yankton (SD) Union & Dakotaian*, May 22, 1869, issue 6, col. A, via 19th Century U.S. Newspapers, Gale Digital Collections. Thomas Hart Benton, speech to the National Railroad Convention, October 16, 1849, as reported in the *Missouri Republican* (published in Black Hawk, CO, for the neighboring city of Central City, CO), October 18, 1849. Transcription provided by Bob Moore, Jefferson National Expansion Memorial, Saint Louis.

5. Benton, speech to the National Railroad Convention; *Daily Central City (CO) Register,* June 22, 1869, issue 281, col. B, via 19th Century U.S. Newspapers, Gale Digital Collections.

6. Nina Silber, *The Romance of Reunion: Northerners and the South, 1865–1900* (Chapel Hill: University of North Carolina Press, 1993); Patricia Nelson Limerick, *The Legacy of Conquest: The Unbroken Past of the American West* (New York: W. W. Norton, 1987); Heather Cox Richardson, *West from Appomattox: The Reconstruction of America after the Civil War* (New Haven, CT: Yale University Press, 2007).

7. J. Valerie Fifer, *American Progress: The Growth of the Transport, Tourist, and Information Industries in the Nineteenth-Century West, Seen through the Life and Times of George A. Crofutt, Pioneer and Publicist of the Transcontinental Age* (Chester, CT: Globe Pequot Press, 1988), 145–46.

8. For one such general description, see Martha A. Sandweiss, "John Gast, American Progress, 1872," in *Picturing United States History: An Interactive Resource for Teaching with Visual Evidence,* n.d., a project of the American Social History Project / Center for Media and Learning at the City University of New York Graduate Center, http://picturinghistory.gc.cuny .edu/item.php?item_id=180, accessed August 2012. John Gast, passport application, July 22, 1865, National Archives and Records Administration Passport Applications, 1795–1905, Collection number: ARC Identifier 566612 / MLR number A1 508, NARA Series: M1372, roll no. 151, via Ancestry.com; Leopold Gast and family, 1850 U.S. Census, Saint Louis, Missouri, roll no. M432_415, page 124A, image 253, lines 9–14, via Ancestry.com.

9. Julius Hutawa and Leopold Gast, *View of the City of St, Louis, Mo. The Great Fire of the City on the 17th & 18th May 1849,* August 1849, Missouri Historical Society Prints & Photographs Collection, Saint Louis; Adam Arenson, *The Great Heart of the Republic: St. Louis and the Cultural Civil War* (Cambridge, MA: Harvard University Press, 2011), chap. 1, esp. pp. 25–26.

10. Josiah Dent, *Lecture on the Mississippi Valley, Delivered before the St. Louis Mercantile Library Association on the 18th February, 1853* (Saint Louis: Chambers & Knapp, 1853), 30–31.

11. Sextus Shearer, San Francisco, to James Bissell, Saint Louis, October 15, 1854, Daniel Bissell Papers, Missouri Historical Society, Saint Louis; Massachusetts Emigrant Aid Company, *Nebraska and Kansas: Report of the Committee of the Massachusetts Emigrant Aid Society with the Act of Incorporation and Other Documents* (Boston: Published for the Massachusetts Emigrant Aid Co., 1854), 18, accessed via Kansas Collection, www.kancoll.org/books/emig_ aid/emigrant.htm; Jefferson Davis, War Department, to Thomas L. O'Sullivan, consulting engineer, St. Louis and Iron Mountain Rail Road Company, October 13 and 20, 1853, documents held in Records of the War Department, Office of the Secretary, Letters Sent, Military Book 35, marked 54–57, 63, by the National Archives and Records Service, in copies held at the Saint Louis Public Library since February 27, 1951. See also discussion in Arenson, *Great Heart of the Republic,* 68–69.

12. Leopold Gast and Brother [August Gast], "Saint Louis, MO. In 1855," stone engraving, Missouri History Museum Photograph and Print Collection, Saint Louis.

13. William Cronon, *Nature's Metropolis: Chicago and the Great West* (New York: W. W. Norton, 1991); Arenson, *Great Heart of the Republic,* chap. 4.

14. James B. Christensen, "Negro Slavery in the Utah Territory," *Phylon Quarterly* 18, no. 3 (Fall 1957): 298–305.

15. Republican Party Platform of 1856, June 18, 1856, via Gerhard Peters and John T. Woolley, the American Presidency Project, www.presidency.ucsb.edu/ws/?pid=29619; Jesse A. Gove and Otis Grant Hammond, *The Utah Expedition, 1857–1858: Letters of Capt. Jesse A. Gove . . . to Mrs. Gove, and Special Correspondence of the* New York Herald (Concord: New Hampshire Historical Society, 1928), as excerpted and described in William Francis Deverell and Anne Farrar Hyde, eds., *The West in the History of the Nation: A Reader* (Boston: Bedford / St. Martin's, 2000).

16. Martha B. Caldwell, "When Horace Greeley Visited Kansas in 1859," *Kansas Historical Quarterly* 9, no. 2 (May 1940): 116, via Kansas Collection, www.kancoll.org/khq/1940/40_2_caldwell.htm; Elliott West, *The Contested Plains: Indians, Goldseekers, & the Rush to Colorado* (Lawrence: University Press of Kansas, 1998), 180; thanks also to Arielle Gorin for sharing these insights from her unpublished research, "Greeley at Gregory Diggings: The *New York Tribune,* Colorado, and Continental Reconstruction." On Gilpin, see J. Christopher Schnell and Katherine B. Clinton, "The New West: Themes in Nineteenth Century Urban Promotion, 1815–1880," *Missouri Historical Society Bulletin* 30, no. 2 (January 1974): 75–88; Hine and Faragher, *American West,* 401; West, *Contested Plains,* 237–38.

17. Fifer, *American Progress,* on origins, 23, 24, 36; on publishing, 64, 66, 90; on Saint Louis, 71. See also Susan Schulten, "The Civil War and the Origins of the Colorado Territory," *Western Historical Quarterly* 44, no. 1 (Spring 2013): 37, 39–40, 44.

18. Schulten, "Civil War," 42–43; West, *Contested Plains,* 238–39. Gilpin had been living in Independence, Missouri. James Whiteside, "William Gilpin," in *Dictionary of Missouri Biography,* ed. Lawrence O. Christensen (Columbia: University of Missouri Press, 1999), 339–40.

19. A. A. Humphreys, *The Virginia Campaign of '64 and '65,* vol. 12 of *Campaigns of the Civil War* (New York: Charles Scribner's Sons, 1883), 387; Stephen Z. Starr, *The Union Cavalry in the Civil War: The War in the East, from Gettysburg to Appomattox, 1863–1865* (Baton Rouge: Louisiana State University Press, 1981), 379; Arenson, *Great Heart of the Republic,* 118. On the telegraph, see Elliott West, *The Last Indian War: The Nez Perce Story* (New York: Oxford University Press, 2009), 95–96, 180–81; on congressional action, see Schulten, "Civil War," 43–44.

20. Fifer, *American Progress,* 119, 127, 129.

21. White, *Railroaded,* 18, 19–20, 30–31.

22. On balancing the truth and myth of Dodge's role, see Wallace D. Farnham, "Grenville Dodge and the Union Pacific: A Study of Historical Legends," *Journal of American History* 51, no. 4 (March 1965): esp. pp. 640–41.

23. White, *Railroaded,* 227–28; Bowman, "Driving the Last Spike: At Promontory, 1869 (Concluded)," 263.

24. Fifer, *American Progress,* chap. 5, esp. pp. 140–41, 148, 168.

25. "Senator Schurz on Suffrage," *Saint Louis Westliche Post* (June 18, 1869), as translated in the *Saint Louis Daily Missouri Democrat,* June 19, 1869, emphasis in original. Found in the James S. Thomas Scrapbooks, in "1869 Scrapbook," Saint Louis Mercantile Library. See also discussion in Arenson, *Great Heart of the Republic,* 187.

26. "West and South—the St. Louis Republican Supporting the Carl Schurz Republicans," *Boston Daily Advertiser,* September 30, 1870, no. 78, col. F, via Gale Digital Collections. See also discussion in Arenson, *Great Heart of the Republic,* 187.

27. L. U. Reavis, *A Pamphlet for the People: Containing Facts and Arguments in Favor of the Removal of the National Capital, to the Mississippi Valley* (Saint Louis: E. P. Gray, 1869), 6–7;

Reavis, *The New Republic; or, the Transition Complete, with an Approaching Change of National Empire, Based upon the Commercial and Industrial Expansion of the Great West Together with Hints at National Safety & Social Progress* (Saint Louis: J. F. Torrey, 1867); Reavis, *A Change of National Empire; or, Arguments in Favor of the Removal of the National Capital from Washington City to the Mississippi Valley* (Saint Louis: J. F. Torrey, 1869); Reavis, *Saint Louis: The Future Great City of the World* (Saint Louis: By the order of the Saint Louis County Court, 1870); Reavis, *The National Capital Is Movable; or, Facts and Arguments in Favor of the Removal of the National Capital to the Mississippi Valley* (Saint Louis: Missouri Democrat Book and Job Printing House, 1871). See also Arenson, *Great Heart of the Republic,* chap. 9.

28. Arenson, *Great Heart of the Republic,* 184.

29. Ibid., 185–86, 189–90.

30. Horace Greeley to Logan Reavis, February 4, 1870, as reprinted in Reavis, *Saint Louis: The Future Great City of the World,* 6, 7; Gorin, "Greeley at Gregory Diggings."

31. "Reavis Nominates Greeley for President," *Milwaukee Sentinel,* April 13, 1871, no. 86, col. B, via Gale Digital Collections. See also Arenson, *Great Heart of the Republic,* 195–96.

32. Arenson, *Great Heart of the Republic,* 195–97; Matthew T. Downey, "Horace Greeley and the Politicians: The Liberal Republican Convention in 1872," *Journal of American History* 53, no. 4 (March 1967): 727–50. Thanks to Stephanie Narrow, author of "The Grip-Sack Guide to George Crofutt," a paper written for History 191D with Stephen Aron, December 6, 2010, for her reminder of the connections between Schurz's time at the Department of the Interior and the allotment process. Gast moved after 1870; see Leopold Gast and family, 1870 U.S. Census, Saint Louis, Missouri, p. 96, lines 35–39, via Ancestry.com.

33. George A. Crofutt, *Crofutt's Trans-Continental Tourist: Containing a Full and Authentic Description of Over Five Hundred Cities, Towns, Villages, Stations, Government Forts and Camps, Mountains, Lakes, Rivers, Sulphur, Soda, and Hot Springs, Scenery, Watering Places, Summer Resorts . . . : Over the Union Pacific Railroad, Central Pacific Railroad of California, Their Branches and Connections by Stage and Water, from the Atlantic to the Pacific Ocean,* 6th ed. (New York: G. A. Crofutt, 1874), 157, emphasis in the original. Crofutt continually revised this guide; this edition was the sixth major revision and the fifth round of minor changes within that edition.

34. Ibid., 157.

35. Ibid.

36. J. Valerie Fifer's authoritative biography *American Progress* claims to draw from all the (seemingly scant) extant collections of Crofutt's words and opinions, but, in more than four hundred pages, Fifer has nothing to say about Crofutt's politics, his engagement with the slavery question, the Civil War, Reconstruction, or the resurgence of American territorial expansion in 1898. On the seemingly hermetic seal between histories of the West and the Civil War, see Arenson, introduction to *Unifying America: Western Perspectives on the Civil War,* ed. Adam Arenson and Andrew Graybill (Berkeley: University of California Press, forthcoming); Arenson, "More Than Just a Prize: The Civil War and the American West," *Western History Association Newsletter* (Fall 2011): 5–7; Schulten, "Civil War," 22.

37. Richardson, *West from Appomattox,* chap. 4; William Gillette, *Retreat from Reconstruction, 1869–1879* (Baton Rouge: Louisiana State University Press, 1979).

38. The rights and reproductions office of the Autry National Center provided data for requests for use of the image for the period of 2006 to February 2013. In that time, the image

had been licensed forty-nine times, including for ten textbooks, eight museum exhibits, and three teacher-preparation websites. Given that the black-and-white engravings of the image are out of copyright, and that dozens of copies of the color image populate the Internet, these forty-nine licensed uses certainly constitute only a small fraction of the uses. Thanks to Marilyn Van Winkle-Kim and Marva Felchlin for their assistance in providing this information in February 2013. Erik Greenberg and Autry National Center, *Manifest Destiny,* app for iPad, released December 7, 2011, iTunes, https://itunes.apple.com/hk/app/manifest-destiny /id485413652?mt=8.

39. White, *Railroaded,* 203–4; Alan Trachtenberg, *Brooklyn Bridge: Fact and Symbol* (New York: Oxford University Press, 1965), 8–9.

40. Sandweiss, "John Gast, American Progress, 1872."

41. Frederick Jackson Turner, "The Significance of the Frontier in American History" (paper presented to the American Historical Association, Chicago, July 12, 1893), as printed in *Annual Report of the American Historical Association for the Year 1893* (Washington, DC: Government Printing Office, 1894), 208. For the connection, see Sandweiss, "John Gast, American Progress, 1872."

42. For an overview of ghosts in the Turner essay, see Patricia Nelson Limerick, "Turnerians All: The Dream of a Helpful History in an Intelligible World," *American Historical Review* 100, no. 3 (June 1995): 697–716: Kerwin Lee Klein, "Reclaiming the 'F' Word, or Being and Becoming Postwestern," *Pacific Historical Review* 65, no. 2 (May 1996): esp. pp. 181–83.

8

EMPIRE AND LIBERTY IN
THE MIDDLE OF NOWHERE

Virginia Scharff

Generally speaking women do not prepare themselves to wear two wedding dresses in a lifetime. But the vagaries of fortune in nineteenth-century America led many American women to marry more than once. "'Til death do us part" signified a partnership contingent on the twists and turns of a highly unpredictable path and could mean a shorter commitment than anyone would foresee.

One such woman was Janet McOmie Sherlock Smith of South Pass City, Wyoming. Chances are, you've never been to South Pass City, Wyoming. There's no particular reason why you should have. It's not on the way from anywhere, to anywhere else. It's beautiful up there, on the edge of the Continental Divide, but not much more scenic than most places in the middle of the high country of the American West, far from towns and cities. If you happen up there to camp, you'll encounter winds so fierce they'll blow your tent clear off its pegs and your steak right off your plate.

Even at their founding peak in the late 1860s, when the construction of the first transcontinental railroad and a gold-mining boom brought fortune hunters to this remote spot on the globe, the three mining camps on the Sweetwater River—South Pass City, Atlantic City, and Miner's Delight, Wyoming Territory—never mustered much more than three thousand souls at the height of the summer mining season. Far fewer people than that lived there in the wintertime, which then, and in most years since, constituted all the usual months as well as most of those we are accustomed to associating with spring and fall. Snow fell early and late, frequently and deep, and when the snow melted, mud season began. Mostly, it was as hard to get out as in. Not many people chose to stay.

FIGURE 8.1

William Henry Jackson, *South Pass, Fremont County, Wyoming,* 1870. Department of the Interior, General Land Office, U.S. Geological and Geographic Survey of the Territories.

Among those who ever ventured there, hoping to make a bundle or at least a stake, the vast majority were transient men of the type associated with battles and barrooms and brawling, men who worked at brutal and generally unrewarding tasks, breaking and hauling rock, drinking up what money they made, and moving along down the road. Long after they were gone, the wind blew through the cracks of the makeshift shacks and disappointed dwellings that sheltered them for so brief a time.[1]

But even in such tough places, some stubborn people take their stand. They do the small things that make big things possible. In the process, they may witness and make history that has surprising, even vast consequences. In the American West, the presence of such determined settlers anchored the claims of a distant government to places sometimes strenuously contested—by indigenous inhabitants, and by various groups of emigrants jostling for power and place. Empires, even or perhaps especially "empires for liberty," in Thomas Jefferson's famous phrase, are built not only with massive weaponry—guns, germs, and steel—but also with the mundane comforts of new homes in hard places, with kettles and blankets, counterpanes and petticoats. Without those tools of domestication, settlement simply doesn't stick.

One of those "stickers," as Wallace Stegner called such persons, was Janet McOmie Sherlock Smith. Janet covered a lot of ground before she even got to South Pass City. She'd been born in Scotland in 1844 to a Mormon convert family, had emigrated to the United States in 1861, and had walked across half a continent to Utah. In 1862 in Salt Lake City, at the age of eighteen and already a skilled seamstress, Janet sewed herself a wedding dress, in the height of fashion, lushly patterned with purple paisley figures.

The dress was made of cotton, the most cosmopolitan and morally tainted textile in American history. On plantations in Mississippi and Alabama, Georgia and Louisiana, and westward into Texas, enslaved people had, for decades, labored their lives away in hot sun and pouring rain, planting and cultivating and harvesting acre after acre of sticky, fluffy bolls. Perpetually under the watchful eye and ready lash of overseers, they dug and hoed, bent and stooped, and dragged heavy sacks of the stuff to be weighed. The cotton gin, the machine that separated fiber from seed, was one of nineteenth-century America's most important inventions, a designed dreamed up by the Connecticut Yankee inventor Eli Whitney and his hostess, plantation mistress Eliza Lucas Pinckney, on a trip he made to the South. The cleaned fiber would be sent north to be spun into thread and woven into cloth in factories like the famous one at Lowell, Massachusetts, where farm girls became factory girls. Bolts of cloth then made their way, by river, rail, and trail, into the hands of traveling peddlers and general storekeepers and Indian traders in far-flung places, including the unknown spot where Janet McOmie selected that gay paisley for her wedding dress. Janet's fabric of choice represented connections among places that were, by 1862, not just far apart but torn asunder by war.

Still, the tender ties of marriage, and the iron links in chains of money, made it possible for Janet to buy a length of cotton fabric to make that treasured dress. She married a fellow immigrant, Briton, and Mormon, Richard Sherlock. For a teenage bride who had already seen plenty of toil and expected more, a delicate white wedding dress symbolized the freshness and frailty of hope while facing the likelihood of hardship.[2]

In the spring of 1868, the Sherlock family, by then including Janet, husband Richard, and three children under the age of four—Margaret (known as Maggie), Peter, and baby Janet (known as Jenny)—took an optimistic gamble. They made the hard trek up the Oregon Trail to the Sweetwater goldfields, in what was still called Dakota Territory. At the point where the Trail met the Sweetwater River, some enterprising soul had set up a ferry, and Richard Sherlock paid seven hundred dollars, a sizeable sum, to buy the ferry and move into a nearby cabin. Now all that remained was to cash in on the flood of fortune hunters due to arrive with the coming of warmer weather.

According to Janet's grandson, James Sherlock, Richard had made the kind of rookie mistake we might read about in Mark Twain's *Roughing It.* The Sweetwater was like most of the shallow, seasonal rivers of the West, not like the deep waterways of Sherlock's native England. Once the mountain snows melted and the spring runoff ended, travelers had no trouble wading across. Financially and emotionally embarrassed, the Sherlocks packed up their gear and headed for the bustling little boomtown of South Pass City.[3]

Aside from abandoning the site of their adventure in poor judgment, the Sherlocks may have had other reasons to move to town. What some people called Dakota Territory, or the Sweetwater goldfields, others, including Shoshone, Crow, Arapaho, Cheyenne, Lakota, and Bannock peoples, claimed as home. As part of the nation's effort to consolidate control of western lands, the United States government was carrying out its program of relocating and concentrating indigenous people, a program that some preferred to prosecute as a campaign of extermination. At the same time, east of the Mississippi, the country was, in succession, straining to the breaking point over the issue of slavery, torn to pieces for four years of war, and painfully struggling to figure out how to reunify what had fallen apart. All kinds of people were in motion, boundaries were fluid, and earnest little families out on their own were vulnerable to the intentions of strangers on the move, nonnative and indigenous alike.

With so many people on the move, claims in flux, and tempers frayed, conflicts were inevitable. It didn't take much more than rumor to ignite terror and the potential for violent confrontation. Even when nothing happened, fear could launch people in any direction.[4] Small wonder that one of Janet's granddaughters, perhaps glad enough to gloss over her grandfather's early miscalculation, remembered the move to town differently from James Sherlock. She recalled an "Indian scare" as the reason for the family's move to South Pass City.[5]

You can't begin to understand what that community was like, without recalling that the Sherlocks had trodden their path to Utah Territory as the American nation was embarking on its great Civil War. The family journeyed to the crest of the Continental Divide even as hundreds of humans uprooted by the war worked their various ways forward on the uncertain footing of national fragmentation and unification. The place the Sherlocks hoped to call home had, at one time or another, been claimed by the governments of Spain, France, Mexico, the Republic of Texas, and a bewildering array of shifting United States jurisdictions, including the territories of Louisiana, Oregon, Utah, Nebraska, and most recently, Dakota. At the time the Sherlocks made their trek, the country they traveled through was still claimed—by occupation, treaty rights, and violence—by half a dozen indigenous groups, most especially the Shoshones, who were negotiating a treaty for a large reservation overlapping the mining district. In July of 1868, the Territory of Wyoming was overlaid onto country the Shoshones claimed, the Mormons coveted, and the Bannocks, Arapahos, Lakota, and Cheyenne contested. The new federal entity was to be governed under the awkward combination of appointed and elected officials, militarization and mobilization, resistance and resignation, that would have been familiar to Southerners undergoing federal Reconstruction.

The Sweetwater settlements would not have existed at all had there been no military presence in the area. The opening of the Oregon Trail and the emigrations of the 1840s went hand in hand with the presence of the United States military, beginning with the explorations of John C. Frémont in 1842 and continuing with the arrival, in 1845, of Stephen Watts Kearny's First Dragoons. Conflict between the Mormons in Utah and the federal government led to the garrisoning of Fort Bridger on the Green River in 1858.[6]

With the outbreak of the Civil War, federal troops were temporarily withdrawn from Utah. But by 1862, Colonel Patrick E. Connor, in command of a column of California militia in Utah, sent two companies of Nevada volunteers to Fort Bridger. As in so many other places, American soldiers also acted as part-time prospectors. There had been rumors of gold in the streams along the Divide since the time of the fur trade. Some of Connor's Nevada men had mining experience from the Comstock boom of 1859, and Connor encouraged his men to prospect for gold. He not only hoped that mines would attract settlers, who would supplant the Indians, but also thought gentile emigrants might help the United States contain Mormon expansion in the region. The soldier-prospectors began to find promising placers along Willow Creek, near what would become South Pass City. When the soldiers came with their picks and their pans, Indian resistance drove them off.[7]

The war in, and for, the West, like the war in the South, was waged not only with troops but also with technology and traffic.[8] Ben Holliday's Overland Daily Stage, from Atchison, Kansas, to San Francisco, began to run in 1861, the same year that the transcontinental telegraph line was completed. The following year, indigenous attacks on the coaches and riders forced Holliday to move his route south, while the governor of Utah

Territory hastened to organize a regiment of mounted rangers and President Lincoln authorized a company of one hundred Ninety-Day Wonders (soldiers who enlisted for three months) to patrol the area west of Independence Rock.[9]

Traffic into the area was picking up as the Union Pacific Railroad inched its way across the continent, headed for a meeting with its Pacific partner and rival, the Central Pacific Railroad. As Wyoming's first territorial governor, John A. Campbell, pointed out in his inaugural message: "For the first time in the history of our country, the organization of a territorial government was rendered necessary by the building of a railroad. Heretofore the railroad had been the follower instead of the pioneer of civilization."[10]

What Campbell meant by *civilization* was open to debate. Along with the railroad came a heterogeneous population of workers and opportunists, of Union and Confederate veterans and deserters, European immigrants, African Americans, Mexican Americans, and Chinese immigrants. Some of the self-appointed apostles of civilization were, to put it bluntly, vicious racists who believed that white supremacy justified any kind of violence. The Indians were justifiably skeptical of the intentions and actions of the invaders. Some native groups staked their claims by raiding, others by asserting their treaty rights and by asking for government protection from their indigenous enemies.

The Shoshones, including the band headed by Chief Washakie, had been devastated by Connor's Bear River campaign of 1863, including the infamous Bear River Massacre, when Connor attacked Shoshone lodges on a snowy January morning, killing nearly 300 men and leaving 160 women and children destitute and frozen in their wrecked village, amid the bodies of their dead.[11] That year, in the Fort Bridger Treaty, Washakie's Shoshones agreed to give the government the right to establish roads, posts, farms, and most important, telegraph and rail lines in Shoshone territory, in return for the promise of a reservation in the Wind River country, the right to hunt off-reservation, and twenty thousand dollars in annuities for twenty years (unilaterally reduced by Congress to ten thousand dollars). By 1865 they were caught between Cheyenne, Arapaho, and Lakota bands trying to prevent them from occupying reservation lands; the emigrant fortune-seekers of the Sweetwater mining region, who coveted the Shoshones' claims to fertile farmlands and potential mines; and the agents of the government, who alternately violated and enforced the Indians' rights. General Connor, for example, had hired soldiers to stake claims on his own behalf in 1864, though Indian raiders once again sent the prospectors fleeing and destroyed the tools they left behind.[12]

By 1865, a somewhat astounding, and confounding, array of people jostled against one another in the middle of nowhere. Washakie had allied himself with the U.S. government and received a silver medal engraved with the likeness of President Andrew Johnson. The Lakota, Cheyenne, and Arapahos despised the Shoshones as wards of the government, and held that Washakie's people should no longer be allowed to hunt on the plains. Hunger and harassment by troops and settlers had forced all these peoples, along with the Bannocks, into what would become Wyoming Territory. That same year, a soldier in the First Battalion Nevada Volunteer Cavalry discovered the Carissa Lode, the richest deposit of gold-bearing quartz that the Sweetwater region would ever see, and reported his findings back to Connor in Salt Lake City. By 1867, the rush was on. The Miner's Delight Lode was located in September, and by October the town site of South Pass City had been laid out. The first buildings were erected, and some miners hauled wood, shot and salted down game, hauled in supplies, and prepared to spend the long winter there in order to be first on the ground in the spring.[13]

That summer, the towns of South Pass City, Atlantic City, and Miner's Delight attracted more and more fortune hunters, along with a newspaper (the *Sweetwater Mines*), a weekly mail delivery, a power-driven arrastre to pulverize quartz, and a six-stamp mill to process ore. Prospective farmers and ranchers were moving into the area, and emigrants flocked in to find work cutting timber and hauling freight. Just as Congress was establishing a Peace Commission to negotiate with the Indians, 150 Lakota warriors assaulted miners working the Carissa and the placers along Willow Creek, and Lakota and Arapaho parties attacked farmers and prospectors in the Wind River valley. The Lakota leader Red Cloud and his allies assailed emigrant parties, mail carriers, and soldiers, burned telegraph poles and stampeded cattle, and laid siege to the hated forts along the Bozeman Road in the Powder River country. The *Sweetwater Mines* and the even more virulently racist *Frontier Index*, the Union Pacific's "press on wheels," railed against "the peace commissioners' pets" and unleashed a torrent of invective against the natives (and, for that matter, against African Americans, Chinese immigrants, and Mexican Americans), while government agents worked to get Indians to cede land. In short, at the moment that the Sherlock family decided to stake its future on South Pass City, it was far from clear which of the many rival claimants to the place would ultimately have the upper hand.[14]

Eighteen sixty-eight was a big year for treaty making, including the famous Fort Laramie Treaty, which allocated reservations north of the Platte River for the Lakota and Northern Cheyenne, closed the despised forts along the Bozeman Trail, and accorded the Indians hunting rights in the Big Horn–Powder River area in return for a railroad right of way through tribal land. The Shoshones and Bannocks, negotiating at Fort Bridger, also signed a treaty ceding a railroad right of way in return for their own reservation in the Wind River country. Washakie, who had claimed all the territory from Salt Lake to Independence Rock, settled for a reservation of nearly three million acres in the Wind River and Popo Agie Valleys. Much of the Sweetwater mining region lay within the borders of the newly established reservation, now the recognized home to Shoshones who had long inhabited the area, Bannocks who had come to the region, and, by the summer of 1869, to Arapahos the government was at pains to accommodate, well, somewhere.[15]

Thus the Wind River Reservation and the Sweetwater settlements were born together, uneasy neighbors with overlapping, not to say conflicting, claims, barely tethered to a distant federal government. In the summer of 1869, the chief agent of that authority was

FIGURE 8.3

Janet Sherlock Smith owned this pair of beaded gauntlets made at the Wind River Reservation, most likely by a Shoshone or Arapaho woman, circa 1880–1910. Donated in memory of Janet S. Payne, Autry National Center, 98.122.1.

the newly appointed governor and superintendent of Indian affairs of Wyoming Territory, one John A. Campbell, a native of Ohio, Union Army veteran, and stalwart Republican. In an era of American politics notorious for corruption and venality, Campbell was that rarest creature, an honest and fair-minded man.

Faced with the incursions of white squatters into Indian land, government failure to erect agency buildings and send annuities, and Washakie's refusal to go to the reservation until the United States kept its promises, Campbell noted that the Indians were destitute and rightfully suspicious that the government had no intention of honoring its treaty obligations to protect their lands and furnish provisions. "The fact that nothing has been done towards carrying out the treaty has led to the impression that the government does not intend to strictly observe it, and that settlers would be permitted to occupy the land," Campbell wrote to Commissioner of Indian Affairs Ely S. Parker. "I believe it to be unwise and wrong to insist on a faithful obeisance of the Treaty stipulations on the part of the Indians without a corresponding faithfulness on our part."[16]

Campbell and other agents of the federal government had their hands full in the vast and volatile reaches of Wyoming Territory, where rumors could start panic, and violence could flow from rumor. Civil War enmities continued to simmer as veterans from North and South moved West. Fortune hunters wanted the government to send more troops to protect them but not restrain them from doing as they wished. Most of the emigrants were white men who hoped to make a bundle, or at least a stake, and to move on. The men of the military and mining and railroad frontiers were agents of American conquest but pretty unreliable as stable occupants. It remained for the minority of "family men" and their wives and children to do the attenuated and tedious job of claiming a permanent home where the buffalo roamed.

White women in particular were expected to "tame" the Wild West, were considered ideal agents of civilization. Victorian Americans believed that "true women" (by which they meant white, middle-class women) possessed an inborn nobility of character. Such women were morally superior to men, willing to sacrifice themselves in the name of social harmony and community improvement, and equipped with a genius for creating comfortable homes in inhospitable places. Out on the Continental Divide, they would be charged with the duty to teach and nurse, cook and clean, and demand from potentially unruly men the kind of "sivilized" behavior that made the likes of Huck Finn want to light out for territories such as Wyoming, precisely to escape the confines of their domesticity.[17]

Men like Governor John Campbell hoped that such women could be recruited to Wyoming as family members who would settle, "uplift" society, and stay. And in the case of South Pass City, a few dogged families, foremost among them Janet and Richard Sherlock and their children, did indeed mean to put down roots. According to her granddaughter, Janet Smith had brought with her some of the things she needed in order to act as a civilizing presence: books by Shakespeare and Robert Burns and Sir Walter Scott, as well as cloth, including that well-traveled, troubling cotton, to make garments for her family. Looking to find a way to make a living, and knowing what a dirty job mining was, the Sherlocks built a bathhouse, a small two-story structure. There were two tubs, one wooden and one metal, and they pumped and heated spring water, charging fifty cents a bath. The bathhouse brought in a fair amount, but not enough to support a growing family, as Janet bore two more children, John (born in 1869) and William (born in 1871). Richard, meanwhile, looked for work to supplement what they made from the bathhouse.

Try to imagine Janet Sherlock dealing with five children and running that bathhouse while Richard was otherwise occupied and out of touch, as he so often was, laboring heavily for wages. Picture Janet handing off cotton towels and hard soap to mining men, who were always filthy, nearly always disappointed in their quest for riches, and often enough springing for a bath because they were on their way to spend some of their hard-earned money drinking in the saloons and carousing with loose women. Whatever else she may have been, she wasn't delicate, and she did not have the luxury of withdrawing from the rough-and-tumble world of men. As she well knew, plenty of those men, and not a few of the women, were up to no good.

South Pass City's wives and mothers had heard sermons and read novels, advice books, and magazines urging them to live up to the ideal of true womanhood, to gently

FIGURE 8.4
Janet Sherlock Smith and H.G.
Nickerson at South Pass City.
Photograph by Grace Raymond
Hebard, 1915. Wyoming State
Archives.

persuade their husbands and sons to eschew the allures of drinking and gambling, of cheating and fighting. Those who made the effort had a tough job. According to the 1870 federal census, South Pass City's population of 460 souls was four-fifths male; and in that settlement alone, there were seven retail liquor dealers, three breweries, and one liquor wholesaler. Newspaper editors throughout the territory liked to recommend their favorite bars in their editorial columns—and no wonder, when the saloons were their biggest advertisers, one ad memorably touting the benefits of their cocktails "taken before breakfast in the morning."[18]

This is not to say that saloons were good for one thing only. Janet would later tell historian Grace Raymond Hebard that she thought South Pass City, even in its wild and wooly heyday, had been a fairly law-abiding town, noting that Methodist-Episcopal services had been held there. She neglected to mention that those services had been held at the Magnolia Saloon, evidently a multipurpose gathering place. But she also noted there had never been a lynching in the town; and according to her descendants, Janet was the hero who had made that claim plausible. When her own brother, George McOmie, was shot and killed by a man named Al Tompkins, a mob gathered in the town's main street to hang the murderer without benefit of trial. As Janet's grandson, James Sherlock, reported, "Grandmother in her devout Christian and characteristically kind and sensible manner, interceded. She said that her loss was already great enough without having this man's blood on her hands."[19]

Elections stirred the pot in places like South Pass City, where keeping order was never easy. In volatile Wyoming, the election season of 1868 saw the most extreme politics of Reconstruction on rabid display. The *Frontier Index* predicted race war if the Republican candidate, former Union general Ulysses S. Grant, won the presidency, exclaiming that "Grant's platform will Africanise and Indianise our whole mongrel region. . . . Four hundred millions of Chinamen . . . [will be] 'knocking at our national door.' . . . Our white laborers and their wives and children will suffer for bread."[20]

As the first candidates ran for the Wyoming territorial legislature in September of 1869, the *Frontier Index* insisted, "A modest woman must often neither see nor hear." But in a tiny town like South Pass City, Janet Sherlock could not help but witness the mob of angry white men who tried to prevent newly enfranchised African American voters from exercising their right to vote. President Grant had filled territorial offices, from the governorship to the judiciary and the office of U.S. marshal, with Republicans like John Campbell. Those federal appointees were determined to enforce black men's rights as citizens, despite the fact that most eligible voters in the territory were Democrats, many of them Southerners, who equated the situation of the South with that of the West. As election day approached, seventeen men in South Pass City signed a circular announcing a mass meeting to "repudiate the Reconstruction policy of Congress, negro suffrage, and the principles espoused by the Radical Republican Party, and who are in favor of equal and exact justice to all sections of the union." When South Pass City voters went to the polls on September 2, fifteen or twenty black men were among them. A territorial justice, John Kingman, a New Hampshire Republican, described the scene:

> Some drunken fellows with large knives and loaded revolvers swaggered around the polls, and swore that no Negro should vote. . . . When one man remarked quietly that he thought the Negroes had as good a right to vote as any of them had, he was immediately knocked down, jumped on, kicked, and pounded without mercy and would have been killed had not his friends rushed into the brutal crowd and dragged him out, bloody and insensible. There were quite a number of colored men who wanted to vote, but did not dare approach the polls until the United States Marshal, himself at their head and with a revolver in hand, escorted them through the crowd, saying he would shoot the first man that interfered with them. There was much quarreling and tumult, but the Negroes voted.[21]

While those voters presumably cast their ballots for Republicans, they were in the minority. The Democratic Party, proclaiming itself the champion of white supremacy and the enemy of black, Indian, Mexican, and Chinese rights, swept the Wyoming territorial elections that year. For its part, South Pass City elected to the territorial council William H. Bright, a Virginian and Union Army veteran who had signed the call for the mass meeting.[22]

The Democrats who traveled to Cheyenne for the inaugural session of the territorial legislature in 1869 disagreed with the Republican governor and federally appointed officials on most things. But all those white men, and for that matter, the black voters who had cast their ballots in Wyoming, found one source of common ground: they all believed that Wyoming belonged to the United States, and that all that was right and good decreed that the indigenous inhabitants of the territory should be displaced, defeated, and confined in order to make way for American settlers. They would adopt all kinds of measures in order to further that common goal, and among those was a series of laws designed to attract more women like Janet Sherlock to Wyoming.

That year, woman suffrage activists had taken to the road to campaign for voting rights across the country. The nation's most celebrated suffragists, including Elizabeth Cady Stanton and Susan B. Anthony, boarded stagecoaches and train cars, climbed into wagons, and carried the crusade into far-flung places from coast to coast. Newspapers covered their speeches in a spirit akin to what Dr. Johnson had said one would experience at the sight of a woman preaching. He had likened it to seeing a dog walk on its hind legs: it was not done well, he said, but one was surprised that it was done at all. Wyoming newspapers were full of stories of their exploits, and two suffrage speakers, Missourian Redelia Bates and the celebrated Pennsylvania Quaker orator Anna Dickinson, even found their way to Cheyenne.[23]

On November 12, 1869, South Pass City's William Bright announced that he intended to introduce a bill for woman suffrage to the territorial council. Some thought his wife, Julia, had put him up to it. Others thought he was joking. Justice John Kingman, a supporter of the measure, recalled that Bright's "character was not above reproach, but he had an excellent, well-informed wife and he was a kind, indulgent husband. In fact, he venerated his wife and submitted to her judgment and influence more willingly than one could have supposed, and she was in favor of woman suffrage."[24]

That year, white supremacy often kept close company with women's rights. William Bright believed that women like his wife were at least as qualified as freedmen to exercise the franchise, and he was not alone. Stanton and Anthony, alienated from the men they had worked with as abolitionists, who were now Republicans counseling that it was not the time for woman suffrage, had forged an alliance of convenience with the racist millionaire George Francis Train, who bankrolled their suffrage newspaper, *The Revolution*.[25]

Even opponents of woman suffrage, like South Pass City legislator Ben Sheeks, believed Julia Bright had put her husband up to introducing the bill. We do know that at least one other woman in South Pass City was openly in favor of the measure, six-foot-tall Esther Hobart Morris, a subscriber to Anthony and Stanton's *Revolution*, soon to gain fame as the nation's first woman justice of the peace.[26]

Captain H. G. Nickerson, the Republican who had lost the election to Bright, told historian Grace Raymond Hebard a story about the origin of the suffrage bill that would attain the status of legend in many places, including Janet Sherlock's memory. Nickerson claimed that before the election, Esther Morris had invited both candidates to a tea party at her house, and there, in front of the town's leading womenfolk, had made both men promise to promote a suffrage bill if they were elected. We may assume that Nickerson told the story in order to claim part of the credit for the measure; there does not seem to be much historical evidence supporting the tale. Janet Sherlock, however, recalled being invited and having to decline because she had to stay at home with a sick child.[27]

In 1869, Wyoming Territory would become the first government in American history to enfranchise women. But the legislature did not stop at giving women the vote. That year, Wyoming lawmakers passed a host of measures they hoped would draw strong-minded, ambitious women to the territory, including a law giving married women control over their property and earnings, and a law mandating that women teachers receive the same pay as their male counterparts. Thus the territorial government promised more liberty, and more power, to women like Janet Sherlock in return for their part in expanding the American empire.[28]

In the end, ailing children and the challenges of daily life mattered more in Janet's life than politics and legal rights. Consider the fact that Janet was pregnant at least seven times between 1864 and 1880, and that she lived through epidemics of both smallpox and diphtheria, taking it upon herself in 1882 to ask her eldest son to send "four points of [smallpox] Virus" from Omaha so that she could vaccinate the other children. Then she and her older daughters had to nurse the younger ones through the scary, painful, and potentially deadly vaccination reaction.[29]

But we are getting ahead of our story. When the Sweetwater boom busted early in the 1870s, most people moved along. The Sherlocks determined to remain. Before long, tragedy struck. In 1873, Richard Sherlock was working at a sawmill on Willow Creek when he caught a cold that turned into fatal pneumonia. Now Janet was a widow with five children to support in a luckless, hard-panned shell of a village. She got herself appointed postmistress of South Pass City, a position she held on to until 1908, and she took over the South Pass Hotel, where the stagecoach stopped. She moved her family into the hotel and ran the post office and a small dry goods store (with all that had changed, cotton thread and cloth remained) out of the hotel office. The year she was widowed, she also took on the position of election clerk in the South Pass Precinct.[30]

Two years later, at the age of thirty-one, Janet sewed herself another wedding dress, a bit behind the latest fashion but more luxurious and more somber than the first, made of silk. That fabric might have been made in China or England, or perhaps in Paterson, New Jersey, the teeming mill town known for its silk manufacture. This second matrimonial garment brought new trade relations and migration patterns, rising cities, and global relations into the middle of nowhere. The dress was heavy and warm and dark,

FIGURE 8.5
Hand-stitched wedding dress
made by Janet Sherlock for her
wedding to James Smith, 1875.
Donated in memory of Janet S.
Payne. Autry National Center,
98.142.4. For a color version of
this image, see plate 12.

appropriate to the life of a respected matron navigating the streets of a muddy little town.
The blue-and-gray-striped silk skirt and bodice were trimmed with brown silk and velvet,
and she wore the garment for her 1875 wedding to James Smith, the man who would be
the father of Janet's two youngest children, Anna, born in 1876, and James Earnest, born
in 1880. Smith was a hard, hardworking, unlettered man who may not have known how
to read or write. Still, together he and Janet and the Sherlock and Smith children ran the
hotel and the mercantile across the street, and they picked up jobs hauling and freight-
ing, cutting wood and mining, when the mines were operating, as the latter did intermittently into the twentieth century. Janet needed a partner, and for twenty years of marriage
the Smiths endured and even prospered, at least as long as the stagecoach from Green
River to Lander, Fort Washakie, and Red Lodge, Montana, stopped in South Pass City

along the way. Jim was inclined to drink and was so tough on Janet's sons from her first marriage that the boys struck out on their own the moment they could, still in their teens. But he was also a responsible and concerned father and provider, and Janet wrote in 1882 that she thanked the Lord that "Jim is still abstaining from Liquor. It makes such a difference on him."[31]

Smith was a Catholic, so Janet converted, but it seems she saw religion less as a question of revelation or doctrine, and more as a matter of right behavior. When her son Peter turned fifteen, he was sent to boarding school at Creighton in Omaha, Nebraska. He had written to the family, announcing a plan to get baptized, and his mother responded, "With regard to you getting Baptized I have not anything to say. I have always made it my study to leave your mind unbiased by my creed." But then she went on at length to explain her own ethical and pragmatic view of religion:

> I have tried to empress it upon your mind that in order to be happy here and here after you must endeavor to do what is right to your fellow man. "To do as you would that others should do unto you." To fear God and try to live by the law that is laid down by Jesus Christ in the New Testament. I never believed in making long prayers. I have made it the rule of my life to only ask God to give me that which I stood in need of, that which he knew would be for my benefit and above all have I asked for Wisdom to lead and Guide me in all my undertakings. To give me strength to overcome temptations and avoid sin. Peter it is not a profession of Religion that will do any one any good. You must be good from principle, from a love of doing good and hateing evil. . . . I do not want you to give up too much of you[r] time to the Study of religion. I want you to go ahead and get an education that will fit you for a useful place in the world.[32]

Janet Sherlock Smith was the sturdiest pillar of her community and the heart of her family. She was the kind of woman who could face down a lynch mob, and who could cut her children's arms and smear in viral matter she hoped would keep them from getting smallpox, even as she knew the vaccine would make them sick. She relied, in turn, on her husband and children, who worked as hard as she did. Her daughters Maggie and Jennie worked endless hours alongside her at the hotel, cleaning and preparing rooms, doing laundry, hauling water and wood, cooking and serving and cleaning up yet again. At the age of thirteen, her son John was raising cattle and hiring out to drive livestock, and on one occasion in 1882 he returned from the Wind River valley two weeks late, prompting his sister Maggie to report, "We were awful uneasy about him on account of the Indians being so bad." By that time, the town was down to four families, though the stagecoach and other traffic made it possible for the Sherlock-Smith clan to hang on by dint of sheer willpower and hard work.[33]

That resolve would be tested again and again by almost unfathomable tragedy. In 1883, cheerful, generous-spirited, and indomitable Maggie Sherlock was, at the age of eighteen, finally supposed to get the education she could not secure in South Pass City.

Her parents were sending her to attend a Catholic girls' academy in Salt Lake. Her mother worried that she would not be able to manage without Maggie, but Jim Smith wanted to see his stepdaughter get her chance.

There had already been a series of storms that winter, and on days when the stagecoach could not make the run, the drivers made use of a team and sleigh. On a fateful day in February, Maggie set out with a young and inexperienced driver named George Ryder. A horrible blizzard blew up. By the time they were found, they had spent nine days out, Ryder was dead, and Maggie Sherlock was "very nearly gone." The people who found her "had to cut her clothing to get her out of the sleigh," and her hands and feet were frozen beyond saving. Her stepfather had spent six days out in the storm looking for her and managed to get her back to South Pass City. But Maggie died on February 21, 1883. Her mother would never be the same. "I tell you Peter, she was brave," Janet wrote to her son in Omaha. "About the last words she said to me was mama I am not afraid. Oh Peter, why she should have died such a death is a Mystery. She was such a good Girl. God knows best what is good for us. If I could only be reconciled to his will but it seems so hard. She was so much comfort to me. More like a companion than a child."[34]

Maggie's death broke something in the Sherlock-Smith family, though they leaned on one another even more than before. Younger sister Jennie took Maggie's place as her mother's strong right arm, and the other children grew up to assert themselves as stalwarts of the ever-dwindling town of South Pass City. The stagecoach stopped running altogether after that horrible winter.

Peter Sherlock, who had hoped to be a lawyer, came home from Nebraska the summer after his sister's death and did not return to school. Instead, he worked at various laboring jobs, often in partnership with his brothers John and Will. In 1887, at the age of twenty-one, he was blinded in a mining accident. After that time, he worked with his brothers, cutting and hauling wood and helping them when they started ranching south of town.

Jim Smith died in 1895, leaving Janet again a widow. Janet's friends and family urged her to take the younger children and go back to Salt Lake, but she refused. John and Peter came back to town to help her run the store. Over the rest of her life, she did consent to spending more time in climes more hospitable than the windswept and snowbound place where she had borne and raised and lost her children. When she died in 1923, she left behind an estate valued at over forty thousand dollars.

Peter Sherlock lived on until 1947, a fixture of the town, keeping the store alive and joining his siblings in holding on to mining interests. The Sherlock-Smith name continued on in the area, but Peter's death marked, for all purposes, the end of the town as a settlement. The family had, however, held on long enough that the landscape they left, a ghost town swaying in the gale, would see new life as a site ripe for historic preservation. The Shoshone and Arapaho people are, of course, still around, living on the Wind River Reservation, coping with the pressures of modern life. And the area is home to a new mining boom that has raised alarms about the practice of fracking and environmental damage in tiny towns like Pavillion, Wyoming. And so it seems that where nineteenth-century Americans saw a war between racially distinct people for control of far-flung places, we now see the heirs of all those peoples living side by side, often uneasily, facing a common uncertain future.[35] Janet McOmie Sherlock Smith's two wedding dresses, like the battered plank buildings of South Pass City, the town she built and kept, have somehow endured to be repaired, refurbished, and preserved. The gowns and the town are markers of memory, symbols of hard-earned empire and unexpected liberty, of love and work and violence and struggle and pride and loss, in the middle of nowhere.

NOTES

1. The best sources on the history of South Pass City and the Sweetwater mining settlements include Lola M. Homsher, *South Pass, 1868* (Lincoln: University of Nebraska Press, 1960); T. A. Larson, *History of Wyoming* (Lincoln: University of Nebraska Press, 1965); James L. Sherlock, *South Pass and Its Tales* (New York: Vantage, 1978); and *Wind River Mountaineer* 7, no. 2 (April–June 1991).

2. Object record 98.142.2, Janet Sherlock Smith wedding dress, Autry National Center of the American West.

3. Sherlock, *South Pass and Its Tales*, iv, 42.

4. Virginia J. Scharff, "South Pass since 1812: Woman Suffrage and the Expansion of the Western Adventure" (master's thesis, Department of History, University of Wyoming, 1981).

5. *Wind River Mountaineer*, 2.

6. "Wyoming Legends: Fort Bridger Historic Site," Legends of America, http://www.legendsofamerica.com/wy-fortbridger.html, accessed June 27, 2014.

7. Robert A. Murray, "Miner's Delight, Investor's Despair: The Ups and Downs of a Sub-marginal Mining Camp in Wyoming," *Annals of Wyoming* 44 (1972): 29–31.

8. For a brilliant study of the Civil War as mobilization, see Yael Sternhell, *Routes of War: The World of Movement in the Confederate South* (Cambridge, MA: Harvard University Press, 2012).

9. Grace Raymond Hebard, *Washakie* (Cleveland: Arthur C. Clark, 1930), 104–6.

10. Larson, *History of Wyoming*, 36.

11. See Ned Blackhawk, *Violence over the Land: Indians and Empires in the Early American West* (Cambridge, MA: Harvard, 2006), 263–66.

12. Hebard, *Washakie*, 109; Marjorie C. Trevor, "History of Carter-Sweetwater County, Wyoming to 1875" (master's thesis, Department of History, University of Wyoming, 1954), 27.

13. Murray, "Miner's Delight," 33; Trevor, "History of Carter-Sweetwater County," 28, 34; Fred D. Stratton, *Early History of South Pass City, Wyoming, and How Women First Received the Right to Vote and Hold Office* (n.p., 1950), 3.

14. Stratton, "Early History," 1; Riley Snow, "Removal of Indians from Wyoming" (master's thesis, Colorado State College of Education, 1936), 2, 9, 84; *Sweetwater Mines,* March 25, 1868, March 28, 1868, April 8, 1868.

15. Arrell Morgan Gibson, *The American Indian* (Norman: University of Oklahoma Press, 1980), 414–15; *Treaty of July 3, 1868, between the Shoshone and Bannock Indians and the United States Government,* ratified February 26, 1869, Wyoming State Archives, Cheyenne, Wyoming; Governor John A. Campbell to Commissioner Ely S. Parker, November 20, 1869, Records of the Office of Indian Affairs, Correspondence of the Office of Indian Affairs, Letters Received, Wyoming Superintendency, 1869–90, microfilm, 1959, National Archives, Washington, DC.

16. Governor John A. Campbell to Commissioner Ely S. Parker, June 10, 1869, Records of the Office of Indian Affairs, Correspondence of the Office of Indian Affairs, Letters Received, Wyoming Superintendency, 1869–90, microfilm, 1959, National Archives, Washington, DC.

17. The classic essay on the Victorian cult of domesticity is Barbara Welter, "The Cult of True Womanhood, 1820–1860," *American Quarterly* 18 (Summer 1966). Linda Kerber, in "Separate Spheres, Female Worlds, Woman's Place: The Rhetoric of Women's History" (*Journal of American History* 75 [June 1988]: 9–39), points out the problems with assuming that Victorians were able or willing to always practice what they preached.

18. *Sweetwater Mines,* June 3, 1868.

19. *South Pass News,* August 1, 1870; Trevor, "History of Carter-Sweetwater County," 93; Sherlock, *South Pass and Its Tales,* 68–69.

20. *Frontier Index,* August 18, 1868.

21. Quoted in Carrie Chapman Catt and Nettie Rogers Shuler, *Woman Suffrage in Wyoming* (New York: Charles Scribner, 1923), 76.

22. Larson, *History of Wyoming,* 70–74.

23. *Frontier Index,* March 6, 24, June 5, November 13, 1868; *Cheyenne Argus,* November 12, 1869; *Sweetwater Mines,* December 5, 23, 1869; *Cheyenne Leader,* November 22, 24, December 2, 10, 1869; *Wyoming Tribune* (Cheyenne), December 4, 1869. See also Larson, *History of Wyoming,* 78–83.

24. Elizabeth Cady Stanton, Susan B. Anthony, Matilda Joslyn Gage, *History of Woman Suffrage* (Rochester, NY: Charles Mann, 1887), 3:730.

25. Ellen Carol Dubois, *Feminism and Suffrage: The Emergence of an Independent Woman's Movement in America, 1848–1869* (Ithaca, NY: Cornell University Press, 1978); Virginia Scharff, "The Case for Domestic Feminism: Woman Suffrage in Wyoming," *Annals of Wyoming* 56, no. 2 (Fall 1984): 29–37.

26. See Virginia Scharff, *Twenty Thousand Roads: Women, Movement, and the West* (Berkeley: University of California Press, 2003), 85–89.

27. Sherlock, *South Pass and Its Tales,* 81.

28. Larson, *History of Wyoming;* Scharff, "Case for Domestic Feminism"; Michael A. Massie, "Reform Is Where You Find It: The Roots of Woman Suffrage in Wyoming," *Annals of Wyoming* 62, no. 1 (Spring 1990): 2–21.

29. *Wind River Mountaineer,* 11–13.

30. Ibid., 28.

31. Ibid., 2–19.

32. Ibid., 18.

33. Ibid., 16, 19.

34. Ibid., 23.

35. Dustin Bleizeffer, "WyoFile Energy Report: EPA Again Delays Pavillion Groundwater Investigation Related to Fracking," WyoFile, last updated January 11, 2013, http://wyofile .com/2013/01/epa-again-delays-pavillion-groundwater-investigation-related-to-fracking/.

9

THE NOT-SO-FREE LABOR IN THE AMERICAN SOUTHWEST

Maria E. Montoya

In a photo from the 1930s (figure 9.1), Deluvina Maxwell sits with the children for whom she cares. One of the little ones is Ida Harris Custer, a distant relation of General George Armstrong Custer, the leader of the Seventh Cavalry. Custer, the larger-than-life Indian killer, met his demise at the Battle of Little Big Horn in 1876 and infamously came to represent U.S. brutality and dominance over Native peoples. How did Deluvina come to be in charge of the care of a Custer descendant? The answer to this question takes us into a tangled web of violence, captivity, slavery, and forced labor that had its origins in the eighteenth century. Yet even as late as the Great Depression, that bundle of rights and limitations had not yet been unraveled into a world of free labor. So, how is it that, more than seventy years after the end of slavery, the descendant of one of the most legendary Indian killers came to be sitting in the lap of a Native American woman who herself had been held in captivity for most of her life?

One of the few issues supposedly settled at the end of the Civil War was the place of free labor in the American political, cultural, and economic system. As Eric Foner tells us, "Sanctified by the North's triumph, the free labor ideology would emerge from the war further strengthened as a definition of the good society, an underpinning of Republican Party policy, and a starting point for discussions of the postwar South."[1] While the ability to contract for one's own labor became law (if not practice) for African Americans across the South, for Indians, Mexicans, and Chinese throughout the American West the meaning of the Thirteenth Amendment was not so clear.[2]

FIGURE 9.1
Deluvina Maxwell with
children in her care, circa
1930s, photographer
unknown. Palace of the
Governors Photo Archives.

Even before the Civil War, many Americans assumed that slavery was unlikely to spread into the American West. In 1857, the Oregon booster George H. Williams wrote, "Isolated as Oregon is by thousands of miles from other slave states, and from all the supports of slavery, an effort to maintain the Institution here would be almost as impotent as the command of the vain Canute to the waves of the ocean."[3] Antislavery advocates pointed out that the landscape and climate precluded the easy spread of plantation slavery into the arid regions of the country. Also, the West had long been associated with the Jeffersonian agrarian ideal of small farmers creating a virtuous republic, or an "empire for liberty" as Jefferson named it, based on family farms and entrepreneurship. Most agreed by the middle of the nineteenth century that both geography and ideology made the spread of African chattel slavery a practical impossibility.

The idea of free labor in the West was also tied to the myth of free land, which had justified the practice of Indian removal and had continually prodded Americans into the western lands. Frederick Jackson Turner expressed in his famous 1892 essay "The

Significance of the Frontier in American History" the idea that the presence of "free" land had created space for the nation to expand. The freedom to labor, without slavery, was the hallmark of the West; the West was also a safety valve for the nation's ballooning population. Turner, like most Americans, was convinced that slavery had been eradicated and had no place in the emerging modern American West. In reality however, the West was home to a complex set of labor relations that often bore a strange and disturbing resemblance to the slavery of the antebellum South.[4]

In the nineteenth-century American West, an intricate weave of peoples lived on and shaped the landscape long before U.S. legal systems showed up to define their work and its value. Native Americans were first interrupted and exploited by Spanish immigrants, who saw Indian labor as one of the few tangible assets on the barren land. The Spanish Crown, and later the Mexican government, defined how and when labor could be exacted from Native communities for the benefit of Spanish, and later Mexican, expansion. By 1824, when Mexico came to control what would eventually become the American Southwest, a complex set of laws and practices ruled how households used Native slave laborers and Mexican *peones,* who worked as unfree men and women, who held no property, and who were bound to the large estates for their livelihood.

Given this mid-nineteenth-century patchwork of legal systems and labor practices, an influx of Asian peoples, mostly Chinese, further complicated the racial, economic, and social worlds of the American Southwest. Unlike the American South and East, where for the most part the racial world could be divided between black and white, the Southwest had a legacy of four ethnic groups (Indian, Mexican, Chinese, and white). To further muddle the matter, while the South embraced a clear definition of how to organize labor—free and slave—the Southwest was characterized by varying degrees of labor autonomy, which ranged from free, to indentured, to enslaved. It was a messy business all along that spectrum.[5] So, while the Thirteenth Amendment outlawed slavery, it was not so clear how best to deal with the bonded labor extracted, in varying degrees, from the Native American, Mexican, and Chinese populations of the region. By looking at six items in the Autry collection, we can explore the complexities of Indian slavery, Mexicano debt peonage, and Chinese "coolie" labor.

Figure 9.2 shows the 1868 facsimile made to announce the passing of the Thirteenth Amendment. Copies such as this would have been publicly displayed across the United States, including California. This very public and ostentatious document proclaimed in boldface that "neither slavery not involuntary servitude shall exist within the United States." The image in the middle of the document was a classic rendering of bringing African Americans, and possibly Native and mixed-race, peoples into the democratic and republican world of the postwar United States. Shackles are replaced by white doves as this group partakes of civilization in the form of reading and family formation. Surely clothing and shoes cannot be far off in their future? This document portrays the ideal behind the passage of the Thirteenth Amendment, but how legible this proclamation and iconography would have been to residents of the American West is not so clear.

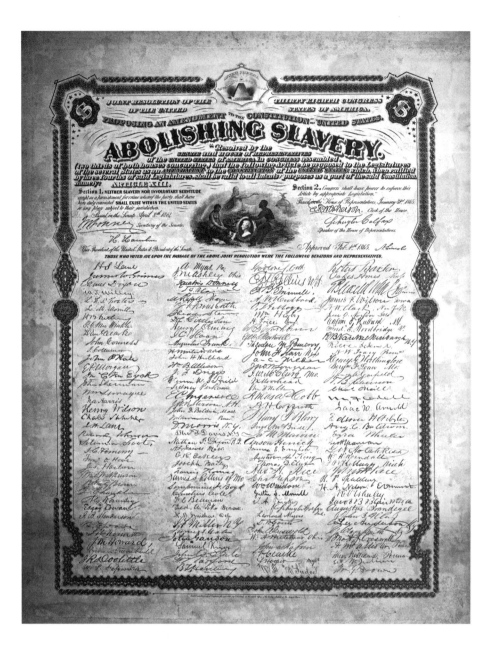

FIGURE 9.2

*Joint Resolution of the 38th Congress of the United States of America, proposing an amendment to the
Constitution of the United States abolishing slavery*, 1868, lithograph. Gift of Mrs. H. Gearing. Southwest
Museum of the American Indian Collection, Autry National Center, 198.G.1.

In the West, the Thirteenth Amendment seemed to create little clarity. The issue of whether slavery was an accepted legal labor system out in the territories was so murky that President Andrew Johnson issued an executive order in 1865. Johnson was responding directly to repeated reports of Indians raiding one another, as well as reports of whites and Hispanos raiding Indian populations or purchasing slaves from these raids. Johnson acknowledged that Native peoples were "reduced to slavery," which violated New Mexico's Organic Act, the law that provided for New Mexico's entrance into the United States as a territory. The executive order, however, did not tie the eradication of the practice of Indian slavery to either the Emancipation Proclamation or the Thirteenth Amendment. Johnson only declared that federal and territorial officials must work to "discountenance the practice."[6] Why wouldn't Johnson invoke either of these two laws? We can surmise that the labor system in the American West was somehow categorically different in the minds of the president and Congress. Consequently the practice of Indian raiding and trading continued well into the early twentieth century. Territorial officials constantly claimed that they were helpless to stop the practice, which was so deeply ingrained in the fabric of Euro-American Hispano society and culture. Hubert Howe Bancroft, writing contemporaneously, noted that there were few military or civil officials who did not own captive slaves, and that slaves were found even in the service of the Indian agents. Laura Gomez notes that Lafayette Head, a former territorial legislator as well as Indian agent, held multiple slaves and justified holding them by saying they could leave at any time they chose.[7]

Perhaps responding to the weakness of President Johnson's executive order, Congress passed a statute in 1867 outlawing debt-peonage labor in the territories. The law also stated that the U.S. military would not be responsible for returning escaped *peones* or slaves to their "owners," because the practice had been outlawed. Antislavery politicians entered into the *Congressional Record* ample evidence of the abuse of labor in New Mexico, and Congress felt the need to deal with the particular case of Indian slavery in the territories.[8] The proclamation affected about 10 percent of New Mexico households, which held slaves or *peones* at the time.[9]

Ideological and cultural tensions came into play in the choice of venue for prosecuting abuse-of-labor cases. Progressive reformers in New Mexico, most of them Anglo, brought these suits before the territorial courts, where federally appointed judges heard the cases and tended to make rulings based on constitutional arguments under the Thirteenth and Fourteenth Amendments. Hispano owners who held detribalized native *genizaros* (slaves), however, preferred local courts, where the issues would be adjudicated as disagreements about property and contract law.[10] In fact, Indian agents complained bitterly about Anglo and Hispano elites, "to the manner born," who consistently flouted the law prohibiting peonage and slavery. In New Mexico there was never a definitive legal and practical precedent that ended the practice of debt peonage. The detention of *genizaros* in intimate settings with Hispanos continued well into the twentieth century.

How Deluvina Maxwell came to still be living with the Maxwell family in the 1930s is a case in point. Deluvina had been one of fifteen household servants, seven of whom were Native Americans, living on the Lucien Maxwell estate in northeastern New Mexico at the end of the nineteenth century; she eventually worked for the Maxwells' granddaughter, who had moved to Albuquerque. Deluvina served in the Maxwells' households from about 1875 until her death in the 1930s. Lucien Maxwell had brought Deluvina to his household as a small girl, after he had purchased her from a group of Utes who had captured her during one of their raids on the Navajos, killing her entire family.

Maxwell gave little Deluvina to his wife, Luz Beaubien Maxwell, as a present. Deluvina was to help Luz and her children, serving the large household. Deluvina grew up with the Maxwell children and became exceedingly close to the girls in the family. She had a brush with Western legend when local officials accused her of aiding the Maxwell children in harboring and protecting Billy the Kid as he hid from Pat Garrett, just before his capture on the Maxwell estate in 1881.[11] It is worth noting that Deluvina's initial captivity and forced labor came a decade *after* the end of the Civil War and the emancipation of slaves in the South. Yet few thought it odd that she remained a servant (paid or unpaid) in the Maxwell family until her death.[12]

Indian slavery and debt peonage was, however, really much uglier and harsher for most who were enslaved. Only some were, like Deluvina, incorporated into the family. Hispano families holding *genizaros* felt a certain moral and religious obligation to intimately connect them to their Christian households. But for most captives, particularly those held under debt peonage, day-to-day life could be horrific. For example, the Territorial Supreme Court had taken up the issue of peonage in *Mariana Jaramillo v. Jose de la Cruz Romero* in an effort to clarify the relationship. Mariana, a thirteen-year-old girl, had run away from her patron, Romero, without repaying the remaining $51.75 left on her debt. In court, she claimed she had been abused at the hands of both Romero and his wife, who kept her as a household servant without pay and adequate shelter and food. Sexual abuse also seemed likely. After hearing her case, the court ruled that Romero could not force her to repay the debt through labor, because she was a minor and thus incapable of making contracts. The court also suspected that the debt belonged to her father, and not her, and she had been sold to Romero to repay the father's debt. Note that the court made its decision based on a contractual argument and not on the issue of constitutionality. As horrific as her story is, Jaramillo was one of the lucky ones who made it into the legal system and was freed by it. Few slaves or *peones* had the ability to take their cases to the territorial courts; most remained stuck in their situations out on the far frontiers of the U.S. legal system.

Most stories of captivity, slavery, and peonage in late-nineteenth-century New Mexico are neither so colorful nor nearly so benign as Deluvina's story, and more closely resemble the experience of Mariana Jaramillo. Throughout the 1850s and 1860s, New Mexico's justices of the peace and territorial courts had struggled to make sense of the peon/

patron relationship, which was a legacy of the Spanish and Mexican legal system inherited by the United States in 1848. Labor relations on the New Mexico frontier were complicated and messy. While peonage certainly was not the same as slavery, neither was it free contract labor. Many observers saw a slavelike relationship, particular as it pertained to women inside Hispano households, though others argued that these were simply contract labor situations with a set beginning and end and an exchange of money for services.[13] Most court cases involved young girls living in difficult circumstances, in families with predatory older men. Others dealt with male field laborers who were not being paid wages for their work, and who found themselves crushed under the multiple burdens of debt peonage, sharecropping, or *partido*. The latter was a practice peculiar to New Mexico, in which families would take on consignment a certain number of lambs. They promised the owner that they would return the lambs as adult sheep, plus a specified increase in the number of animals, in a certain amount of time. Whatever extra yield the family attained through good care and management of the animals was their profit. It was not always a successful venture for a family, and many ended up in debt to the owners when they could not return the right number of animals. What all these cases had in common was that at no time did the courts invoke the Emancipation Proclamation or the Thirteenth Amendment as a reason to end unfree labor practices. Peonage and forced labor, some of it closely akin to slavery, persisted well into the twentieth century in the West.[14]

Labor questions were often bound up with ideas about religion and the conquest of land and peoples. When the Spanish came to the New World, they arduously pursued religious conversion of Native peoples who were, by the way, pretty happy with their own set of religious practices. These converts were known as *genizaros*, Native Americans who had been captured and enslaved but also incorporated into Hispano households as Christianized servants. The intertwining of Catholic conversion with labor systems wove a web of power, salvation, and paternalism between *genizaros* and their masters and mistresses. This relationship between religion and labor was not limited to those held in captivity. The intimate connection between land, religion, and labor wed agriculturally based communities to a tight web of shared relationships.

We can view this connection between religion, land, and labor in the folk artworks known as santos, which were found in almost every New Mexican household. Because priests and churches were relatively scarce in the isolated communities, Hispano households used santos as a way of recognizing religion within their homes. San Ysidro, or San Isidro as he is known in Europe, was the patron saint of farmers, *peones*, and day laborers, and a particular favorite of New Mexican agricultural families. Isidro, born in 1070 to a poor family in Madrid, worked for a large hacienda owner as a farmer and day laborer. He married Maria Torribia and they had one son. Isidro was known for his devotion to God and to his work, but his coworkers often complained that he came late for work everyday because he stopped every morning for Mass. When the don found Isidro at morning mass instead of working the fields, he returned home determined to fire Isidro

FIGURE 9.3
José Aragon, *St. Isidore (San
Ysidro)*, 1820–35. Richard and
Dorothea Casady Collection,
Southwest Museum of the
American Indian Collection,
Autry National Center,
4094.G.7.

when he came in late. But when the don returned to his estate, he found an angel plowing Isidro's fields for him. Indeed, although Isidro seemed to work much less than his coworkers, his output was always three times the work they completed. His angels sent by God eased his burden.

Isidro's miraculous life has been associated not only with labor but also with water. Two miracles revealed his powers and connections with God. When Isidro and Maria's only son fell into a well, facing certain death by drowning, a miracle occurred. In response to the parents' fervent prayers, waters in the well burbled up and brought their son safely to the surface. In gratitude, Maria and Isidro pledged to live a pious life of continence and celibacy. One day, as Isidro worked the field during a drought, he tapped the earth with his plow while in prayer and drew up a fresh spring of abundant water. The place became a holy site marked later by Queen Isabella after her husband, King Ferdinand, recovered from an illness after drinking the spring water. Throughout their lives, God blessed both Isidro and Maria with more miracles and physical signs of God's pleasure in them. The Catholic Church eventually elevated both to sainthood after their deaths.

Ysidro, as he was commonly known in New Mexico, became the favorite patron saint of small rural communities, farm laborers, and workers from New Mexico's Spanish *entrada* to the present day.[15] Every spring on his Saint Day, May 15, communities bring their San Ysidro santos, *bultos,* and *retablos* out of their homes and churches and walk them through the fields so that the saint might bless the fields and bring bounty in the coming season. In the recent days of severe drought, the parading of San Ysidro through the fields has a particularly intense feel in these communities.

San Ysidro is beloved by farmers and workers because he represents hard work and the contingencies of making a living off the land. Ysidro is never carved to look opulent and, in New Mexico, is always portrayed as a *pobladore* or peon. San Ysidro represents not only the honor in working hard but also the honor in working hard for a master or patron. He was the perfect icon for a region that relied on peon labor and enshrined the mutual obligations between farm owner and farmworker.

These cultural practices, as well as the folk art that has been embedded in New Mexico rural life, evoke a romanticism that has lasted well into the twenty-first century. Even after the practices of debt peonage and keeping *genizaros* ended in New Mexico, this labor system came to be romanticized as part of New Mexico's own Spanish fantasy heritage. The relationship between patron and peon was often viewed as one of mutual understanding and need, with little consideration for the power dynamics at work.[16]

Ernest Blumenschein's painting *New Mexico Peon* reflects this romanticism. Like San Ysidro, Blumenschein's *Peon* represents the nobility of hard work on the land. The artist, however, also invokes melancholy, portraying the workingman as tired; he is slouching a little and is somewhat disheveled, amid what appears to be a bountiful field and home. It is this man's hard work, probably ill compensated, that allows for the relative success of his employer. The lighting and feeling of the image does portray a romanticized notion of the relationship between farmworker, landowner, and the products of that relationship. Blumenschein's *Peon* has little to do with New Mexico of the 1930s and early 1940s, the period in which the artist painted it. At that time, the state would have been feeling the impact of modernization and industrialization on its rural communities, but the painting looks backward to an era when individual peons worked within the context of paternalist households.

Blumenschein, a native of Pittsburgh, had grown up in Ohio and studied in Paris and New York before coming to Taos, in 1898, on a sketching trip from Denver to Mexico. He had been trained in the most modern of schools and places, and he brought with him a particular kind of cosmopolitanism that New Mexicans had not yet been exposed to in their art. Like other early-twentieth-century artists and cultural critics who came to New Mexico, such as Bert Phillips, Georgia O'Keeffe, and Mary Austin, Blumenschein rejected modernist tropes and instead latched on to the ideal of the primitive that he imagined to be embodied in the people and landscape of New Mexico. In 1915, Blumenschein, Phillips, and others created the Taos Society of Artists. It eventually included twenty-one members, and it lasted until 1927. The purpose of the Society was to promote the artists' work, as well as to say something profound about the place of New Mexico, and Taos in particular, within the array of American modern art.

When Blumenschein first visited Taos, he wrote, "The month was September, and the fertile valley a beautiful sight, an inspiration for those who ply the brush for happiness. The primitive people of this out-of-the-way region were harvesting their crops by sunlight and by moonlight. Brown people they were, both Mexicans and Indians, happy people with happy children, in a garden spot protected by mountains."[17] Blumenschein, like his fellow Society members, believed that he needed to uplift the view of both Hispano *peones* and Native Americans among mainstream Americans. As Blumenschein commented,

FIGURE 9.4

Ernest Blumenschein, *New Mexico Peon*, 1930–42. James R. Parks Collection. Autry National Center, LT2011–43–1. For a color version of this image, see plate 13.

"We had to write this little about the Pueblo inhabitants, if only to counteract the impression so common in our country that our Indians are not quite respectable."[18] This romantic vision of peonage obscured the day-to-day experience of those working on the farms of Hispano landowners.

In New Mexico, ideas about free labor were tangled in a web of relationships connecting religion, power, paternalism, and family. Outside of New Mexico, both the federal government and reformers assumed that something qualitatively separated the practice of Indian slavery and debt peonage from the practice of antebellum Southern slavery. In reality, the daily experience of forced and uncompensated labor that Indian, *genizaro,* and Hispano men and women endured had much in common with the predicament of the enslaved. Free labor, like free land, was a western myth perpetuated by those who wanted to put the stain of slavery behind them at the end of the nineteenth century.

As the discovery of gold and the expansion of railroads brought thousands of immigrants into the West, and into California in particular, the array of labor relationships became even more complicated. Chinese immigrants willingly did the backbreaking and dangerous work of mining and building the railroads for the expanding U.S. economy. Chinese labor, which was often erroneously equated to "coolie" labor (labor that was forced, unfree, akin to slavery), had long been seen as an alternative to African slavery in the Caribbean sugar plantations. From the very beginning of Chinese immigration to the United States, American law and daily practices treated the Chinese differently. American companies viewed the Chinese as mobile and pliable laborers who would not make permanent homes in the United States but would instead work for a few years, send home money, and eventually return to their home provinces. American workers, however, viewed them as a threat because they were tainted with the label of unfree, or coolie, labor, which threatened the free white laborers of the American West. White workingmen saw in the Chinese what they feared they would become if they did not protect their free-labor status.

Chinese workers arrived via the Pacific Mail Steamship Company, which sold them tickets on credit. Many of them came by way of labor contractors who recruited men to build the transcontinental railroads in the mid-1860s. But many also came as coolies because they had been captured and forced into slavery or because they had been forced into signing unfair labor contracts, making them beholden to the labor contractors and the companies. While some of these contracts were made freely, labor contractors captured, bound into service, and shanghaied Chinese men, shipping them off to Cuban sugar plantations, Mexican mines, and the shores of California. Some historians have compared these immigrants' "Pacific Passage" to the "Middle Passage," which took black slaves from Africa to the Americas, and to the horrors of the Middle Passage—the crowded and dirty conditions aboard ship. Once in California, the Chinese laborers were bound to contractors and then isolated in Chinatowns, where they had little recourse if they were not paid, or if they suffered harsh conditions or were injured.[19]

Chinese immigrants, unlike European immigrants and Mexicans who had been incorporated into the citizenry by the Treaty of Guadalupe Hidalgo, were not eligible for citizenship, and U.S. and California officials tightly regulated their immigration. In 1862, at the height of the Civil War, Congress passed an "anticoolie" labor law, which prohibited the importation and immigration of most Chinese laborers, whom they considered to be uniformly unfree. As Moon-Ho Jung argues, however, this antislavery law was also the first in a series of anti-immigration laws aimed at the Chinese.[20] Moreover, American law discouraged the Chinese from creating stable families and home lives in the American West, as the immigration of Chinese women was all but prohibited by the Page Act of 1875. The act barred anyone from bringing laborers "without their free and voluntary consent, for the purpose of holding them to a term of service," a measure directed particularly at women, whom the government treated as intrinsically immoral, potential prostitutes. The Page Act, although marred by racist undertones, served as an early anti-trafficking law to keep out vice and protect immigrant women. But anti-immigration laws were meant to ensure that Chinese workers gained no toehold in the United States. In 1855, just about 2 percent of the Chinese population was female, and by 1890 that number had risen to only 4 percent.[21]

So within this context of tight immigration controls and deep prejudice, Chinese men had few options but to work long, hard hours in hope of sending enough money home and returning one day to their families in China. The work was arduous and extremely dangerous. Mian Situ's painting *The Powder Monkeys* captures the intensity and extremity of the work Chinese laborers endured while building the railroad bed across the Sierra Nevada. Paid little more than a dollar a day, these workers cut through the most difficult canyons to create a rail bed wide enough for the train to pass along safely. As you can see in the background of the painting, men were lowered in baskets to drill holes into the rock wall, in which they placed dynamite sticks. Workers would then light the dynamite and be pulled up as quickly as possible by fellow workers, missing the blast if all went well. The death rate on these work crews was extremely high. Working conditions were torrid in summer and freezing in the winter, when the men worked through snowdrifts to complete their portions of the railroad as quickly as possible.[22]

Even as California businesses depended on the labor of the Chinese, white workers felt threatened by a labor force that often worked for below-market wages. Under pressure from the Democratic Party and workingmen's advocates, the California State Legislature passed its own Anti-Coolie Act in 1862, which levied a license fee of $2.50 on all "Asiatics" who wanted to work in the coalfields or for the railroad or to "conduct business." Most Chinese earned only $4 to 5 a month, but they had no choice but to pay the tax. Chinese workers continued to be persecuted and had little ability to engage in free labor or demand fair contracts. Then, in 1879, the State of California added this provision to its constitution: "The presence of foreigners ineligible to become citizens of the United States is declared to be dangerous to the well-being of the State, and the Legislature shall discourage their immigration by all the means within its power. Asiatic

FIGURE 9.5

Mian Situ, *The Powder Monkeys, Transcontinental Railroad, Cape Horn, 1865*, 2001–2, oil on canvas. Autry National Center, 2002.3.1. For a color version of this image, see plate 14.

coolieism is a form of human slavery, and is forever prohibited in this State, and all contracts for coolie labour *[sic]* shall be void. All companies or corporations, whether formed in this country or any foreign country, for the importation of such labour *[sic]*, shall be subject to such penalties as the Legislature may prescribe."[23] In this instance, California led the nation in anti-Chinese legislation, but in 1882 the U.S. Congress caught up and passed the Chinese Exclusion Act, which denied the Chinese access to U.S. citizenship.

Even as late as the 1890s, local, state, and federal governments severely limited the mobility and power of the Chinese. The Page Act, the Chinese Exclusion Act, and later the Geary Act all constrained Chinese immigrants' ability to choose where, how, and with whom to live and work in the United States. In 1892 the Geary Act required that all Chinese residents carry a resident permit at all times. If authorities caught someone without the permit, they could deport him or subject him to a year of hard labor. Chinese residents could not give testimony in a court of law and could not post bail when brought

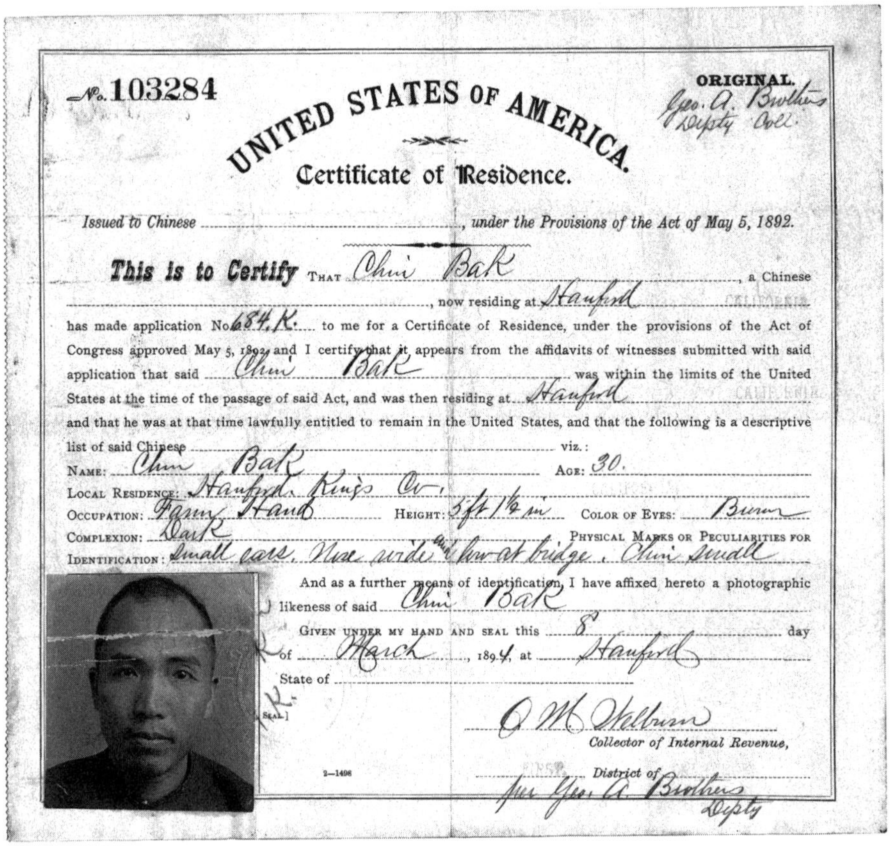

№. 103284

ORIGINAL. Geo. A. Brothers Dep'ty Coll.

UNITED STATES OF AMERICA.

Certificate of Residence.

Issued to Chinese ...., *under the Provisions of the Act of May 5, 1892.*

This is to Certify THAT Chin Bak, a Chinese, now residing at Hanford California has made application No. 684 K. to me for a Certificate of Residence, under the provisions of the Act of Congress approved May 5, 1892, and I certify that it appears from the affidavits of witnesses submitted with said application that said Chin Bak was within the limits of the United States at the time of the passage of said Act, and was then residing at Hanford California and that he was at that time lawfully entitled to remain in the United States, and that the following is a descriptive list of said Chinese viz.:

NAME: Chin Bak AGE: 30.

LOCAL RESIDENCE: Hanford, Kings Co.

OCCUPATION: Farm Hand HEIGHT: 5 ft 1½ in COLOR OF EYES: Brown

COMPLEXION: Dark PHYSICAL MARKS OR PECULIARITIES FOR IDENTIFICATION: Small ears, Nose wide & low at bridge, Chin small

And as a further means of identification, I have affixed hereto a photographic likeness of said Chin Bak

GIVEN UNDER MY HAND AND SEAL this 8 day of March, 1894, at Hanford

State of

[SEAL]

O. M. Welburn
Collector of Internal Revenue,
District of
per Geo. A. Brothers Deputy

2—1498

FIGURE 9.6
Certificate of residence for Chin Bak, Hanford, California, dated March 1894. Autry National Center, 87.59.356.

to jail or court. The Certificate of Residence issued to Chin Bak of Hanford, California, pictured in figure 9.6, was issued in 1894 with his photo attached to the corner. Any government official who wanted to check his status would know that he was who he said he was. Every day, when Chin Bak left his home for work or maybe to simply go down to the store, he would have to carefully fold this document and keep it safe in his pocket. Any authority at any time could stop him and ask to see the paper that stood between this man and deportation.

The situation of the Chinese at the end of the nineteenth century was not unlike what African Americans faced, both ante- and postbellum, in the South. Slave codes, and then later black codes instituted in the post-Reconstruction South, severely limited the mobility of African Americans as they looked for work and tried to create or re-create family life. This series of laws aimed at both curbing Chinese immigration and limiting the power they had over their own working and family lives once they had settled in the

United States. Such laws inflicted an unfair burden on immigrant workers. Not until 1941 did rules governing Chinese immigration ease, making Chinese immigrants eligible for citizenship. Yet for almost a century Chinese families made their way to the United States, contributed to the growth and development of the American West, and did so without the benefits of American citizenship and labor laws that could have protected them from slavery-like conditions in their work settings.

Documents like Chin Bak's residency permit reveal to us the gray areas between citizens and noncitizens, just as the photo of Deluvina shows us the slippery slope between free and forced labor. Often historians have tried to simplify complex sets of relationships into black-and-white dichotomies. You are either a citizen or you are not. You are either a free laborer or you are not. The reality, however, turned out to be much messier and more complicated.

NOTES

1. Eric Foner, *Reconstruction: American's Unfinished Revolution, 1863–1877* (New York: Harper and Row, 1988), 29.

2. A number of scholars have written about this problem of free labor in the American West. Please see Howard R. Lamar, "From Bondage to Contract: Ethnic Labor in the American West," in *The Countryside in the Age of Capitalist Transformation* (Chapel Hill: University of North Carolina Press, 1985); Gunther Peck, *Reinventing Free Labor: Padrones and Immigrant Workers in the North American West, 1885–1930* (Cambridge: Cambridge University Press, 2000). For a more recent discussion, see Stacey L. Smith, *Freedom's Frontier: California and the Struggle over Unfree Labor, Emancipation, and Reconstruction* (Chapel Hill: University of North Carolina Press, 2013).

3. George H. Williams, letter to the editor, *Oregon Statesman* (Salem), July 28, 1857.

4. Frederick Jackson Turner, "The Significance of the Frontier in American History," *Rereading Frederick Jackson Turner* (New Haven, CT: Yale University Press, 1999).

5. See Moon-Ho Jung, *Coolies and Cane: Race, Labor and Sugar in the Age of Emancipation* (Baltimore: Johns Hopkins University Press, 2006). Jung argues that the presence of coolies complicated the black/white and slave/free binaries in the South.

6. See the original text of Johnson's order: Andrew Johnson, "Executive Order," June 9, 1865, available online at Gerhard Peters and John T. Woolley, American Presidency Project, www.presidency.ucsb.edu/ws/index.php?pid=72246.

7. Laura Gomez, *Manifest Destinies: The Making of the Mexican American Race* (New York: New York University Press, 2007), 108–9; James F. Brooks, *Captives and Cousins: Slavery, Kinship, and Community in the Southwest Borderlands* (Chapel Hill: University of North Carolina Press, 2002), 346. See also Pekka Hämäläinen, *The Comanche Empire* (New Haven, CT: Yale University Press, 2008).

8. Cong. Globe, 39th Cong., 2nd sess., 239–40 (January 3, 1867).

9. The Peonage Abolition Act, ch. 187, sec. 1, 14 Stat. 546 (enacted March 2, 1867), codified at 42 U.S.C. §1994. Regarding the debate over the law, see James Gray Pope, "Contract, Race, and Freedom of Labor in the Constitutional Law of 'Involuntary Servitude,'" *Yale Law Journal* 119 (April 25, 2010): 1474, 1485–87; Gomez, *Manifest Destinies*, 108.

10. Gomez, *Manifest Destinies*, 110.

11. There are numerous books on Billy the Kid, but the following specifically mention Deluvina's role after his death: Jon Tuska, *Billy the Kid: His Life and Legend* (Albuquerque: University of New Mexico Press, 1994), 103–4; Robert M. Utley, *Billy the Kid: A Short and Violent Life* (Norman: University of Oklahoma Press, 1989), 160–61, 192, 194. For a fictional account, see Larry McMurtry, *All for Billy* (New York: Simon and Schuster, 1988).

12. See Ned Blackhawk, *Violence over the Land: Indians and Empires in the Early American West* (Cambridge, MA: Harvard University Press, 2006), 1–10. Blackhawk describes the violence used on Native peoples as they were torn from their homes and brought into Anglo and Hispano households.

13. See Brooks, *Captives and Cousins*, in general, but particularly p. 352.

14. See Maria E. Montoya, *Translating Property: The Maxwell Land Grant and the Conflict over Land in the American West, 1840–1900* (Lawrence: University of Kansas Press, 2005), 63–68.

15. For a general discussion about the role of santos in New Mexican culture, see Charles M. Carrillo, *Saints of the Pueblos* (Albuquerque: LPD Press, 2004); Mary Martha Weigle, *Los Hermanos Penitentes: Historical and Ritual Aspects of Folk Religion in Northern New Mexico and Southern Colorado* (Philadelphia: University of Pennsylvania Press, 1973).

16. Regarding the role of paternalism and slavery in general, there is a long literature and complex historiography. For an example, see Eugene Genovese, *Roll Jordan Roll: The World the Slaves Made* (New York: Pantheon, 1974). See also my fuller discussion about paternalism and *peones* in *Translating Property*, 65.

17. Blumenschein quoted in George W. James, *New Mexico: The Land of the Delight Makers: The History of Its Ancient Cliff Dwellings* (New York: Forgotten Books, 2012), 374–75. See also Amy Scott, *Taos Society of Artists: Masters and Masterworks* (New York: Gerald Peters Gallery, 1998).

18. James, *New Mexico*, 376.

19. See Jung, *Coolies and Cane*, 28–33, for one example.

20. Ibid., 37.

21. Ronald Takaki, *Strangers from a Different Shore: A History of Asian Americans* (Berkeley: University of California Press, 1989), xx.

22. The literature on Asian American labor history is immense. For a sampling, see Ronald Takaki, *Pau Hana: Plantation Life and Labor in Hawaii, 1835–1920* (Honolulu: University of Hawai'i Press, 1983); Erika Lee, *At America's Gates: Chinese Immigration during the Exclusion Era, 1882–1943* (Chapel Hill: University of North Carolina Press, 2003); Chris Friday, *Organizing Asian-American Labor: The Pacific Coast Canned-Salmon Industry, 1870–1942* (Philadelphia: Temple University Press, 1995).

23. State of California, Constitution, Article XIX, sec. 4 (1879).

10

AFTER ANTIETAM
Memory and Memorabilia in the Far West

William Deverell

Is there anything that ties together the West and the Civil War so well as the carved halves of a steer's horns?

You cannot make this sort of thing up. Carolyn Brucken, curator at the Autry National Center, wrote me about the wild artifact pictured here. There's more than first meets the eye. This is, Brucken writes, an "electric lamp that seems to decoratively merge the West and the Civil War. It is described as having a cast-iron body with a buffalo at the center and two decorated steer horns affixed to either side of the lightbulb sockets. One steer horn is carved with a scene of an Indian attack on a stagecoach; the other steer horn is

FIGURE 10.1

Electrical lamp with carved steer horns, circa 1891. Acquisition made possible by Mr. James H. Hoiby. Autry National Center, 91.2.1. For a color version of this image, see plate 15.

FIGURE 10.2
Left: Detail of a carving of the battle of Antietam. *Right:* Detail of a carving of an American Indian attack on a stagecoach.

carved with a battle scene of Antietam." Imagine that. Scrimshaw commemoration of the keystone sites of nineteenth-century American warfare: the Civil War and the postwar, final, and far-western chapter of indigenous resistance to brutal conquest born of service to manifest-destiny exhortations and certitudes.

It is entirely worth a closer look. See figure 10.2 for the zoom on the Antietam horn and the Indian attack. The lamp has a patent date from the spring of 1891. But Brucken assumes that someone modified the fixture's original body by adding the carved steer's horns. Outsider folk art meets fin-de-siècle electrification meets frontier violence meets Civil War horror meets . . . meets what? Nostalgia? Celebration? Commemoration? Some amalgam of all? What a thing made of nineteenth-century processes, dreams, and events!

Annie Powers, who has made the closest study of this odd object, writes that the lamp, despite its heft, was meant to be mounted on a wall. A pair of electric lightbulbs would have been inserted into holes drilled into the base of each horn; the lamp's light would have bathed the two battle scenes.[1] I admit to looking to see if the carvings hinted at any figure of George Armstrong Custer, probably the American *most* identified with both Antietam and the West, but he doesn't seem to be represented here.

There is no provenance. Alas. No artist, no owner, no donor. No "I carved this because it depicts my life." No "that's me." No matter. The horn is so evocative, so strange, and so compelling a material thing that it grabs and focuses our attention in this brief essay on facets of the war and the West. The sheer materiality of the horned lamp is exuberant validation of some kind of link between the West and the war, and it prompts us to think about retying threads connecting the far West to the war and its aftermath. Cleaving the West from the war and the postwar, which is the usual scholarly and pedagogical tendency, obscures far more than it illuminates. In the West: gold and overland migrations and narratives. In the East: *Uncle Tom's Cabin* and the coming crisis. In the West,

railroads crest mountains. In the East, soldiers ready for battle. The twain—or at least the lowercase twain—do not meet. East and West remain, in popular reckoning, apart.

In all its tangible weirdness, the lamp gives us an opportunity to contemplate deeper connections existing between West and war. Let us steer our attention back to the halves as a whole, laying eastern and western ends of a cow's horns the full breadth of the nation: a transcontinental horn of memory and memorabilia.

Walk first down one side of our odd lamp, the longhorn of the Civil War at its darkest. The horn takes us to mid-September 1862, to the cornfields of northern Maryland and to famed Burnside's Bridge running across Antietam Creek. Here the armies of North and South fell upon and tore one another to pieces over twelve hours of hellish combat. Nothing like this had ever happened in America. After Antietam ended, Oliver Wendell Holmes received a messenger at his Boston home in the middle of the night. Holmes's namesake son has been wounded at Antietam, shot through the neck, and is lying somewhere in a makeshift hospital, possibly a barn near the crossroads village of Keedysville. Twenty-one-year-old Oliver Wendell Holmes Jr., future justice of the United States Supreme Court, is one of the nearly twenty-five thousand men who fell that day.

The senior Holmes went in search of his son, traveling south as quickly as possible in the company of another anxious father and a surgeon. A famed physician himself, Holmes feared the worst, knowing all too well the dangers of such a wound and the threats, seen and unseen, posed by Civil War medical care and convalescence. The men said little to one another on the train, preferring to ride in the silence of their fears. Stopping in Philadelphia, Holmes rushed to a house belonging to the aristocratic Hallowell family. Norwood Penrose Hallowell, one of the family's three soldiering sons, was a friend and Harvard classmate of the younger Holmes; "Pen" Hallowell would later serve as an officer in the

Fifty-Fourth Massachusetts, the famed African American regiment led by Robert Gould Shaw. Filled as it was with abolitionist sentiments and Republican sympathies, it was to this very mansion that Massachusetts senator Charles Sumner had come to recuperate after being viciously caned by South Carolinian Preston Brooks on the Senate floor in 1856.

The younger Holmes's friend, Pen Hallowell, is already at home, his arm nearly shot off at Antietam. Others rest there, too (the mansion will be a convalescent ward for Union wounded throughout the war). But Holmes Jr. is not with them. The paternal search party must go south, to the battlefield and its field hospitals. Leaving Philadelphia, the train takes on others searching for soldier kin. As the men wait on the platform of the Baltimore train station, a telegraphic messenger hands a message to one of Holmes's companions, notifying him that the son he searches for has died. Holmes feared the sorrow of a similar conclusion to his search. "I knew what he had lost," he wrote.

At Frederick, the travelers transfer to a carriage—the railroad tracks and bridges had been blown up. Holmes is told a rumor that his son is dead. Two men ask if they can ride along toward the battlefield. Having judged "that they were neither Rebels in disguise, nor deserters, nor camp-followers, nor miscreants, but plain, honest men on a proper errand," Holmes invites them along. One is a Moravian, chaplain in a Pennsylvania regiment he is looking to rejoin. The other is a sober "New Englander of respectable appearance, with a grave, hard, honest, hay-bearded face, who had come to serve the sick and wounded on the battle-field." For whatever reason, Holmes never refers to either by name, calling this New Englander "the Philanthropist" and the other "the Chaplain."[2]

The anxious search continued: The driver, Holmes, an officer's wife, the Chaplain, and the Philanthropist. Crossing through farmland, they face a sad and poignant scene: the road is full of straggling and wounded soldiers, the human toll of the terrible battle that forever drove home the grim and obvious fact that the Civil War was not a farce, not a lark, not to be over with quickly. The Civil War was brutality unimaginable. Soldiers of both North and South, the dead and the alive, now took separate journeys radiating out from the bloody contest and its "carnival of death." The suffering so moved Oliver Wendell Holmes—as of course it would, his words a dirge: "The slain of higher condition, 'embalmed' and iron-cased, were sliding off on the railways to their far homes; the dead of the rank and file were being gathered up and committed hastily to the earth; the gravely wounded were cared for hard by the scene of conflict, or pushed a little way along to the neighboring villages; while those who could walk were meeting us. . . . It was a pitiable sight, truly pitiable."[3] The line of wounded had become nothing but a "great caravan of maimed pilgrims." Some in the bloody parade would surely die. Some would live, and the "wounds they bore would be the medals they show their children and grandchildren by and by."[4]

The description is vivid, awful, and sad, and one expects that Holmes never forgot the spectacle of so many shattered young men tramping painfully past him, especially because he tried to scan every face in search of his son.[5] At one point, Holmes stands in the bed of the wagon in which they are traveling, and speaks "of the beauty of the scenery, and of the terrible strife being enacted, and its consequent horrors—using his best

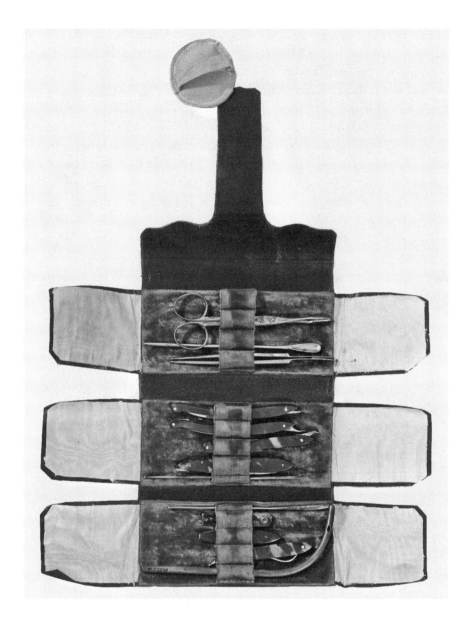

powers of description."[6] The Philanthropist hands peaches over to the soldiers, and he
even offers up some of Holmes's liquor (which Holmes carried "as a medicine in case of
inward grief") to a "poor fellow who looked as if he needed it."

The travelers arrive in Middletown. The officer's wife finds her wounded husband,
now one-armed, the amputation site raw at his maimed shoulder. The Chaplain wanders

off in search of his unit. Holmes and the Philanthropist retire to guest quarters, sharing a bed in which Holmes's companion sleeps peacefully through the night, while Holmes tosses, fretting over the fate of his boy.

This "hay-bearded" man fascinated Oliver Wendell Holmes. He wrote a good deal about his companion's character and benevolence. He was a "really kind, good man, full of zeal, determined to help somebody, and absorbed in his one thought[,] . . . a purely benevolent errand." Quick to assist with the care of the wounded (look again on the prone scrimshaw soldiers crawling across our lamp), the Philanthropist made himself useful in the makeshift hospitals and clinics carved from churches and homes that immediately filled up with ten thousand Union soldiers and, here and there, a Confederate among them.

Having failed to find young Holmes in Middleton, the search party rides out toward Keedysville. Holmes carries with him a letter of introduction to Dr. Jonathan Letterman, the chief surgeon of the Army of the Potomac. Letterman had just intro- duced his new system of care for the wounded, involving battlefield triage decisions and the use of ambulances to fetch the wounded from where they fell. Antietam was unmitigated horror, but without Letterman's innovations, it would have been even worse.[7]

On this leg of the five-hundred-mile journey, Holmes has brought with him a bale of oakum, or tarred hemp, in case he encounters Dr. Letterman (one wonders if he brought it with him all the way from Boston). There had been recent medical literature, which Holmes had certainly seen, suggesting that oakum could be a substitute for more com- monly used lint on festering wounds.[8] At Keedysville, Holmes hears reliably that his son is alive, that he is on his way up toward Philadelphia. Again in the company of the Chap- lain and the Philanthropist, Holmes goes off in search of him, retracing his route after first inexplicably detouring to see the parts of the Antietam battlefield where fighting had been its most fierce. The party picks its way across fields strewn with material and detri- tus from the clash—dead horses, canteens, scraps of paper, belt buckles, hats, many of them blood-stained. Puddles of blood congealed in the hot sun. At one mass grave, a rough board made do as a headstone, an angry epitaph scrawled upon it: "We buried eighty damned rebels in this hole."[9]

Holmes parts company with his two companions. The Chaplain continues the search for his regiment; the Philanthropist goes in search of other wounded to care for. Holmes keeps his itinerant vigil, trying to find his boy here and there—moving in and around Maryland and Pennsylvania in search of him. At last he is discovered, alive and convales- cent. The reunion is met and the journey ended when father and the son rendered prodigal by his war and his wounds return home to Boston. "Fling open the window- blinds of the chamber that looks out on the waters and towards the western sun! . . . So comes down another night over this household, unbroken by any messenger of evil tidings,—a night of peaceful rest and grateful thoughts; for this our son and brother was dead and is alive again, and was lost and is found."[10]

Holmes's companion on the anxious search for his son was a man named Horatio Nelson Rust, whom Holmes had called "the Philanthropist." He lived a life east to west, navigating the spaces, memories, and histories inscribed in our lighted steer's horns. Born in New England in 1828, Rust came of age under the tutelage of a blacksmithing father committed to abolition and social reform. In later years, he also credited a visit to the enslaved prisoners aboard the *Amistad* with helping foster a lifelong commitment to civil rights and humanitarian causes.

In 1857, at work as a druggist in Collinsville, Connecticut, Rust met and befriended John Brown. Shared abolitionist sympathies quickly cemented a friendship personal and political. Horatio Rust helped John Brown raise money for his antislavery crusade in Kansas, and he played a key role in securing the one thousand pikes that Brown had first planned for use in Kansas but which he later decided ought to be distributed to slaves bent on insurrection. That friendship lasted just two years, until Brown's execution for his role as prime mover in the farcical raid on the Harper's Ferry arsenal. But Rust's devotion to Brown's memory and the Brown family lasted a lifetime, and it is that devotion that helps drive our story east to west, from Antietam all the way to Southern California, where memory and memorabilia, and Horatio Rust, together resided.

At the outbreak of the war, Rust, who had hoped to become a doctor, volunteered his services to the Union cause. This was not unusual, although historical awareness of noncombatant volunteers is sorely lacking. Dispatched to the front, he spent a good portion of the war years working as a medical aide—driving the horse-drawn ambulances devised and organized by Jonathan Letterman, aiding at surgeries and amputations, dressing wounds, helping to transport the wounded to field units or back home. He would return even to the battlefields of Antietam two years later, where he would be surrounded again by the war wounded.[11]

Horatio Rust lived a very busy life. Following his humanitarian efforts on the battlefields of the worst clashes of the Civil War, he characteristically threw himself into a number of occupations and avocations: archeologist, Indian agent, educator, horticulturalist. From his ministrations to the wounded of the Civil War, we track Rust first to Chicago, where he was a salesman and a volunteer active in organizations helping settle and support freed slaves. "I am pleased to know that you are well and busy in doing good service to humanity, as always," Holmes Sr. wrote to Rust in the early 1880s, "for it is your instinct and your calling."[12]

Abolition, John Brown, freedpeople, and, curiously, memorabilia tied to such causes and their actors: this is what drove Horatio Rust after the war. He arranged a speaking tour by the Reverend Josiah Henson, Harriet Beecher Stowe's model for Uncle Tom. Fascinated throughout his entire life by Native American history and artifacts, Rust participated in numerous archeological investigations and digs, and he regularly trekked across the West and Midwest on solo expeditions, finding artifacts, studying the people who made them, and then selling or giving away much of what he dug up. All this as the final resistance of Native peoples (look to the other end of horn) faced crushing violence meted out by those same soldiers who had survived the Civil War.

Because of his interest in indigenous peoples and their history, Horatio Rust was drawn to the West and Southwest, and he loved one part of it in particular. In the early 1880s, Rust traveled to Southern California from Chicago, looking for land to buy and cultivate. He made a beeline to Pasadena, "the objective point of our journey."[13] In search of "good soil, pure water, a better climate . . . and a respectable community," Rust found what he was looking for in the new town just northeast of Los Angeles, nestled against the San Gabriel Mountains.[14] The village was tiny, perhaps five hundred people lived there; it had a single grocery store, one school, one blacksmith, no hotel or board-inghouse. But Rust liked what he saw. Within a year, having purchased a large plot of citrus-growing land at the southern edge of Pasadena, he and his large family lived there, at one of the very centers where the West and the Civil War intersected in the last third of the nineteenth century.

Ever tied to the Civil War by experience and memory, Horatio Rust maintained regular contact with veterans and veterans groups. Such sinews were not uncommon in Reconstruction and post-Reconstruction eras, although we might imagine that they meant even more to the Philanthropist. When the Grand Army of the Republic held its reunion in Northern California in 1886, Rust traveled to a rail station in the California desert to meet the veterans as they came west, on their way to San Francisco; his hospitality, complete with fruit, wine, and lemonade, gave the former soldiers "a truthful knowledge of the advantages which our country offers them and their friends for settlement."[15]

A year later, Rust even took the fruit of California to Union veterans far away. A booster to the core, champion of California soils, sunshine, and produce, Rust presided over an exhibit of California fruit in Saint Louis that coincided with the next Grand Army of the Republic reunion. He sent a load of grapes to the veterans free of charge, and a local newspaper commented on the booster tactic aimed directly at those who had served. "Everyone of the veterans who has a cluster of these grapes, or tastes of the other luscious fruit, will have a definite appreciation of what the charming climate of California can produce, such as no reading or advertisement of any kind could convey. The whole plan is unique, and will, under the management of Major [the title was honorific from the war] Rust and his colleagues, add perceptibly to the boom that Southern California is already enjoying."[16]

But it was John Brown, John Brown's family, and material artifacts of their lives that occupied Rust's attention more than grapes. He spent fifty years in close contact with various members of the large family (Brown had twenty children); gathering family memorabilia, weapons, photographs, and autographs; and working to raise money for the care of the sons and daughters of John Brown and urging them to come west to settle and start anew. At the center of Horatio Nelson Rust's West was Pasadena, and he single-handedly made Pasadena a national center of John Brown nostalgia and memorabilia by way of fervent postwar curatorship.

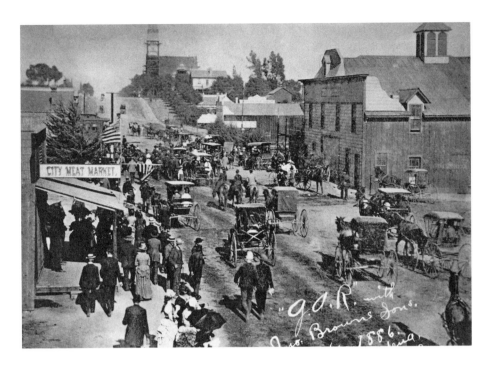

FIGURE 10.4

An 1886 Grand Army of the Republic convocation in downtown Pasadena, with John Brown's sons in attendance. Courtesy Pasadena History Museum.

John Brown Jr. wrote to Rust in 1884, explaining that his brother Jason, shy and modest, but "genuine all through," was thinking seriously about relocating to Southern California.[17] Rust jumped to the task, urging Jason to do so and offering to help set him up in horticultural work. Before long, Jason, his brother Owen, their sister Ruth Thompson, and their brother-in-law Henry Thompson had settled in Pasadena. Rust had everything to do with this, just as he was likely responsible for bringing Jason Brown along on one of the Grand Army of the Republic train trips. In 1886, when Rust met the westbound train carrying members of the Grand Army of the Republic, at Barstow, with California wine and fruit, Jason Brown shook hands with an old Confederate soldier who, dressed in his gray Confederate States of America uniform, greeted the son of antislavery's crusader "in brotherly affection."[18] That clasp is hard to believe, even though the historian David Blight has taught us to expect it.

Like her Philanthropist benefactor, Ruth Brown Thompson is buried in Pasadena's Mountain View cemetery, not far from where she lived out her final days (and alongside five hundred or more Civil War veterans who also sought solace and renewal in Southern California). Let's linger, if figuratively, by her grave and contemplate her later life.

Ruth Brown was raised in the chaotic household in which everything revolved around her father's increasingly violent, millennial antipathy toward the South, slaveholders, and the institution of slavery. One of Brown's nearly two dozen children, Ruth lived a life inextricably shaped—and inevitably shaken—by her father's devotion to the antislavery cause and his fierce methods of expressing it.

Ruth Brown married Henry Thompson, a close confidante and ally of her father's, one of three Thompson brothers caught up in the widening gyre of Brown's actions in Kansas in the 1850s. It was Henry Thompson and his brother-in-law Owen who wielded their swords with grim efficiency in the infamous Pottawatomie Massacre in late May 1856, where forces loyal to Brown and abolition hacked five proslavery men to death.[19] Days later, Henry Thompson was shot through the lungs at the Battle of Black Jack, when pro- and antislavery forces fought a pitched battle. Some consider the Battle of Black Jack to be the first battle of the Civil War.[20]

By the late summer of 1859, Henry's brothers William and Dauphin, several of Ruth's brothers, and others who had fallen under their leader's spell went east to plan and then take part in the crazed raid on Harper's Ferry. Henry Thompson was not with them, at least in part because his wife feared for his safety when he was engaged in what Thompson termed "the enterprise." As Ruth wrote her father: "I should like to have him go with you if I could feel that he would live to come back."[21] This was hardly a promise that her father could make.

Ruth Thompson was prescient. During the Harper's Ferry attack, at which townsfolk and U.S. soldiers counterattacked Brown's motley group of would-be insurrectionists, William Thompson was thrown into the Potomac by drunken townspeople, who then riddled his body with gunfire. Blue-eyed and baby-faced Dauphin Thompson died when a United States marine ran him through with a bayonet. Two of Ruth's brothers were also killed. As he lay mortally wounded, Oliver Brown begged his father to shoot him, whereupon John Brown insisted his son die like a man.

After that awful event, after John Brown's hanging, and years after the Civil War, Ruth Brown Thompson and her husband did what Horatio Rust did. They moved all the way across the nation to Pasadena, arriving on Thanksgiving Day 1884. They stayed for the rest of their lives, living what the newspapers curiously referred to as "a relatively peaceful life in Pasadena."[22]

Not long after their arrival, two of Ruth's brothers, Owen, who'd been at Harper's Ferry, and Jason, who had not, also arrived in Southern California. They homesteaded some hardscrabble land in the foothills above Mountain View Cemetery.

Described as "mentally astray for some time," Owen died broke in the late 1880s at the home of his sister. His last words were: "It is better to be in a place and suffer wrong than to do wrong." Owen Brown was among the last of the Harper's Ferry raiders to die. A local obituary turned that event toward biblical narrative, saying that Owen had escaped the slaughter of the Harper's Ferry raid by flight "through mountain fastnesses and swamps and forests and sassafras leaves." He kept going west and then, once he'd made it all the way to Pasadena, he and his brother climbed north into the mountains overlooking the small town.[23] They ended up in their succession of tiny cabins, objects

LAS CASITAS VIEWS.   MOUNTAIN HOME OF JOHN BROWN'S SONS.   F.H.Rogers, Photo, L.A. Cal'a.

FIGURE 10.5

Photograph of the Brown brothers at their cabin above Pasadena, 1880s. Little Round Top, named for the famed battle site at Gettysburg, rises in the background. The Asian man in the background is unidentified. Courtesy Pasadena History Museum.

of curiosity, their huts a destination for sightseers. Owen and his brother Jason began homesteading (sort of) high in the San Gabriel Mountains overlooking Pasadena, clearing some land and working the few acres of a little ranch. Jason also helped tend the wild animals at the nearby animal park owned by Civil War balloner Thaddeus Lowe. Old and feeble by the 1880s, the two brothers with long beards and faraway eyes did not say much; as novelist Russell Banks wrote in the voice of Owen, it got to a point where he "stayed silent altogether."

Death brought a spotlight to Owen Brown and to these connections between Pasadena and the Civil War. Two thousand people attended Owen Brown's funeral, organized by trusted family friend Horatio Rust. The pallbearers, old abolitionists who had come west after the war, bore the casket from the funeral parlor to the tune and strains of "John Brown's Body," with its chorus of "glory glory hallelujah, his soul is marching on." "It is quite remarkable," Owen's obituary in *The Pasadena Standard* noted, "that there should be found in Pasadena so many men who were associated with John Brown in his mighty work, which heaved up the nation and made the entering wedge for the overthrow of slavery thirty years ago."[24] Nearly ten years later, ever mindful of artifacts, Rust arranged to place a stone at Owen's grave atop the mountain where he had retreated; the ceremony drew whites and African Americans alike, all paying respects to the old antislavery warrior and, in this way, to the Philanthropist as well.

FIGURE 10.6
Written in Horatio Rust's hand on the back of this photograph, circa 1899: "Picture taken as we set the stone at Owen Browns [sic] grave on a spine of the Sierra Madre Mountains south [actually north] of Pasadena." Brown is in the inset; Rust, wearing a beard, is standing in line with the tree. Reproduced with permission of the Huntington Library, San Marino, California.

The reclusive, odd Brown brothers and their older sister did not just fall into Pasadena. They did not simply choose their mountain hideaway because it was so far away from Harper's Ferry, from Bleeding Kansas, from their father's Virginia execution, though I am sure that distance formed part of their reasoning for living out their final days in Southern California. The brothers were hermits, strange. They even got lost—for four acorn-eating days—on their own mountaintop. But they'd seen a lot of death by then. It behooves us to see them, even to see postwar Pasadena more generally, through a prism of harm borne of the violence of the Civil War.[25]

The West, and especially Southern California, beckoned to the Brown brothers. It drew them away from the boosterism that swept through post–Civil War America, to a place that became, if briefly, a more egalitarian corner of the world in regard to race and redemption. Their lives—and the lives of all their siblings—represent the complexities and human costs of the ongoing American projects of empire and liberty. *Liberty* had been the watchword of their father's life, and thus theirs, but the toll that the pursuit of it had taken on all their lives could hardly have been more obvious. And thus, to the postwar West they went, carving out a tiny sliver of space in the far western corner of empire so that they could be left alone with memories and traumas.

Ruth Brown Thompson had a different trajectory once she came to the same place. It was she who understood the American West as a place, chastened by the Civil War, where postwar healing could happen. She ran a tiny convalescent hospital, ministering to the sick and apparently doing so across the racial divides that were otherwise solidifying as the century waned. She cared for white and black alike. A tiny Confederate hospital two miles away cared for wounded sons of the South; and the Soldier's Home, on the west side of Los Angeles, adjacent to what is now UCLA, took in veterans of the Mexican and Civil Wars (Union only). All three hospitals and others like them, large and small, filled up.

In old age, Ruth Brown Thompson lived at the south end of Arroyo Boulevard in Pasadena, on the eastern side of the Arroyo Seco canyon, and cared for her frail husband. Their little cottage draped in vines and roses had two portraits of her father prominently displayed, one a photograph of a younger John Brown, the other a famed print of the bearded zealot not long before his execution.[26] Wealthy, and a magnet for tourists, the Pasadena that was a product of post–Civil War American prosperity, grew up around them.

When Ruth Thompson died in the early twentieth century, the crowds returned. At her funeral, held in a big church in central Pasadena, people wandered amid floral arrangements, basketry, and other garden funerary decorations. Two gigantic American flags draped the choir screens, and ivy wreaths and palm fronds were hung in profusion. The local chapter of the women's auxiliary to the Grand Army of the Republic, the Women's Relief Corps, sent fifty representatives.

Children from the Garfield School, where Ruth Thompson's daughter Mary taught the sixth grade, and which had been renamed in honor of the assassinated President James Garfield, sent a basket of flowers. Garfield's widow, Lucretia, who lived nearby in South Pasadena, sent carnations. The Afro-American League of Pasadena sent a wreath of violets and hyacinths. Flowers lay on the casket. Like her husband before her, Ruth Brown Thompson was buried in Mountain View Cemetery.

As old men, the Brown brothers were passive observers of the world, cramped into their little cabin atop the San Gabriel Mountains. But their sister Ruth was different. Where her brothers chose escape and mountaintop isolation, Ruth Brown Thompson was very much both *in* and *of* the post–Civil War West.

Horatio Nelson Rust died two years after Ruth Brown Thompson, and he is buried not far from her in Mountain View. Nearby lies Union veteran John Ransom, author of a searing diary account of his incarceration at the notorious Confederate-run prison at Andersonville, Georgia. Ransom's migration westward also describes that migratory arc tying the Civil War to the postwar West and, once again, directly to Southern California, directly to Pasadena.

And perhaps with those journeys, the weird, inexplicable horned lamp of violence becomes oddly explicable? Maybe that big electrified horn, which the editor of this volume, Virginia Scharff, rightly considers "jarring," casts light on postbellum journeys of fact, of memory, and of memorabilia? Perhaps, as in scrimshaw, our understandings of the nation are illuminated if we insist upon tying East to West, tip to tip, bound by slavery and war and conquest, linked by violence fraternal and violence genocidal, but linked also by memorabilia and commemoration. And linked, as well, by a fervent postwar search for redemption amid all the vines and flowers, all the vistas of distance and of memory.

NOTES

1. Annie Powers, "The Riddle of the Lamp: Identity, Progress, and Modernity in Late Nineteenth Century America" (unpublished manuscript, 2013). Annie Powers is a doctoral student in the history department at University of California, Los Angeles, and I am indebted to her and her work in this essay. Her research places the lamp deeply within the context of the iconography of Civil War and western conquest material and visual culture. William Deverell also thanks Virginia Scharff and David Igler for their insightful readings of this paper.

2. Holmes, *The Writings of Oliver Wendell Holmes* (Boston: Houghton Mifflin, 1891), 8:28–29.

3. Ibid., 29–30. The "carnival of death" quote is on p. 32.

4. Ibid., 8:30.

5. He wrote of later being in the battlefield's makeshift hospitals: "Many times as I went from hospital to hospital in my wanderings, I started as some faint resemblance,—the shade of a young man's hair, the outline of his half-turned face,—recalled the presence I was in search of. The face would turn towards me, and the momentary illusion would pass away, but still the fancy clung to me." Ibid., 8:36.

6. From Horatio N. Rust's reminiscences of Antietam, published in the *Easthampton (MA) News*, October 13, 1899; see the Horatio Nelson Rust Collection, "Personal Articles" scrapbook, p. 120, Huntington Library, San Marino, CA.

7. Jonathan Letterman never got over the horrors of the war. He maintained a deep, abiding grudge against General George Meade, Union commander at Gettysburg, for Meade's refusal to allow Letterman's ambulances and medical evacuation units to get any closer than three miles from the Gettysburg battlefields, which rendered them useless. See William Deverell, "Redemption Falls Short: Soldier and Surgeon in the Post–Civil War Far West," in *Civil War Wests: Testing the Limits of the United States,* ed. Adam Arenson and Andrew Graybill (Berkeley: University of California Press, forthcoming).

8. See *Medical and Surgical Reporter* 9, no. 8 (November 1862): 198–99.

9. Rust, reminiscences of Antietam.

10. Holmes, *Writings,* 77. The younger Holmes would suffer terrible wounds again, and he would write poignantly of his struggle to keep mind and body together in his darkest periods of the war. "These last few days have been very bad. Many a man has gone crazy since this campaign begun [sic] from the terrible pressures on mind and body. . . . I hope to pull through but I don't know. Doubt demoralizes me as it does any nervous man. I cannot now endure the

labors and hardships of the line." See Mark Micale's fine essay "Medical and Literary Discourses of Trauma in the Age of the American Civil War," in *Neurology and Literature, 1860–1920*, ed. Anne Stiles (New York: Palgrave Macmillan, 2007), 187–88.

11. See Albert D. Rust, *Record of the Rust Family* (Waco, TX: self-published, 1891).

12. Oliver Wendell Holmes, letter to Horatio Nelson Rust, April 19, 1881, Horatio Nelson Rust Collection, Huntington Library.

13. See Horatio Nelson Rust, diary no. 23, "Trip to California," Horatio Nelson Rust Collection, Huntington Library.

14. Jane Apostol, "Horatio Nelson Rust: Abolitionist, Archeologist, Indian Agent," *California History* 58 (Winter 1979–80): 304–15, quote from Rust on p. 306.

15. Ibid., 309.

16. Ibid., 307.

17. Jason Brown, though against slavery, objected to many of his father's violent tactics.

18. Might we see this as even odder than a longhorn lamp tying Antietam to frontier violence? See untitled, undated clipping in Rust, "Personal Articles" scrapbook, p. 66.

19. The swords were probably given to Brown by Lucius Bierce, the grandfather of Ambrose Bierce, a wounded Civil War veteran and acerbic California writer. See Carey McWilliams, *Ambrose Bierce: A Biography* (1929; reprint, Hamden, CT: Archon Books, 1967), xxii–xxiii.

20. On Bleeding Kansas as the first battle of the Civil War, see the essay by Jonathan Earle in this volume.

21. Ruth Brown Thompson to John Brown, April 21, 1858, Territorial Kansas Online, www .kansasmemory.org/item/4827.

22. That qualifier *relatively* is tantalizing, but I have yet to find any instance or evidence of disruption, other than Ruth and Henry Thompson's slide into penniless.

23. See also Ralph Keeler, "Owen Brown's Escape from Harper's Ferry," *Atlantic Monthly* 33 (March 1874): 342–65.

24. Matt Horman, "Pasadena's Abolitionist Heritage," Hometown Pasadena, October 15, 2009, http://hometown-pasadena.com/history/pasadenas-abolitionist-heritage/5931. At Owen Brown's death, in addition to his sister Ruth and brother Jason, four of his six other surviving siblings lived in California.

25. On the Brown brothers getting lost atop their mountain, see Horatio Nelson Rust, untitled newspaper clipping regarding Owen Brown's funeral, n.d., in Rust's "Obituary Scrapbook," Horatio Nelson Rust Collection, Huntington Library.

26. See "'This Soul Is Marching On': The Prologue to the Drama of the Civil War," *Los Angeles Times*, July 18, 1897.

11

"YOU BROUGHT HISTORY ALIVE FOR US"
Reflections on the Lives of Nineteenth-Century Diné Women

Jennifer Denetdale

Several years ago the director of the Navajo Nation Museum, Manuelito Wheeler, invited me to co-curate an exhibit on Diné leaders of the nineteenth century, based upon my study *Reclaiming Navajo History: The Legacies of Chief Manuelito and Juanita*. Manuelito Wheeler, who is from Coyote Canyon, New Mexico, was named for the prominent nineteenth-century Diné leader Manuelito. My book examined an important segment of Navajo history through the lives of the latter Manuelito, who is known best to the Diné as Hastiin Ch'il Hajin (Man from Black Weeds) and one of his wives, known as Juanita, and whose Diné name was Asdzáá Tł'ógi (Lady Weaver). Interestingly, but perhaps not surprisingly, the leader Manuelito looms large in Navajo histories created for the general public, while very little was known about Juanita. Through oral history, I was able to illuminate Navajo women's lives in the nineteenth and early twentieth centuries. The exhibit focused upon my maternal great-great-great-grandparents Hastiin Ch'il Hajin and Asdzáá Tł'ógi and their roles during the American conquest of the Diné in the nineteenth century.[1] The exhibit used photographs, textiles, and text to raise questions about traditional Navajo leadership in the nineteenth century, including women's leadership, and the role of memory in perpetuating traditional Navajo values.

A *Navajo Times* article about the exhibit highlighted two items of material culture borrowed from the Autry National Center in Los Angeles, California.[2] These items had been collected by George Wharton James, who claimed that my great-great-great-grandmother Asdzáá Tł'ógi had given the objects to him after they became friends.[3] The *biil eh'* (woven dress) and *dahaastłoo* (saddle blanket) are attributed to her and were most

FIGURE 11.1

Biil eh' (woven dress) worn by Asdzáá Tł'ógi (Lady Weaver), also known as Juanita Manuelito, circa 1868. The George Wharton James Collection. Southwest Museum of the American Indian Collection, Autry National Center, 421.G.1115. For a color version of this image, see plate 16.

FIGURE 11.2

Dahaastłoo (saddle blanket) woven by Asdzáá Tł'ógi, 1895–1905. The George Wharton
James Collection. Southwest Museum of the American Indian Collection, Autry National
Center, 421.G.1108. For a color version of this image, see plate 17.

likely of her manufacture. Dated to the 1870s, these two items were from the decade
when Diné struggled to recover from the trauma of the Long Walk and incarceration at
the Bosque Redondo reservation at Fort Sumner, New Mexico; our exhibit was the first
time the dress and blanket had been back in their Diné homeland.

Over the course of eighteen months, hundreds of Diné and other visitors viewed
them. Anthropologists and other scholars have used items like these with the intent of
preserving a sense of the Navajo past, to illuminate Navajo life in the nineteenth century,
and to encourage appreciation of the economic and artistic contributions that Navajo
women have made to their societies. However much these collections might help others
understand Navajos, past and present, these pieces that once belonged to my great-great-
great-grandmother provided yet another avenue for talking about what is culturally

important to us as Diné. These items returned to Diné country opened space for renewed storytelling, particularly about Navajo forms of *k'e,* or kinship, and formations of local communities and family. The exhibit also gave us a chance to think about traditional leadership and Navajo women's places as leaders in our society.

Some of my earliest discoveries about my great-great-great-grandmother were photographs of her, with the first probably taken in 1868. One of the earliest photographs of Juanita is a classic studio pose, where she stands next to a prop covered by a print cloth that is also used in the only known photograph of the peace leader Barboncito. In this photo, she is young, probably in her twenties.[4] I also discovered my grandmother's public Navajo name, Asdzáá Tł'ógi, in census records at the St. Michaels Mission in Saint Michaels, Arizona.[5] Asdzáá Tł'ógi, translated as "Lady Weaver," indicates that like most Navajo women of her time, she was a weaver. Her name also indicates her matrilineal clan, the Tł'ógi, or Weaver, clan, and suggests historical and cultural ties to Zia Pueblo, a tribal nation north of Albuquerque, New Mexico. Like my grandmothers, I identify as a Tł'ógi woman who is born into the Áshįįh (Salt) clan, who are my fathers.

The dress and the saddle blanket that had once belonged to my great-great-great-grandmother came to my attention during the course of my research and the subsequent publication of my Diné history. Much of what we know and recover about Native women resides in oral history and other culturally based forms, so understanding our history requires knowing local communities and, in my personal case, getting to know my clan relatives. Privileging oral history shows the persistence of Navajo forms of organization that center on women's places in Navajo society. Inevitably, contradictions between Native oral history and American written sources lead many researchers to question the value of oral histories as sources to illuminate gender roles. However, rather than measure oral history against the standards of written documentations, we might think about what these contradictions say about cultural processes—Native engagements with colonialism, and the persistence of Diné values concerning culture and gender.[6]

For example, my great-great-great-grandmother is best known by her Mexican name, Juanita. When I began looking for her in the historical record, I consistently came across two details about her: she had been a Mexican slave who married Manuelito and came to be regarded as his favorite wife. Photographs of my great-great-great-grandparents span at least three decades, from the 1860s to the 1880s, showing them together. Portraits of them were taken at places where Manuelito was meeting with American officials who were stipulating or enforcing federal policies for Navajos. Photographs of leaders like Barboncito and Manuelito were taken when they traveled to meet American representatives of the federal government.[7] The series of photographs I discovered indicate that Juanita traveled with Manuelito, across several decades, to important political proceedings, suggesting that he valued her presence. My grandmother's story refers to an event in Navajo history in which Navajo male leaders, the Indian agent William Arny, translators, and Juanita traveled to Washington, D.C., to meet with President Ulysses S. Grant in order to secure Navajo landholdings in the northern section of their territory in 1874.[8]

Navajo leaders were concerned about Navajo lands being invaded by white settlers along the northeastern border, around the San Juan River, and wished to speak to the president about ensuring Navajo land claims. Historian Herman Viola notes the Navajo delegation's presence in Washington, D.C., in February of 1874 and suggests that the trip was self-serving and merely an opportunity for the Navajo leaders to sightsee.[9] However, Navajo leaders, like other indigenous leaders, expected to meet with the president of the United States to address their concerns and grievances. Tribal leaders' expectations to meet with another head of state reflect their conviction that their relationships with the United States were based upon a nation-to-nation model. The delegation began its journey on November 15, 1873, in Santa Fe, New Mexico, where they boarded the train to travel across the country. Reaching their final destination, the Navajo leaders met briefly with the president but were unable to bring their matter of land claims before him. They spent weeks in the capital hoping to meet again with the American president. Although no written records exist to note Juanita's presence as part of the delegation, she is captured in several photographs by Charles Bell.[10]

Importantly, her presence, her voice, her thoughts are also recorded through the stories that my matrilineal clan relayed about their grandmother's travels. During my interviews with my maternal grandparents, my grandmother Faye Yazzie informed me that our grandmother provided her husband with counsel, and that he often sought out her counsel in matters of state. Faye relayed a story of our grandmother going to Washington, D.C., with an otherwise all-male Navajo delegation, because "her husband, Manuelito, wanted his wife, Juanita, to go on the trip because she spoke well and maybe she could persuade the president to let the Navajos keep their lands. Manuelito said the president's back was 'stiff' and perhaps Juanita's words could soften [persuade] him." My interviews with my maternal grandparents, the descendants of Juanita and Manuelito, not only yielded rich information about their grandmother's place in Navajo history but also reminded me that clan relationships are still very important.

The photographs I shared with my grandparents have also spurred present-day Navajo interest in history. As a result of my interviews with my grandparents, and my research, my relatives began to pay attention to the matrilineal genealogy I had constructed with the assistance of my grandparents. In particular, my children's generation began recognizing kin relationships and how they are related to each other through their grandmothers. Before my visits and interviews with my grandparents, I had known them from afar. Hence, one of the most valuable aspects of working in my community has been the recognition of and respect for kinship ties, which is the basis for *k'e*, Navajo people's practice of how we relate to each other as human beings and how we relate to the nonhuman beings, who are no less significant than humans. Navajo traditional teachings center on matrilineality so that we acknowledge kinship to each other through women, through mothers and grandmothers. The photographs, then, encouraged a remembrance of Navajo teachings about matrilineality.

FIGURE 11.3
Asdzáá Tłʼógi (Lady Weaver),
unidentified photographer, circa
1877, albumen print. Braun
Research Library Collection,
Autry National Center,
A.152.198.

In my earlier project, I hoped to learn more about my great-great-great-grandmother, about her life as the wife of a prominent leader. Through her story, I had hoped to illuminate Navajo women's lives in the nineteenth century. What I did learn was that across several centuries, non-Indian observers noted the respect and authority accorded to Navajo women. For example, I came across an American military officer's comments about a Navajo peace leader's wife when she rode into the fort looking for her relative who had been stolen by slave raiders. After speaking with her, he reported, "She is a woman well known and influential among her people, intelligent for an Indian, and though past middle age active and vigorous."[11] Such observations of Navajo women's roles and the influence they have within their communities and extended families often lead to questions about women's lack of presence in the present-day Navajo government, particularly in

the Tribal Council and in the offices of president and vice president of our Navajo Nation.[12] My exploration of Juanita's place in her society, then, has led to questions about gender and traditional leadership: in what ways were Navajo women seen as leaders before the American invasion of their lands after 1846? How have cycles of colonialism shifted women's roles?

In an effort to illuminate and recover traditional Navajo gender roles, scholars have scoured the historical record for glimpses of women's places, drawn insights from traditional creation narratives, applied principles of ideal womanhood to contemporary women's roles, and written narratives that highlight notable Diné women.[13] Building on previous scholarship, we have made use of material culture, including photographs and textiles to augment more conventional methodologies. Through examinations of material culture, we explore the intersections of history and Navajo storytelling, even as we engage with the ongoing consequences of settler colonialism. Despite centuries of violence intended to eliminate the Diné, traditional principles shape Navajo women's roles today, in ways we are only beginning to interrogate, evaluate, and in some cases, reaffirm. Our dialogue is ongoing, and our work is unfinished.

At the time I began my foray into Diné women's history, I was faced with the formidable task of making sense of seemingly disparate bits of information and material culture: how could I make a whole out of bits and pieces, fragments—a dress, textiles, photographs, bits of written sources, and stories from my clan relatives? Hoping to create coherence, I struggled with the erasures, losses, ruptures, and silences in the history of Navajo women's lives, and with the continuing sanitizing of the history of the United States' efforts to dispossess Diné. As I worked through my research and talked to Diné, I reflected on the ways in which our losses reverberated in our nation and communities. Chickasaw scholar Jodi Byrd uses the term *cacophony* to describe how American conquest overwrites, erases, and rewrites the culture, politics, and representations of Indians.[14] The violence used to dispossess and disenfranchise indigenous peoples continues to be ignored, as discursive practices treat the history of U.S.-Diné relations as an artifact of the past, even as we continue to press for the sovereignty of the Navajo Nation. And yet, against all odds, I find inspiration and energy in the power of stories. As we remember, and as we speak, our stories traverse colonized spaces. Our stories affirm what it means to be indigenous and Diné in the twenty-first century.[15]

Against, through, and in spite of such silences, refusals, and denials, I worked to create a narrative that would honor our ancestors for defending their lands, for as I have often said, surely our grandfathers and grandmothers were thinking of the future, of us, when they stood their ground against incredible odds.

It took a long time to arrange to borrow the items for the Navajo exhibit. After more than a year of correspondence between the Autry and the Navajo Nation Museum, Robert Johnson, the Navajo Nation Museum's cultural educator, drove to Los Angeles in a Navajo Nation van to pick up the items. The Autry museum described my grandmother's dress as one of very few remaining from the early Navajo reservation period. Kathleen Whitaker's *Southwest Textiles: Weavings of the Navajo and Pueblo* (2002) included both of the pieces by my grandmother. Typical of publications on southwestern and Navajo textiles, this volume is lavish with photographs of textiles as it describes the weavings by wefts and warps, provides dates, and sometimes supplements the color plates with photographs of Native peoples that represent the period.

According to Whitaker's descriptions, the textiles reflected their maker's willingness to incorporate all kinds of materials at hand, even as she preserved traditional design elements and methods of manufacture. The *biil eh'* was made with churro wool, from sheep that Navajos had prized and which were replaced with what federal officials deemed hardier sheep. Panels of the dress used dyes of indigo (a dark blue dye derived from a plant), lac (a scarlet dye from the resinous secretions of insect species), and cochineal (a crimson coloring, also derived from insects). The panels of black-brown were natural.[16] The dress shows much wear—on the lower half of the back panel, pieces of cotton fabric and colored calico are stitched on the inside and outside to patch unraveling and thinned spots. The stitching is made with white thread and loops along the edges of the patches. Whitaker identifies my grandmother's textile as a "Navajo single-style saddle blanket" woven between 1895 and 1905. The textile has machine-spun string warp, and the weft is made of handspun wool. The blanket is fringed with tufts of goat hair, and in the center is a star of red, indigo, gold, orange, and green.[17]

As we prepared to exhibit the dress and blanket, we followed the specifications of the curator of the Autry's Southwest Museum of the American Indian, who accompanied the textiles to the Navajo Nation. Because the Navajo Nation Museum respects Navajo traditional practices, and because we had been advised about precautions to take with respect to the two items, the director enlisted a medicine man to conduct a private ceremony for the museum staff and my immediate family. Many events on the Navajo Nation require prayers for protection and well-being. The medicine man, a young man, walked around the exhibit and shared his thoughts as he used what he saw to inform his prayer. He commented on how Manuelito had been a warrior who spent his life defending the land and the people. My mom was so pleased with the proceedings, the return of the dress and the saddle blanket, the prayer, and the exhibit. Later she told me that our grandmother was pleased that we honored her.

As I looked at the dress that my grandmother had woven, I imagined her deft fingers moving across the back and front panels, stitching in squares of calico to strengthen the worn, fragile fabric. She must have treasured the dress to put so much care into preserving it, I thought. Much later, I became acquainted with Navajo weaver Gilbert Begay. One day, he shared with me the story of his visit along with other weavers to view my grandmother's *biil*. He was fascinated by the pattern on the border of the dress. He said she had used a double-weave technique that he had not seen before, and which weavers did not use anymore. I was entranced by the conversation. Gilbert's weaver's eyes saw something I did not see. My father also made comments, particularly on the saddle blanket. In great detail, he explained what he saw in the star design. We have a word for the time when the morning star is the colors depicted in the weaving. His narrative affirmed the vast sacred and ceremonial knowledge possessed by women as weavers. The process of weaving held within it traditional Navajo teachings about the importance of k'e and what kind of relationships we should have with the natural world, the earth and the skies, and each other.[18]

In the space of the Navajo museum, other spaces that I also inhabit came together—the space of academia; Navajo national space, where a collective memory is created and re-created; and my personal family's and clan memories. In the place where we honored our ancestors and remembered their sacrifices and their determination to persist as a people, academia, tribal nation, community, and family merged. As we remembered our grandparents—our traditional leaders who struggled to affirm sovereignty for their people—we expressed appreciation, gratitude, and a desire to know more about the Navajo past. After the prayer and a preview of the exhibit, my father said to me, "Hwiin yoo la," telling me that I have made some worthwhile contributions! It was nice to hear my father approve of the ways in which I was using my education for positive change for Navajo people. Many descendants of Manuelito and Juanita, along with a primarily Navajo public, were present for the reception that officially opened the exhibit to the public. One of my cousins, Tabitha Manuelito, said to me with enthusiasm, "You brought history alive for us!"

The photographs of my great-great-great-grandparents were an amazing find, especially because, for the most part, photographers of Navajos did not name the individuals, nor did they indicate places photos were taken; they also were not consistent about dates. In my initial efforts to recover narratives of my grandmother, I began with the assumption that she was a Diné woman, for I had been told from childhood that I am a Diné woman who comes from a long line of Navajo grandmothers. Not until I was a young woman did I pay closer attention to the stories my mother would tell me about my grandmothers. One day, I realized she was talking about the wife of the prominent leader Manuelito. Although some of my grandparents and other relatives have acknowledged that our grandmother was a Mexican slave, there were few who knew any details regarding this aspect of her identity.

At different times my fellow Navajos have asked me if indeed my grandmother had been a Mexican slave and, if so, why I was presenting her as a Navajo woman. Other questions related to how she became a member of the Tł'ógi, or Weaver, clan if she was in fact a Mexican woman. Since publishing *Reclaiming Diné History*, I have heard, through conversations with my clan relatives, that indeed our grandmother had been a Mexican slave. However, this bit of information deserves scrutiny, and a plunge into the history of the Southwest raises questions about constructions of nineteenth-century race ideology, slave raiding, and the process of belonging in Navajo communities.

How did a woman who is said to have been a Mexican and then a slave of Navajos come to live among the Diné, marry a man who led the resistance against American invasion of the Diné Bikéyah (Navajoland), and become accepted as a Diné woman? Born around 1845, Asdzáá Tł'ógi lived in an era when captive-taking was an important component of the regional economy. As scholars have shown, although indigenous societies practiced forms of captive-taking, the practice intensified under Spanish rule in the late fifteenth and sixteenth centuries in the Southwest. Slave-taking was a constant feature of the Southwest, and it intensified under Spanish rule and then American occupation after 1846. Anthropologist David Brugge's perusal of Spanish Catholic Church records shed light on how captives were incorporated into Hispanic societies in northern New Mexico. Baptismal records, dating between 1770 and 1868, list women and children from different tribal groups, their estimated ages, the Spanish names they were given, and the households in which they were indentured.[19]

In narratives recorded by the Work Projects Administration in the 1940s, historian Estevan Rael-Galvez discovered traces of Navajos who had been captured for the slave trade and sold to Hispanic households. One woman was captured in Navajoland and taken with her child into northern New Mexico, where she lived out her life as a servant to a Hispanic family. During her capture her husband and older child were killed by the slave raiders. When she attempted to run away from her master, her child was taken away from her. Captured as a young woman, the only thing this woman remembered of being Navajo was her name, "At'eed BaHózhó," which translates as "Happy Girl." Known to the children in the Hispanic household as "Yoyo Mah," she never returned to her homeland.[20] Brugge also showed that Navajos and other "savage" tribes were targets of the escalating trade in captives. Records indicate that raiding Navajo communities for slaves peaked in 1863 as the U.S. military forced Navajo surrender and then began rounding up the prisoners for removal to the Bosque Redondo reservation.[21]

Navajo history and oral tradition also offer glimpses of captives who were incorporated into Navajo society. Brugge points out that Navajos incorporated captives into their communities and families in distinctive ways that indicate flexibility, and that some captives were able to change their fortunes by using their individual skills and talents. It appears that my grandmother was such a person. In the 1880s, twenty years after Navajos had been freed from their American prison camp at Fort Sumner, Navajo agent Dennis Ríordan reported that Navajos had among them some three hundred slaves, and he complained that slaves he had "freed" from their Navajo masters refused freedom and "beat a hasty path back to the hogans of their masters." In his study of slave-taking in the Southwest, historian James Brooks references Juanita, who was "owned" by Manuelito, and suggests that she was one of Manuelito's slaves who was offered her "freedom."[22]

If my grandmother had been taken as a slave, she must have been very young, for by 1868 she was photographed in the European convention of portraiture of important and distinguished persons.[23] The few records I could find about her past indicated more complications. During my examination of primary documents in the Navajo Land Claims papers, I discovered a handwritten genealogy of one of Manuelito's sons, known as Naalsoos Neiyéhí (Mail Carrier) or Manuelito no. 2. This genealogy showed the families of two of Manuelito's wives, both of whom resided in Tohatchi. My grandmother was the "first" wife. In this genealogy, next to my grandmother's name, was a note in the corner: "Her grandmother was Zia." The comment speaks to the stories of my grandmother Joan Kinsel, who said that my grandmother—Juanita's and Manuelito's daughter—often traveled to Zia Pueblo to trade with their Zia relatives.[24]

My grandmother's name, Asdzáá Tł'ógi, or Lady Weaver, indicates a number of things: that she was a weaver, and that she was from Zia Pueblo or had kin ties there. Thus, the history of slave-taking and the incorporation of captives into Navajo society raise questions about modern Navajo identity and how tribal peoples made exchanges; my grandmother's story indicates that Navajos and Pueblo peoples had cultural exchanges that included trade, intermarriage, and alliances. That my matrilineal clan is Tł'ógi reminds us of that history made by women. My grandmother came to claim Tł'ógi as her matrilineal clan when she and her family stopped at Zia Pueblo when returning from the Bosque Redondo reservation in 1868, so I am a Tł'ógi woman, born for Ashíí.[25] I've come to appreciate the ways in which Navajo women like Juanita were able to traverse the difficult terrain of the nineteenth-century Southwest, a time of great upheaval for the Diné, who were determined to retain their territorial lands in the face of American colonial rule.

Juanita traveled extensively with her husband, appeared with him in photographs that spanned three decades, from the 1860s to the 1890s, and was by his side during political meetings between Navajo and American leaders. Her dress, the saddle blanket of her manufacture, the photographs of her, including the one in which she is seated next to the textile on a loom, all indicate that she was a Navajo woman. That she was photographed with her husband raises questions about her relationship to her husband and suggests roles that Navajo women may have had when the male leadership met with their American counterparts. Recent oral histories indicate the influence that women had during the negotiation of the treaty of 1868, which allowed the Navajo people to return to their homeland after their imprisonment at the Bosque Redondo reservation from 1863 to 1868. My interpretation of Asdzáá Tłʼógi's role in the leadership of the Navajo Nation is further supported by documents and oral histories that come to us across the decades and from places far from Diné Bikéyah.

When I first took a faculty position in the history department at Northern Arizona University in 2008, a Diné teacher visited me in my office. He showed me a map of nineteenth-century New Mexico Territory and pointed to a statement printed at the site of the Bosque Redondo reservation in northwestern New Mexico. The statement indicated that on one of the evenings, after a day of attempts to negotiate a treaty between Navajos and Americans, Navajo male leaders met with General William Tecumseh Sherman and Samuel Tappan. At the meeting a large gathering of Diné woman had beseeched the Americans to send their people home. Many years later, in the summer of 2010, I was poring through archival documents at the Newberry Library in Chicago when I discovered a cache of oral interviews with Diné from the 1950s. One in particular captured my attention: the interview with Pete Price, a medicine man from the western region of Navajoland. Price shared a story about the Long Walk, the negotiation of the treaty of 1868, and women's influence on its negotiation.

According to Pete Price, during the negotiations the Navajo headmen and American officials would periodically walk out of the building in which they had been talking and into a crowd of Navajo prisoners. These prisoners anxiously awaited word from their leaders, who were urging the Americans to agree to Navajo terms. At the negotiations, Sherman offered the Navajos relocation east, to Indian Territory. The lead negotiator on behalf of the Navajo people, Barboncito, was adamant: the Navajos desired to return to their homeland.[26] Price relayed that the People "heard, instead of returning to their ancient homes, they were to be taken still farther east. They were displeased with the idea, so the wise men of the tribe got together and planned for a meeting with the white man." Price continued: "After the men of the tribe had failed, the women went to the white men, cried and pleaded to be allowed to go back to their home in the west. The women were successful in their efforts to change the American military officer's mind. General Sherman relented, agreeing that the Navajo people should return to their home land, saying, 'You are right, the world is big enough for all the people it contains and all should live at peace with their neighbors.'"[27] Price's oral history offers historical evidence of Navajo women's participation in political decisions that affected all the Navajo people, and requires us to reflect on how the imposition of American democracy has undermined Navajo women's former authority in decision making, economics, and spirituality.

A third weaving attributed to my grandmother made the journey to Washington, D.C., with the 1874 Navajo delegation. As the wife of a respected headman, Juanita accompanied the all-male delegation and remained by her husband's side. Their son also traveled with them. The Navajo male leaders desired to meet with the president as part of their strategy to retain Navajo lands. They were fully aware that Navajo lands had been severely reduced with the treaty of 1868 and knew that aggressive Hispanic and white ranchers were continually looking to claim their lands. They hoped to convince the president to affirm their landholdings, particularly in the northern section around the San Juan River in northwestern New Mexico. The delegation left Navajoland in November of 1873 and returned in February of 1874. My grandmother was the only woman to accompany the delegation. The Indian agent Arny seemed to have used her presence as an attraction to sell Navajo arts and crafts, hence the photograph of her alongside the agent, with the textile in the background as a prop. The weaving may have been used to exhibit Navajo skill at weaving, and most likely Juanita was also part of the "display." Textile scholar Kate Kent Peck names this textile as one of the first pictorials woven by a Navajo woman. The top of the textile depicts an American flag of red, white, and blue, and the lower half is an "eye-dazzler," so named because of the bright colors used.[28]

What could this unfinished textile tell me about Navajo women? Perhaps it marked yet another moment of "cultural change" and of the shifts that Navajos were seeing in the late nineteenth century. In other stories that my grandmother Faye Yazzie relayed to me, Asdzáá Tł'ógi accompanied the delegation of male leaders at the request of her husband, who looked to his wife for advice and counsel. He even entreated her to speak directly to President Grant on behalf of the Navajo people. Faye said that during the months in the east, the Navajo leaders become lonely and hungry for Navajo food, whereupon my grandmother would share the foods she brought: dried corn, venison jerky, and piñon nuts that had been made into a paste. Across time and space, stories like Faye's remind us of the central place that women have in our Navajo communities: Women are the mothers and grandmothers who provide the sustenance for life. They are the caregivers, the nurturers, of the Navajo people, and their care extends far beyond what is considered the acceptable place for women in a democratic society. Navajo women's care extended to the cares of the Navajo Nation.

After eighteen months in their homeland, my great-great-great-grandmother's dress and saddle blanket made the return journey to California. Navajo Nation Museum curator Clarenda Begay and I returned the items in a tribal van. My concerns about how to stitch together fragments of stories, images from photographs, material culture that has

FIGURE 11.5

Charles Milton Bell, *Portrait of Juanita in Native Dress; Blankets, Weaving Implements and Governor Arny Nearby, 1874*. Department of Anthropology, Smithsonian Institution, catalogue no. 2405.

survived into the twenty-first century, and stories from the Navajo people and my kin relatives come together in a community where kinship is affirmed, and where we once again extend prayers and appreciation for our ancestors, for our grandmothers and grandfathers, who surely must have thought about us, about the future. They had no doubt that we would continue to create a path to the future for the next generations of the Na'hokah' Diné—the Earth Surface People—another name for the Diné.

I remain inspired by and appreciative of the multiple forms of remembering the importance of Diné history and culture. I take to heart the ongoing challenges to resist continued U.S. colonialism and its relentless assault on the Navajo people, as do so many Navajos. I sometimes have lunch with my aunt Vivian Arviso, a stately Navajo woman who was Miss Navajo years ago. We get caught up, and she shares her efforts to create a Navajo-based curriculum for Navajo schoolchildren. In 2013, it remains difficult to find teaching materials that are Navajo-centered and that will instruct Navajo children in Navajo cultural values. As a member of the Miss Navajo Council Association, which is made up of former Miss Navajo pageant-title holders, she is busy finishing up details for the Hero Twins Symposium, an event intended to convey traditional Navajo male roles to boys and young men. In September of 2013, I agree to present at a symposium honoring Navajo women in Window Rock, Arizona, and am inspired by the other presenters, who affirm the wisdom of our ancestors. On another day, I laugh heartily, long, and loud as I listen to *Star Wars* in the Navajo language. There is sheer joy in hearing the language in something as ordinary as a Hollywood movie like *Star Wars*.

On any given day, Diné will contact me and want to share their family and clan stories, an oral history project they are interested in creating, or just discuss Navajo history with me. I am gratified that my fellow Diné want to know more Diné history, as I continue to raise questions around critical issues that face us in the present. What has it meant to explore the lives of Navajo women like Juanita, whose Diné public name was Asdzáá Tł'ógi, or Lady Weaver? How does scholarship generated in academia, in a place that many Diné consider to be foreign, move back and forth between the academy, the Navajo Nation, and Navajo communities and families? As a researcher, I not only have gained an appreciation for the roles Navajo women have played throughout history, in the formation of nation, community, and family, but also have thought a lot about the ways in which storytelling is renewed when academia, community, and kinship inform its processes.

NOTES

1. Cindy Yurth, "'A Sense of Pride': Chief Manuelito Exhibit Opens at the Navajo Nation Museum," *Navajo Times*, August 27, 2010, http://navajotimes.com/entertainment/culture/0810 /082710manuelito.php#.UoakmBXn-Uk.

2. Cindy Yurth, "Wooshdéé, biil!: Juanita's Descendants Welcome Home Her Weavings," *Navajo Times*, September 2, 2010, http://navajotimes.com/news/2010/0910/090210rug .php#.UoajyBXn-Uk.

3. George Wharton James, *Indian Blankets and Their Makers* (Chicago: A.C. McClurg, 1914), 118.

4. *Juanita*, 1868. National Anthropological Archives, Smithsonian Institution, neg. no. 55770.

5. We, the Diné, often do not make distinctions across generations of grandmothers. Hence, my great-great-great-grandmother is also referred to as my grandmother.

6. As a novice researcher, when I first began my research on indigenous oral tradition and history, I found the works of Julie Cruikshank, Angela Cavender Wilson (now Waziyatawin), and Winona Stevenson Wheeler very useful to understanding the persistence of traditional philosophies and values. See Julie Cruikshank, "Images of Society in Klondike Gold Rush Narratives: Skookum Jim and the Discovery of Gold," *Ethnohistory* 39 (Winter 1992): 20–41; Angela Cavender Wilson, "Grandmother to Granddaughter: Generations of Oral History in a Dakota Family," in *Natives and Academics: Researching and Writing about American Indians*, ed. Devon A. Mihesuah (Lincoln: University of Nebraska Press, 1998); Waziyatawin Angela

Wilson, *Remember This! Dakota Decolonization and the Eli Taylor Narratives* (Lincoln: University of Nebraska Press, 2005).

7. James C. Faris includes the photograph of Barboncito in his study of Navajo photographs. See *Navajo and Photography: A Critical History of the Representation of an American People* (Albuquerque: University of New Mexico Press, 1996), 31.

8. Bill P. Acrey, *Navajo History: The Land and the People* (Shiprock, NM: Department of Curriculum Materials Development, Central Consolidated School District No. 22, 1994), 82–87.

9. Herman J. Viola, *Diplomats in Buckskin: A History of Indian Delegations in Washington City* (Bluffton, SC: Rivilo Books, 1995).

10. See Jennifer Nez Denetdale, *Reclaiming Diné History: The Legacies of Navajo Chief Manuelito and Juanita* (Tucson: University of Arizona Press, 2007), photographs on pp. 112 and 113. Charles Bell took several photographs of Juanita, including portraits with the Indian agent William F. Arny, 1874 (neg. no. 2405), and the Navajo delegation, Washington, DC, 1874 (neg. no. 2410-C), National Anthropological Archives, Smithsonian Institution, Washington, DC.

11. Captain E. Butler, Fifth Infantry, to Brevet Major Cyrus H. DeForrest, July 29, 1866, Frank McNitt Collection, New Mexico State Records Center and Archives, Santa Fe, quoted in *Santa Fe Gazette*, August 4, 1866.

12. Jennifer Nez Denetdale, "Chairmen, Presidents, and Princesses: The Navajo Nation, Gender, and the Politics of Tradition," *Wicazo Sa Review* 21, no. 1 (Spring 2006): 9–44.

13. In one of the first investigations I conducted of Navajo women in the literature, I discovered that Navajo women were mostly written about by feminist anthropologists who attempted to understand how Navajo women's status had shifted: many non-Indian observers commented that Navajo women seemed autonomous in comparison to their white counterparts. However, not until the 1980s, with the publication of Irene Stewart's life story as told to anthropologist Mary Shepardson, was attention paid to Navajo women and leadership in the Navajo tribe and then the Navajo Nation. See Jennifer Denetdale, "Representing Changing Woman: A Review Essay on Navajo Women," *American Indian Culture and Research Journal* 25, no. 3 (2001): 1–26; Irene Stewart, *A Voice in Her Tribe: A Navajo Woman's Own Story*, ed. Lowell John Bean and Thomas C. Blackburn, with a foreword by Mary Shepardson (Socorro, NM: Ballena Press, 1980); Jennifer Nez Denetdale, "Chairmen, Presidents, and Princesses," 1–26.

14. Jodi A. Byrd, *The Transit of Empire: Indigenous Critiques of Colonialism* (Minneapolis: University of Minnesota Press, 2011).

15. I appreciate the scholarship of anthropologist Patrick Wolfe on the processes of colonialism that always seek to destroy and eliminate indigenous peoples. As he notes, invasions of indigenous peoples' lands and territories is not an event but a structure. See "Settler Colonialism and the Elimination of the Native," *Journal of Genocide Research* 8, no. 4 (2006): 387–409.

16. Kathleen Whitaker, *Southwest Textiles: Weavings of the Navajo and Pueblo* (Seattle: University of Washington Press, 2002), 56–57.

17. Ibid., 206, 207.

18. For contexts in which Navajo women's knowledge of weaving is informed by the sacred creation narratives and history, see Paul G. Zolbrod and Roseann Willink, *Weaving a World:*

Textiles and the Navajo Way of Seeing (Santa Fe: Museum of New Mexico Press, 2001); and Bennie Klain, dir., *Weaving Worlds* (Austin, TX: TricksterFilms, 2008), DVD.

19. David M. Brugge, *Navajos in the Catholic Church Records of New Mexico, 1694–1875* (Tsaile, AZ: Navajo Community College Press, 1985).

20. Estevan Rael-Galvez, "By Any Other Name: A Story of Slavery and Her Legacy," Ché (What You Call Your) Pasa, June 26, 2012, http://chewhatyoucallyourpasa.blogspot.com/2012/06/slavery-time-and-other-things-in-land.html.

21. Brugge, *Navajos in the Catholic Church Records of New Mexico*, 97. See also the graph in the front of the book, which indicates that in the years of the American war on Navajos, there was a significant increase in the number of Navajo women and children taken as slaves.

22. Ríordan quoted in James F. Brooks, *Captives and Cousins: Slavery, Kinship and Communities in the Southwest Borderlands* (Chapel Hill: University of Carolina Press, 2002), 287.

23. Denetdale, *Reclaiming Diné History*, 109. Peter Iverson includes the photograph of Barboncito in his Navajo history. See *Diné: A History of the Navajos (*Albuquerque: University of New Mexico, 2002), 61. See also James C. Faris, *Navajo and Photography* (Logan: University of Utah Press, 2003).

24. Denetdale, *Reclaiming Diné History*, 151.

25. Ibid., 143–47.

26. Martin A. Link, ed., *Navajo Treaty—1868* (Las Vegas: KC Publications, 1968).

27. Pete Price, local leader and medicine man, oral history interview, n.d., Fort Defiance, Arizona, Ayer Modern MS, box 24, folder 231, Newberry Library, Chicago.

28. Denetdale, *Reclaiming Diné History*, 99–101.

CONTRIBUTORS

ADAM ARENSON is associate professor of history at Manhattan College and author of *The Great Heart of the Republic: St. Louis and the Cultural Civil War.*

DURWOOD BALL is associate professor of history and editor of the *New Mexico Historical Review* at the University of New Mexico.

KENT BLANSETT is of Cherokee, Creek, Choctaw, Shawnee, and Potawatomi descent and is assistant professor of history and American Indian studies at the University of Nebraska, Omaha.

CAROLYN BRUCKEN started at the Autry National Center in 2003, where she is the curator of Western Women's History.

JENNIFER DENETDALE is a citizen of the Navajo Nation and associate professor of American studies at the University of New Mexico.

WILLIAM DEVERELL is professor of history and director of the Huntington-USC Institute on California and the West at the University of Southern California.

JONATHAN EARLE is dean of the Honors College at Louisiana State University.

JOHN MACK FARAGHER is Howard R. Lamar Professor of History at Yale University.

DANIEL LYNCH is a doctoral candidate in U.S. history at University of California, Los Angeles, researching the convergence of Southerners and Californios in nineteenth-century Southern California.

MARIA E. MONTOYA is associate professor of history and the author of *Translating Property: The Maxwell Land Grant and the Conflict over Land in the American West.*

VIRGINIA SCHARFF is distinguished professor of history and associate provost at the University of New Mexico and chair of Western Women's History at the Autry National Center.

BRENDA E. STEVENSON is professor of history at University of California, Los Angeles, and author of books on slavery, the family, the justice system, and American women.

INDEX

Abel, Annie Heloise, 96, 103n33
abolitionism, 5, 52, 103n15, 181
Adair, Florella Brown, 55, 64n21
Adair, Samuel, 55, 64n21
African American rights, 130, 131, 150–51, 159,
    172
African Americans, 145, 146
Afro-American League of Pasadena, 186
Alta California, 6, 106, 110–11
American history, "epic moments" approach to,
    1–2
American Progress (novel; Fifer), 138n36
American Progress (painting; Gast), 6, 124 *fig. 7.2*;
    as Liberal Republican vision, 124, 133–35;
    licensed uses of, 138–39n38; omissions of,
    135; understanding meaning of, 124–27
American Revolution, 71
Ames Manufacturing Company (MA), 112–13
Amistad (slave ship), 181
amputations, 179–80, 179 *fig. 10.3*
Anaheim (CA), 110
Angola, 22n9
Anthony, Susan B., 151
Anti-Coolie Act (CA; 1862), 170

Antietam, Battle of (1862), 175–76, 177–80, 177
    fig. 10.2, 181, 188n5
anti-immigrant legislation, 170–72
Antitreaty Party (Cherokee political party), 90,
    101n5
Antonia (slave), 23n15
Apache Indians, 78, 78 *fig. 4.6*, 105, 114, 115, 116
Appomattox Court House, Lee's surrender at
    (1865), 97
Arabia (steamship), 54–55, 63–64n18
Arabia Steamboat Museum (Kansas City, MO),
    64n18
Aragon, José, 166 *fig. 9.3*
Arapaho Indians, 75–76, 128, 143, 144, 145, 146,
    147 *fig. 8.3*, 155
Arenson, Adam, 6
Arizona, 44, 67–68, 108, 111
Arkansas, 67, 91, 92, 96, 103n15
Arkansian, The, 92
Army Corps of Topographical Engineers, 29, 31
Army of the West (USA), 41, 76–77
Arny, William, 193, 203 *fig. 11.5*
Articles of Confederation, 3–4
Arviso, Vivian, 203–4